CW01371709

1 MONTH OF FREE READING

at
www.ForgottenBooks.com

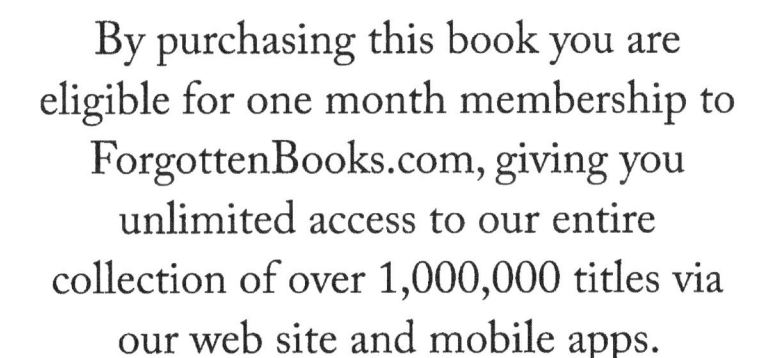

By purchasing this book you are eligible for one month membership to ForgottenBooks.com, giving you unlimited access to our entire collection of over 1,000,000 titles via our web site and mobile apps.

To claim your free month visit: www.forgottenbooks.com/free137989

* Offer is valid for 45 days from date of purchase. Terms and conditions apply.

ISBN 978-0-332-13562-5
PIBN 10137989

This book is a reproduction of an important historical work. Forgotten Books uses state-of-the-art technology to digitally reconstruct the work, preserving the original format whilst repairing imperfections present in the aged copy. In rare cases, an imperfection in the original, such as a blemish or missing page, may be replicated in our edition. We do, however, repair the vast majority of imperfections successfully; any imperfections that remain are intentionally left to preserve the state of such historical works.

Forgotten Books is a registered trademark of FB &c Ltd.
Copyright © 2018 FB &c Ltd.
FB &c Ltd, Dalton House, 60 Windsor Avenue, London, SW19 2RR.
Company number 08720141. Registered in England and Wales.

For support please visit www.forgottenbooks.com

PRESENTED
TO
THE UNIVERSITY OF TORONTO
BY

H. H. Langton Esq.

THE
WAR SPEECHES
OF
WILLIAM PITT
THE YOUNGER

OXFORD UNIVERSITY PRESS
LONDON EDINBURGH GLASGOW NEW YORK
TORONTO MELBOURNE BOMBAY
HUMPHREY MILFORD M.A.
PUBLISHER TO THE UNIVERSITY

Photograph, Emery Walker

WILLIAM PITT

(From the painting by Hoppner in the National Portrait Gallery)

THE
WAR SPEECHES
OF
WILLIAM PITT
THE YOUNGER

SELECTED BY

R. COUPLAND, M.A.
TRINITY COLLEGE, OXFORD

OXFORD
AT THE CLARENDON PRESS
1915

WILLIAM PITT

THE
WAR SPEECHES
OF
WILLIAM PITT
THE YOUNGER

SELECTED BY

R. COUPLAND, M.A.
TRINITY COLLEGE, OXFORD

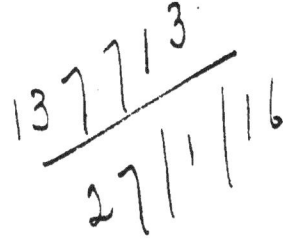

OXFORD
AT THE CLARENDON PRESS
1915

DA
522
P45
1915

CONTENTS

	PAGE
INTRODUCTION	ix

PRELUDE (1783–1793).
1. The Fruits of the American War (February 21, 1783) . 1
2. The Commercial Treaty with France (February 12, 1787) 8
3. The Prosperity of the Nation (February 17, 1792) . . 15

THE WAR: FIRST PHASE (1793–1797).
1. French Ambitions and the Liberty of Europe (February 1, 1793) 24
2. The French Declaration of War (February 12, 1793) . 52
3. War Finance (March 11, 1793) 78
4. On a Motion for Peace (June 17, 1793) 91
5. The Jacobin Government of France (January 21, 1794) . 103
6. On a Motion for a Separate Peace (March 6, 1794) . . 112
7. The Folly of a Premature Peace (December 30, 1794) . 116
8. The War Policy of the Government reviewed and defended (May 10, 1796) 134
9. The Defence of England against Invasion (October 18, 1796) 162
10. Belgium: the Price of Peace (December 30, 1796) . . 173
11. The Mutiny in the Fleet (June 2, 1797) 189

The War: Second Phase (1797–1802).

1. The Renewal of the War: an Appeal for National Unity (November 10, 1797) 199
2. Strength the only Basis of Security (December 5, 1797) . 229
3. The Spirit of 'Mercantile' Britain: an Example to Europe (December 3, 1798) 232
4. At War with Armed Opinions (June 7, 1799) . . . 244
5. Buonaparte (February 3, 1800) ✓ 246
6. The Watchword: 'Security' (February 17, 1800) . . 284
7. Sea-Law and the Neutral Powers (February 2, 1801) . 288

The War: Third Phase (1803–1806).

1. The Impossibility of Peace (May 23, 1803) . . . 304
2. The Undesirability of a Change of Government during War (June 3, 1803) 308
3. The Arming of the Nation (July 18, 1803) . . . 310
   i. The maximum of effort needed (July 22, 1803) . 321
   ii. The need of trained officers (July 22, 1803) . 323
   iii. The protection of London (July 22, 1803) . . 325
   iv. The magnitude of the danger (July 22, 1803) . 328
   v. A permanent system of defence (June 18, 1804) . 330
   vi. The new era (April 25, 1804) 332
   vii. A 'mosquito' fleet (March 15, 1804) . . . 333
   viii. A case of treason? (June 22, 1804) . . . 336
4. Before Trafalgar (June 20, 1805) 338
5. The Concert of Europe (June 21, 1805) . . . 343
6. The Last Speech (November 9, 1805) 349

Index 355

NOTE

Most of the speeches in this volume have been reprinted from *The Speeches of William Pitt*, a collection edited by Mr. W. S. Hathaway, and published in four volumes in November 1806, ten months after Pitt's death. A second edition in three volumes with several speeches omitted was published in 1808. The remainder have been taken from *The Parliamentary History* up to 1803 and *The Parliamentary Debates* from 1804 onwards.

Unfortunately, the reporting of speeches in Parliament in Pitt's time left much to be desired. But, if it was immeasurably inferior both in accuracy and in completeness to that of the present day, it was far better than that of the previous generation. Exact records of Chatham's oratory are very few indeed (*vide* Williams, *Life of William Pitt, Earl of Chatham*, vol. ii, p. 335). Till 1771 the unauthorized publication of Parliamentary debates was held to be a breach of privilege, but thenceforward, though the principle was never abandoned by Parliament, the presence of newspaper reporters was permitted. The introduction of shorthand writing for the purpose in 1802 greatly improved the quality of the reports.

The History and *The Debates* were mainly compiled from these Press reports, and Mr. Hathaway's collection was largely drawn from the same source. But, as he states in his preface, some of the speeches he included were actually revised by Pitt himself, and others were collated and corrected by members of Parliament who had heard them delivered and were well acquainted with the style of their author. If, therefore, the reader detects a certain unevenness in the quality of the following selection, he may rest assured that the more important speeches, at any rate, are reasonably accurate.

The Introduction and Notes are much indebted to the writings of M. Albert Sorel, Mr. H. A. L. Fisher, Mr. C. Grant Robertson, and Dr. J. Holland Rose; they have also enjoyed the advantage of being read by Mr. Grant Robertson in proof.

*It is not to be thought of that the flood
Of British freedom, which, to the open sea
Of the world's praise, from dark antiquity
Hath flowed, 'with pomp of waters, unwithstood',
Roused though it be full often to a mood
Which spurns the check of salutary bands,
That this most famous stream in bogs and sands
Should perish; and to evil and to good
Be lost for ever. In our halls is hung
Armoury of the invincible knights of old:
We must be free or die, who speak the tongue
That Shakespeare spake; the faith and morals hold
Which Milton held.—In everything we are sprung
Of Earth's first blood, have titles manifold.*
WORDSWORTH (in 1802).

I do not believe that England ever will or can be unfaithful to her great tradition, or can forswear her interest in the common transactions and the general interests of Europe.
GLADSTONE (in 1869).

INTRODUCTION

I

WILLIAM PITT, the younger, became Prime Minister in December 1783. At that moment the fortunes of the British Commonwealth had reached their lowest level. The American War, in which France, Spain, and Holland had been leagued with the insurgent colonies against Great Britain, had recently closed with a humiliating peace. The secession of the American colonies from the Commonwealth was now an acknowledged fact. Our position in India was undermined by administrative abuses and threatened by French intrigues. Ireland was seething with discontent. The national finances were in a desperate condition: the funded debt was well over £200,000,000, and the 3 per cent. government stock stood at 57. No wonder that jealous continental Governments believed that a final decline of British power had at last begun. It seemed as if Britain, crippled and friendless, could never recover her place among the leading States of Europe.

To all appearance, indeed, the better part of the work achieved by Chatham was in ruins. Its restoration, so far as restoration was now possible, was the task which lay before his son. He brought to it great gifts of intellect and character—a swift comprehensive mind, eloquence, patience, unbending courage, intense devotion to his country, and, most useful of all, a capacity to face facts as they are and to shape policy in accordance with the lessons of experience. The spirit in which he began his life's work was typical of it all. 'Let us examine what is left', he said in 1783,[1] 'with a manly and determined courage. . . . The misfortunes of individuals and of kingdoms that are laid open and examined with true wisdom, are more than half redressed.'

It was to examining and redressing the misfortunes of the Commonwealth that Pitt devoted his first nine years of power. The administration of the East India Company's territories was improved by an increase of government control. The peculiar difficulties of the political situation in Canada were adjusted for the time by a compromise between the claims of the British Canadians and the rights of French Canadian nationality. And the first British settlement was planted in Australia. But Pitt gave most of his mind to problems nearer home, and the greatest achievement of those nine years was his restoration of the national finances. So successful was he in this his most congenial task, that at the end of the period the revenue was maintaining a steady annual surplus averaging half a million, a great part of the unfunded national debt had been funded and nearly eleven millions of the funded debt written off, and the 3 per cents. had touched 97.

In other directions his hopes were disappointed. His scheme for healing the old feud between Britain and Ireland by establishing the principle of commercial equality between the two countries was thwarted by a combination of mercantile and party interests. His proposals for parliamentary reform were defeated and dropped, and he fought in vain for the abolition of the slave trade. But it was simply a question of times and seasons to renew with success his policy of moderate reform and to render complete and final the economic

[1] *The Speeches of William Pitt* (1806 edition), vol. i, p. 58.

Introduction

recovery of the nation, provided that one condition could be guaranteed. The one condition was peace. Without peace, retrenchment and reform, then as always, were alike impossible, and, because his whole heart was set on nursing the country back to its old strength by means of retrenchment and reform, no British statesman ever sought peace and ensued it more ardently than Pitt.

To that end British foreign policy from 1783 to 1792 was wholly directed. The field of its operations was unpromising. Europe had been swept by constantly recurring wars for centuries, and the four great military Powers, France, Prussia, Austria, and Russia, were still controlled by absolute monarchs, whose chief ambition was, as the fate of Poland showed, to heighten the prestige of their dynasties and extend their hereditary possessions by territorial aggrandizement at the expense of weaker continental States. The three chief combinations were an *entente* between Austria and Russia with an eye to mutual gains at the expense of Poland and Turkey; a Bourbon-Hapsburg alliance between France and Austria; and a 'family compact' which bound together the Bourbon rulers of France and Spain. Prussia stood aloof, ready to pick her own profit from the quarrels of her neighbours.

Confronted by so strained a situation, the first duty of Britain was to look to her own defences. The army Pitt considered as of secondary importance in the event of a European conflagration, and in spite of the lessons of the American War he left it unreformed; but he took immediate advantage of the restored finances to strengthen the navy. 'The relieving by every such means', he said in 1786,[1] ' as my duty will suffer me

[1] *Speeches*, vol. i, p. 295.

to adopt, the burdens of the people and removing that load of debt by which it is oppressed, is the grand and ultimate end of my desire. . . . But let it be well understood how far the objects of necessary defence and of public economy can be reconciled and let the bounds that divide them not be transgressed. Let it be well weighed what a certain security for a lasting peace there is in a defencible and powerful situation and how likely weakness and improvidence are to be the forerunners of war.' But it was clear that, if British statesmen aimed at the maintenance of peace in Europe, they must break down the isolation in which Britain found herself in 1783 and seek new friendships on the Continent—for two reasons. *First,* because her friendlessness invited attack. The American colonies were lost to her, but she still had colonies to lose in Canada and the West Indies, and her position in India was far from unassailable. It was not forgotten, moreover, that for a few critical weeks in 1779 and 1780 the British navy had lost command even of the Channel. It would be a strong temptation, therefore, for any maritime rival, if Britain remained without a friend in Europe, to make an effort to break her sea-power once for all, and capture her colonies and trade in East and West. *Secondly,* because Britain in isolation, however peaceful her intentions, could exert but little influence towards preventing the aggressive and conflicting ambitions of the great military States from kindling a general conflagration in Europe.

It was characteristic of Pitt's direct and sanguine temperament that he should look for friendship in the one quarter where most of his contemporaries denied its possibility. France was the traditional enemy of England. The most dangerous rival of the Commonwealth for a century past, she had recently, by means of her fleets, her armies, and her gold, enabled the Americans to accomplish its disruption; and she was credited with designs for stripping it of the colonies and dependencies which still remained to it. But to Pitt the doctrine of eternal enmity seemed as unreasonable as it was wicked. In spite of the injury France had done us—the greatest injury ever inflicted by a foreign Power on the destinies of Britain—he harboured no thoughts of resentment or designs of revenge. His whole desire was to live with France, not to fight her. The very neighbourhood of the two Powers seemed to him to demand the burying of the hatchet. He realized, moreover, that economically the two countries were complementary, the one mainly agricultural, the other rapidly becoming industrial: and he believed that both would benefit in many ways from the mutual intercourse of the two peoples. He was influenced, also, by his personal sentiments. It was unusual in those days for British ministers to see much of foreign lands, but Pitt had visited France in 1783, and his sympathy with the French people remained unbroken even under the strain of the ensuing war. In the heat of the struggle he repeatedly declared it was not against the French people that we were fighting, but against their system of government.[1] Actuated by these motives he negotiated in 1786 a Commercial Treaty which not only offered considerable economic advantages, but was intended to prepare the way, by the breakdown of tariff barriers and the encouragement of friendly intercourse, to a political *entente*. In an alliance between France and England, Pitt hoped to find the best preventive of aggression and the strongest safeguard of peace in Europe.

[1] See pp. 202-5, 226, 231, &c.

More than a century was to pass before his prophetic vision could be realized. At the time, the ambitions of the Bourbon monarchy, despite the menace of bankruptcy and revolution, prevented a whole-hearted agreement. An opportunity of aggrandizement was afforded by the distracted state of Holland, where the provincial oligarchies were attempting to overthrow the Stadtholder, the hereditary head of the central executive, and to set up a Republic. If their aim could be attained by French assistance, France would exert a dominating influence over the new Republic, and control the Dutch seaboard and the Dutch fleet. The republican party was therefore assisted by French subsidies, and when in 1787 it became clear that the Stadtholder had a majority of the people behind him, and when the republican cause was rendered still more desperate by the advance of a Prussian army to support the Stadtholder, who had married a sister of the Prussian king, a war between France and Prussia was narrowly averted. The storm blew over; but the danger had been due in the first instance to French designs, and Pitt was forced to find some other basis of security than a French *entente*.

The Dutch crisis had provided the required elements, and in 1788 a Triple Alliance was formed between England, Prussia, and Holland. The combination of the Prussian army with the Dutch and British fleets proved an effective instrument for peace. It enabled Pitt in 1790 to obtain without a war the withdrawal of the Spanish claim to a monopoly of trade and settlement up the whole western coast of North America—a claim which, if maintained, would have blocked the natural expansion of Canada to the Pacific. It was the influence of the Triple Alliance that prevented Russia from crushing Sweden in 1789, and led to the restoration of peace and the balance of power in the Baltic. It was the influence of the Triple Alliance that averted war between Prussia and Austria in 1790, and constrained Austria to make peace with Turkey in 1791 and Russia to do likewise in 1792.

There had been checks and disappointments in foreign as in domestic policy, but in 1792 Pitt could look back with legitimate satisfaction on the record of his first administration. He had restored his country not only to internal strength but also to its place in the front rank of European States, and he had successfully employed its renewed power and prestige for the maintenance of peace. His first wish now was that the peace would last long enough for his work to be rounded off and solidified, and he was sanguine enough to estimate its probable duration at roughly fifteen years. Yet, before one year had elapsed, five Powers were at war, and England was among them. With one brief and precarious interval, she was now to fight continuously for over twenty years; and Pitt himself was to die, nine years before peace was finally restored.

II

By the irony of fate, Pitt's dream of peace was shattered by the development of events in the very nation on whose friendship, fostered by commercial ties, he had based a few years previously his chief hopes of maintaining the stability of Europe. Against the forces engendered by the French Revolution the commercial interdependence of France and England was as impotent an argument for peace as the bankruptcy of France itself.

The earlier stages of the Revolution were watched by Pitt with keen and not unfriendly interest. If he did not go the length of Fox, who, with genuine if impulsive enthusiasm, described the fall of the Bastille (July 14, 1789) as 'much the greatest and best event that has happened in the world', he was just as far removed from Burke, who, in language equally rhetorical, denounced the Revolution and all its works. It was difficult, indeed, for an unprejudiced Englishman and a passionate admirer of the British Constitution,[1] not to sympathize with an effort, so largely inspired in origin by the example of British history and the doctrines of British writers, to free the French people from the bonds of feudal tyranny, to set limits to the absolute despotism of the Bourbon kings, and to establish a constitutional system of government. The Prime Minister of a friendly State was naturally slow to express opinions on the internal affairs of France, but early in 1789 Pitt made it clear to the French ambassador that, now French designs on Holland were abandoned, his attitude to France was as cordial as when he had set on foot the negotiations for the Commercial Treaty. He assured him that 'France and England had the same principles, namely, not to aggrandize themselves and to oppose aggrandizement in others'. After the fall of the Bastille, again, he expressed through the Foreign Minister the earnest desire of the British Government 'to cultivate and promote that friendship and harmony which so happily subsists between the two countries'. And in 1790, the year of Burke's impassioned outburst, Pitt openly referred to the situation in France in the House of Commons as follows:[2]

[1] See pp. 21, 29, 72, 172, 243, &c.
[2] *Parliamentary History*, vol. xxviii, p. 351.

'The present convulsions of France', he said, 'must sooner or later terminate in general harmony and regular order.... Whenever the situation of France shall become restored, it will prove freedom rightly understood, freedom resulting from good order and good government; and thus circumstanced, France will stand forward as one of the most brilliant Powers in Europe ; she will enjoy just that kind of liberty which I venerate, and the valuable existence of which it is my duty, as an Englishman, peculiarly to cherish ; nor can I, under this predicament, regard with envious eyes, an approximation in neighbouring States to those sentiments which are the characteristic features of every British subject.'

But it was impossible for the French people, bound down for ages past under the despotism of the *ancien régime*, to attain at one sudden stroke to the enjoyment of such political liberty as Englishmen enjoyed after centuries of gradual development and slow habituation to the practice of self-government. The attempt, indeed, inspired by utopian ideals, to compress the work of centuries into a hasty series of legislative measures was the fundamental cause of the tragedy which presently involved all Europe ; to the inevitable breakdown of that attempt the disastrous change in the character and aims of the revolutionary movement was mainly due.

The failure of the National Assembly to satisfy the aspirations of the people, the spread of disorder in the provinces, the march of the mob on Versailles, and the forcible removal of the King and the Assembly to Paris —these alarming symptoms of 1789 were followed in 1790 by a period of delusive calm. Never were the prospects of re-establishing order under a constitution seemingly brighter. Then, in 1791, came the ill-timed flight of Louis XVI to the frontier, and his capture and return to what was practically imprisonment in Paris. The effect of his action on the peaceful progress of constitutional reform was bad enough, still worse was its effect on the relations of France with foreign Powers. The crowned heads of Europe had been vigorously solicited by the royalist French *émigrés* to send their armies to the rescue of their fellow ruler, to stamp out by force the ill-organized agitation of the revolutionary leaders, and to restore the absolute monarchy in all its ancient power. But George III of England, whatever his private inclinations, was bound to neutrality by Pitt; Catharine II of Russia was absorbed in her designs on Eastern Europe; the only available champions of Louis XVI were Frederick William II of Prussia and Leopold II of Austria. Hitherto these monarchs had turned deaf ears to the appeals of the *émigrés*, but the humiliating and possibly dangerous position of the French royal family after the return from Varennes now impelled them to come forward as the protectors of monarchy in Europe. Leopold, moreover, was seriously concerned for the safety of his sister, Marie Antoinette, the French queen. But they were mainly influenced by other than personal or dynastic motives. The sovereignty over certain provinces on the Upper Rhine was already in dispute. The armies of the central Powers might achieve more for their employers than the easy task of reimposing the Bourbon despotism on a country paralysed by anarchy. A little fishing in troubled waters might well result in territorial acquisitions. In the summer of 1791, therefore, Leopold and Frederick William concluded an alliance, and at the Conference of Pillnitz they declared their readiness to employ their forces in conjunction with those of the other sovereigns of Europe in order to re-establish the position of the French king.

This cautious declaration was by no means a decisive step on the part of Austria and Prussia towards war, but the threat it contained drove French sentiment violently in that direction. Already inflamed by the provocations of the emigrant nobles encamped on the frontier, the French people detected in the Declaration of Pillnitz the proof of an intrigue between Louis and his brother monarchs. Naturally, so far from frightening them back to their old respect for royalty, it strengthened the growing desire for a Republic. And those who, like the Girondin party, believed that a constitution over which the old master of France retained authority, however limited, was unworkable, now welcomed war as a means of driving Louis into the open and ensuring the abolition of the monarchy. Thus constitutional and patriotic motives were intertwined, and the first seeds were sown of the doctrine that the cause of civil liberty depended on triumphs in the field of battle and that the mission of the French Revolution extended beyond the bounds of France. When, therefore, in 1792 the attitude of Austria and Prussia became more menacing, it was an easy task for the Girondin Ministry to bring about a definite rupture. On April 20 France declared war on Austria. On July 24 Prussia, in support of her ally, declared war on France. Thus opened the most sanguinary period of war ever known to Europe before 1914.

War had been desired by Brissot, one of the Girondin leaders, as a trap for the king, and it soon more than fulfilled the object he assigned to it. The wilder forces of the Revolution at once began to get the upper hand at Paris. In the Assembly the Girondins, caught in their own trap, lost influence to the Jacobins; in the streets the mob was supreme. On August 10, the Tuileries was sacked, the Swiss Guard slaughtered, and the royal family imprisoned. In September, some fourteen hundred men, women, and children, who had been seized on the mere suspicion of noble birth or royalist leanings, were massacred at the gates of the prisons by gangs of hired assassins. In December, Louis XVI was put on his trial, and on January 21, 1793, he was executed.

This ghastly change in the character of the internal revolution was accompanied by a change as ominous in the character of the war. It seemed at the beginning as if the raw French troops might be unable to hold back a disciplined army or prevent the invaders reaching Paris. But the moral effect of the Prussian retirement at Valmy in the Argonne (September 20, 1792) transformed the situation. The over-cautious Brunswick, distracted by news of Russian interference in Poland, retreated to the Rhine. By the desperate valour of the French the Austrians were driven from Jemappes near Mons (November 6, 1792); and the armies of the Revolution rapidly overran the Austrian Netherlands and Liège in the north, and Nice and Savoy, which belonged to the Kingdom of Sardinia, in the south. The occupation of those districts confirmed the idea that the strategic frontier of the Alps and the Rhine was appointed by a law of nature as the boundary of France, while the swift discomfiture of the Austrian and Prussian armies inspired the belief that the hostile monarchies were rotten at the core and that their peoples only waited the coming of their republican brothers to throw off the yoke of kings and

Introduction xxi

accept the doctrines of the Revolution. A war of self-defence had thus quickly become a war of liberation. Started by a few republican politicians in order to overthrow their king, it was now regarded with enthusiasm by the mass of the French people as a national crusade.

Plain evidence of the change was afforded by the decrees of the ' Convention '—the new National Assembly which had inaugurated its first session on September 21, 1792, by the proclamation of the Republic. In 1789 the first Assembly had declared that wars of aggrandizement were forbidden. But on November 19, 1792, the Convention passed a decree offering the protection of France to any people which rose against its Government; and on December 15 another decree declared that ' wherever French armies shall come ' the existing régime shall be abolished, the property of the Government and its adherents confiscated, and a new Government established on the French model.[1] That this policy implied ' wars of aggrandizement ' was recognized clearly enough by the Belgians, who at first had welcomed the invaders as their liberators from Austrian rule, but soon changed their minds when heavy contributions were exacted for the support of the French army, and uncongenial republican institutions imposed on them in place of the old provincial administration they desired. What the French brought was not liberty, but a new domination masquerading in its name. The pretence was soon to be discarded. In January 1793 the annexation of the Austrian Netherlands to the French Republic was decreed; in October 1795 it was carried into effect.

[1] See pp. 37, 40–43, 144, 249.

III

That the development of a dangerously aggressive spirit in France was totally unexpected by Pitt is clear enough from his belief, expressed early in 1792, in the prospect of peace for fifteen years to come.[1] More conclusive than his words was his action in slightly reducing both the land and sea forces. His continued sympathy with France was demonstrated, moreover, by his reception of Talleyrand, who had been sent to secure British neutrality, if not support, in the impending war with the central Powers. That shrewd diplomatist reported that the attitude of the British Government was friendly, but he added that the best way for France to maintain the friendship was to show her strength. 'It is with a fleet', he said, 'that you must speak to England.' Talleyrand's report was highly gratifying to the Girondin Ministry. They were on the brink of declaring war on Austria, a step which would probably bring Prussia and possibly other enemies into the field. But, if only England would stand aside, they were prepared to face all Europe.

And yet the first step they took on the outbreak of war was precisely the step most likely to awaken suspicion and anxiety in England. They invaded the Austrian provinces in Belgium, despite the fact that the prevention of a domination of the Low Countries by any of the stronger neighbouring Powers had always been a cardinal precept of British foreign policy. The result of French intrigues in Holland five years previously, which had jarred so harshly on the harmony established at the time of the Commercial Treaty, was convincing evidence that the traditional attitude of British Governments was

[1] See p. 16.

Introduction

unchanged. Further, Britain had acknowledged Austrian rule over part of Belgium by the Treaty of Utrecht in 1713, and had recently confirmed it by the Convention of Reichenbach in 1790. Of these facts the French diplomatists were well aware, and they strove to disarm suspicion by assurances that the invasion was dictated by strategic necessity, and that France had no intention whatever of retaining possession of the provinces after the war. They also pointed out the advantages to England of an Anglo-French Alliance, and suggested that the two Powers in coalition could defy the rest of Europe, divide the spoils of Spanish America, and dominate the world. If these fanciful proposals were intended to keep Pitt from joining the central Powers, they were quite unneeded. Prussia had already drifted away from her partners in the Triple Alliance, because her aggressive designs in Central Europe, and particularly on the Austrian Netherlands, had been opposed by England, and now, in the spring of 1792, she was preparing, in collusion with Austria, to aid Russia in crushing the Polish patriots and in absorbing their country. Since the integrity of Poland had stood in the forefront of Pitt's policy, he was little likely to join hands with its destroyers. He accepted, therefore, the French assurances that the Austrian Netherlands would be evacuated at the close of the war, and declared that his Government would maintain a strict neutrality.

Such was the attitude of England when, with the summer, came the change, described above, in the whole aspect of the Revolution. The series of events which culminated in the September massacres shocked public opinion in England, and alienated some of the sincerest friends of the revolutionary cause. But Pitt rightly held that he was not officially concerned with internal disturbances in France, as long as they did not affect her foreign policy, and he resisted all attempts to deflect Britain from the neutral course he had marked out for her.

But the men who had been responsible for the war-policy of France were unable to control the winds they had unloosed. It was soon imperative for any one who desired to exercise political power, however anxious he might be to retain British friendship, to run before the gale and to foster rather than to check the rising spirit of national aggrandizement, which, inflated by the rapid progress of French arms, welcomed a new enemy in England as merely one more antiquated monarchy for the irresistible forces of the Revolution to overthrow. Whom the gods wish to destroy, they first make mad. Only blind self-confidence can account for the deliberate provocation to neutral England which immediately preceded the delivery of the general challenge to all the Governments of Europe in the decree of November 19. On the 16th, two decrees were published. The first instructed the French generals to pursue the retreating Austrians into any country in which they might take refuge. It was an open threat to violate the neutrality of Holland, and Holland was not only an object of special interest to England for the same reasons as Belgium, but was actually her ally. The second decree was a still more direct defiance. It declared that the River Scheldt between Antwerp and the sea, where it passes through Dutch territory, should in future be freely navigated; and a week later French men-of-war sailed up the river to bombard the citadel of Antwerp, which France desired to occupy and use as a naval port. Now the right to navigate the Scheldt had been exclusively reserved to Holland ever since the Treaty of Münster in 1648; Britain had guaranteed the reservation by treaty as recently as the Anglo-Dutch Alliance of 1788, and it had been recognized by France herself in no less than five treaties since the Peace of Utrecht in 1713. It was soon evident, moreover, that the Revolutionary ministers were not satisfied with tearing up treaties signed by the representatives of the French monarchy, but intended to undo the recent settlement of Holland and set up a Dutch, in addition to a Belgian, Republic. On the fall of Antwerp (November 28) it was reported from The Hague that an unopposed passage through the Dutch fortress of Maestricht was being demanded for the French army; and the Dutch envoy in London formally appealed to the British Government for help.

War was now inevitable. Honour and self-interest alike demanded it; and if Pitt, in his desperate desire to preserve from ruin the fruits of nine years' labour for his country, still clung to the last faint hopes of peace, he admitted that a rupture could not be avoided unless the French Government were willing to revoke the November decrees. But the ministers in Paris knew well enough that, in the present temper of the people, the acceptance of so humiliating a demand would have abruptly closed their political career; and the decrees remained in force. More than that, as if to put the certainty of war beyond all question, they embarked on a course of action which no independent State could tolerate. Their readiness to come to blows with Britain was partly due to a belief that the country was ripe for revolution. Certain Jacobin clubs in England, setting what they supposed to be the cause of liberty and fraternity among all mankind above the immediate and indisputable claims of citizenship, were undoubtedly prepared, at least as far as speech and writing went, to favour the cause of France and disparage that of their own country. With these malcontents the French ambassador and his agents did not scruple to intrigue, and when addresses were presented by them to the Convention, congratulating it on the triumph of liberty in France and holding out prospects of England shortly following her example, they were received with acclamation and published to the world by official decree. In Ireland also the agents of France attempted to stir the smouldering discontent into flame. On December 31 this amazing agitation reached its climax, when the French Minister of Marine, who had already begun to discuss with his colleagues a plan for the invasion of England, dispatched a letter to 'the friends of Liberty and Equality' in British seaports, announcing the imminent descent of French forces on the coast to overthrow the tyranny of the British Government. 'We will hurl thither fifty thousand caps of liberty, we will plant there the sacred tree.'[1]

War was now obviously a question of days, but the interval was crowded with further provocations. On January 12, 1793, two days after the Executive Council had decided to carry on their designs in the Low Countries and thus practically to initiate the war, Brissot derided the impotence of the British Ministry, and declared it an easy task for France to raise a rebellion in Scotland and in Ireland, and to liberate India from her chains. On the 21st, Louis XVI went to the scaffold; and as a result, the French ambassador, having lost his official status as the representative of the French Court,

[1] See pp. 47-48.

was requested to leave England. On the 31st, Danton swept the Convention to its feet with the famous phrase, 'Let us fling down to the kings the head of a king as gage of battle,' and carried without opposition a decree for the annexation of the Austrian Netherlands to the French Republic. Next day France declared war on Great Britain and Holland.

IV

Pitt's statement of the issues for which England fought can be studied in detail in his speeches, but if one sentence may be quoted as summing up the case, it is this : 'England will never consent that France shall arrogate the power of annulling at her pleasure, and under the pretence of a natural right of which she makes herself the only judge, the political system of Europe, established by solemn treaties and guaranteed by the consent of all the Powers.'

In the defence of this position Pitt had at his back the mass of public opinion and a great majority in Parliament. But complete unanimity was as yet impossible. The Jacobin clubs were too deeply committed to the Revolution to support the Government. More unfortunate was the irreconcilable attitude of Fox. A sincere enthusiast for freedom and a lover of peace as earnest as Pitt himself, he had greeted the fall of the Bastille as inaugurating the triumph of both ideals. Convinced that the ambitions of the Bourbon monarchy were the greatest danger to European peace, he had vigorously opposed Pitt's policy of winning the friendship of France by means of the Commercial Treaty. He had even subscribed to the doctrine that France and England must be enemies for ever. But the moment that the power of the Bourbons was broken by the Revolution, he passed to the other extreme. He now saw in France the evangelist not only of freedom, but of peace, among all peoples. To him the advance of Austria and Prussia was a wanton aggression, inspired by the hope of dismembering France, and his chief quarrel with Pitt was that he had failed to prevent that sinister alliance or stop the war by the armed mediation of England. Thus prejudiced he closed his eyes to the real nature of the change which came over the Revolution after Valmy and Jemappes. He excused the crimes of the autumn as the inevitable result of the Austro-Prussian attack, inflaming the ardent spirit of the French people to the madness of desperation in defence of the freedom they had so hardly won. He rejoiced in the triumphs of the French army as the vindication of the Revolution and the chastisement of greedy despotism.

Fox was justified in suspecting the motives of the Powers which planned the rape of Poland and the obliteration of Polish nationality. But he was wrong to suppose that Britain could have restored peace by single-handed intervention between the combatants. As a matter of fact, Pitt actually invited Russia, though he kept it secret at the time, to mediate jointly with England;[1] but, as nothing came of it, he wisely maintained neutrality till France forced him into war. Fox's mistake was his failure to see, as Pitt saw, the real nature of the new militant temper of France. The decrees of November and December and the policy adopted in Belgium were proof that France was now bent not merely on defending her own revolutionary system but on forcing it on other peoples. Theirs was a crusade to propagate, not freedom, but their own conception of freedom, and the

[1] See p. 253.

Introduction

institutions in which alone, as they imagined, freedom was enshrined. Englishmen, for instance, were only to be free on condition that they donned the red caps and saluted the sacred tree prepared for them by the French Minister of Marine. It was 'liberty by compulsion'. As Pitt truly put it, 'all Europe was to learn the principles of liberty from the mouth of the French cannon'.[1] And indeed the astounding contradiction was stated quite as clearly by the Revolutionary leaders themselves. 'Woe to the people', said Cambon, 'that shall try to free itself if it does not at the same instant break *all* its chains!' 'We must establish the despotism of liberty', cried Marat, 'to crush the despotism of kings!'

France was in the first throes of a fever which was not to reach its climax for a decade, and was only to be cured in the end by prolonged and wholesale loss of blood. Unhappily she had no physicians to check it at the onset. Her political leaders were, indeed, largely responsible for its existence. They had found themselves face to face with an impossible task—to create a workable constitution without deposing a vacillating king and an intriguing queen, to satisfy the popular demand for a literal application of Liberty, Equality, and Fraternity, and to restore order and prosperity in a bankrupt and hungry land. They realized that, as soon as their failure became apparent, they would be swept away and replaced by others no more competent than themselves. From this *impasse* war seemed the only escape. The more patriotic of them hoped to find in it a solution of some of their immediate problems. It would probably lead to the removal of the tiresome obstacle of monarchy. It would certainly divert popular attention from politics

[1] p. 38; cf. pp. 251-252.

at Paris to the fortunes of the battle-field, and leave them undisturbed to straighten out the tangle of administration. In that section of the people, at least, of which the armies were composed, it would establish order, and, if things went well, the problems of their pay and food might be solved by the pillage of their enemies. To foster the war-spirit seemed, therefore, the truest patriotism to those who identified the welfare of France with the final triumph of the Revolution. As Louvet, the Girondin, afterwards expressed it, 'Without war the Republic would not have existed.' But they can scarcely have realized that war, so far from permanently removing their difficulties, would raise others yet more difficult to handle. They hoped to hold their own against Austria and Prussia, but were they prepared from the beginning to rouse and defy all Europe? Did they suspect how hard it might prove to control the appetite for conquest, if once their armies were bitten with success? Did they appreciate the further problem of dealing with disbanded soldiers on the morrow of a peace?

Most of the more self-seeking leaders were also bent on war. They desired power at any price, and they realized that in war-time France could not be controlled by a popular assembly. A small, strong, and secret executive would be the natural form of government, and they themselves would be its members. Up to a point their calculations were correct. The war doomed France to that tyranny of secret committees which reached its acme in the Terror. But it needed a mind as clear as Robespierre's to foresee the logical conclusion of the process. If, he asked himself, the conduct of policy in time of war were safer in the hands of few than many, would it not be safer still in the hands of one than of

Introduction xxxi

w? And, if the centre of interest were shifted from
vil to military affairs, what was to prevent the centre
f power shifting from the civil to the military authority?
or the protection of the State from the dangers of war
he public would look first to generals, not to statesmen;
nd, in the disorganized and unstable condition of society,
he favourite of the army would find the road to a dictator-
hip in France as easy as it ever was at Rome.

The first signs of the movement towards the Caesarism,
which Robespierre dreaded, had already appeared when
England was drawn into the war. The main causes of
he rupture have already been stated. It has been
pointed out that the Revolutionary Government was
he aggressor, and directly challenged England; that Pitt
was bound to accept the challenge for the vindication of
treaty, the independence of the Low Countries, the safety
f the British Isles, and the stability of Europe; that, if
he had still shrunk from precipitating his country into
he horrors and losses of war, from interrupting his chosen
life-work and hazarding the gains already won, no further
efforts on his part to persuade the French Ministry to
set a limit to their conquests would have availed against
the crusading ardour of the French people. But one
further significant preventive of peace has not yet been
mentioned. Early in December 1792 a member of the
Convention stated in a private letter the opinion current
in the Girondin circle that peace would be a danger to
the Republic because 'it would be hazardous to recall
an army, flushed with victory, and impatient to gather
fresh laurels, into the heart of a country, where commerce and manufactures have lost their activity, and
which would leave the disbanded multitudes without
resources or employment'. In the same key, Maret,

the French envoy, who had been sincerely working for peace in London, confessed to an English friend: 'Peace is out of the question. We have three hundred thousand men in arms. We must make them march as far as their legs will carry them, or they will return and cut our throats.' In other words, it was no longer in the power of the Executive, still less of the Convention, to decide the question of peace or war. The first stage had been already reached in the process which was to culminate in the coronation of Napoleon.

V

'How could we ever be so deceived', asked Romilly, the champion of reform in England, on the news of the September massacres, 'in the character of the French nation as to think them capable of liberty?' Modern France is a sufficient refutation of a charge so sweeping. But Romilly would have been literally correct if he had denied the capability of the French or any other people to pass at a stride from absolute monarchy to orderly self-government. Burke, like Robespierre, perceived the inevitable result of attempting the impossible. In words which stand out for their prophetic insight from much indiscriminate violence in the *Reflections*, he foretold not only that 'some popular general, who understands the art of conciliating the soldiery and who possesses the true spirit of command, shall draw the eyes of all men upon himself', but also that the new despot would probably exercise 'the most completely arbitrary power that ever appeared on earth'.

That such indeed was the outcome of the Revolution was determined by the law that it is a slower business to build up than to pull down. The *ancien régime* was

Introduction

totally demolished. A solid constitutional structure could not be conjured into immediate existence to take its place. The interval was the opportunity for autocracy to re-establish itself with powers even more absolute than it had previously possessed; for with the old monarchy had gone to limbo the various minor limitations which custom and experience had respected. France, indeed, was as a house swept and garnished when the spirit of despotism returned to dwell there, and it took to it seven other spirits more wicked than itself.

There was much truth, then, in Napoleon's own profession that his elevation from lieutenant of artillery to Emperor of the French was a simple matter, due to the peculiarity of the times. The opportunity was there; and he seized it by methods as old as 'tyranny' itself.

The familiar story may be briefly told. Under the pressure of war, the Committee of Public Safety had little difficulty in concentrating within its own hands the whole authority of the State. Local self-government was greatly reduced, and at Paris the Convention soon became an obedient machine, the ministers mere ciphers. But the abuses of the Terror provoked a reaction. Robespierre fell, the Convention raised its head, put the Committee in its proper place, exiled or guillotined the leading Terrorists, and recalled to its ranks the survivors of the old Girondin party. But the reaction went still further, and the authority of the Convention was scarcely restored when it was threatened by a formidable royalist rising. It happened that Buonaparte, who had recently proved his skill as an artillery officer at Toulon, was in Paris, and by his guns the Convention and the Republic were maintained (October 5, 1795).

Both, however, were to perish by the sword they had

drawn. The constitution established by the Convention was defective. It was so framed that disputes were bound to occur between the two Legislative Chambers and the five Directors who constituted the executive; and no machinery was provided for settling such disputes. The inevitable soon happened. The royalist reaction persisted, and in the summer of 1797 it was supported by a majority in both Chambers, while four of the five Directors were Jacobins. Buonaparte, meanwhile, had established his military fame by the wonderful campaign in Italy; he had also secured the personal allegiance of his soldiers. He was therefore in a position to act no longer at the bidding of the Government but on his own account, and he dispatched one of his generals to Paris to crush the royalists. His troops surrounded the Chambers, and arrested their reactionary leaders (September 4, 1797), and the *coup d'État* was followed by a new period of terrorism.

The constitution remained unchanged, but the Directory and the Chambers alike were now overshadowed by the informal authority of Buonaparte, with his devoted army in the background. They viewed with relief, therefore, his departure for Egypt in the spring of 1798, but in the autumn of the following year, hearing that the Republic was in difficulties with the Second Coalition, he slipped away from Cairo and returned to Paris to find the Directory and the Chambers once more at open strife. For the third time the course of the Revolution was determined not by the will of the people but by force of arms (November 10, 1798). Each *coup d'État* had marked a stage in the growth of Napoleon's power and prestige, and now at last he was strong enough to grasp the prize he had waited for. The Constitution of 1795 was suspended and a provisional triumvirate of three appointed to prepare a new one. Napoleon contrived that it should leave all real authority in the hands of the triumvirs or Consuls, that of these the First Consul should be indisputably supreme, and that the First Consul should be himself. On December 15, 1799, the new Constitution was promulgated, and Napoleon endorsed it with the declaration that the Revolution was now at an end. It was indeed. The wheel had gone full circle, and in the place of the Bourbon monarchy stood the despotism of Napoleon, without its dignity and old traditions, but with more unlimited authority and with greater military force behind it.

It now only required to give it the outward forms and symbols of monarchy, and to stamp it as the permanent Government of France by making it hereditary. The first youthful glow of revolutionary enthusiasm had been quenched by the prolonged chaos it had created, and the French people, exhausted, bankrupt, disillusioned, were easily reconciled to Napoleon's thinly veiled repudiation of the principles of 1789 by his continued triumphs in the field and his supremely efficient re-organization of the whole structure of the State. Nothing should be denied, they felt, to the only man who can at once win us glory abroad and give us order at home. Thus in May 1802 a *plébiscite* resulted in a proportion of over 100 to 1 in favour of making Buonaparte First Consul for life. Two years later the mask of republican titles was finally discarded when a decree was passed declaring with a significant contradiction of terms that ' The Government of the *Republic* is vested in an *Emperor* who will assume the title of Emperor of the French ', that the Emperor is Napoleon Buonaparte, and that the imperial dignity is hereditary. On December 2, 1804, he was crowned in Notre-Dame.

Napoleon had achieved his ambition. It remained to consolidate his power by the familiar methods of autocracy. He saw clearly enough that his dynasty, however hedged about by bayonets, could not be permanently secure unless it could count in the last issue on the goodwill of the people. The only way to train a whole nation to be loyal was to shape to that end the education of its children. ' The essential thing ', he wrote in 1805, ' is a teaching body . . . like that of the Jesuits of old. . . . Unless men are taught from childhood, as they should be, to be republicans or monarchists, Catholics or infidels, and so forth, the State will never make a nation ; it will rest upon shifting and insecure foundations, and will be for ever exposed to disturbance and change.' He therefore constituted an Imperial University, divided into provincial academies under the control of a Grand Master at Paris appointed by himself. Public teaching was forbidden to any one who did not possess the University degree as the sign-manual of political orthodoxy.

The minds of the children would thus be moulded into allegiance to his name and throne, but it was also desirable to protect their fathers from corruption. At the head of the intellectual hierarchy was the Institute, founded in 1795 as a centre for the encouragement of research and the interchange of ideas. One of its three classes, that of ' moral and political science ', naturally contained men whose minds worked with dangerous freedom on the problems of politics. That class was therefore suppressed in 1803, and in 1807 Napoleon decided that the Institute as a body was as much the agent of the Emperor as his new University. ' The

Introduction

Institute cannot refuse what is asked of it,' he wrote. 'It is bound by the terms of its constitution to respond to any demands made upon it by the Ministry of the Interior.'

There were other hot-beds of ideas that needed careful watching. In 1806 he elaborately regulated in twenty-five areas under a strict censorship all the theatres of the Empire. He had already muzzled the Press. Sixty of the seventy-three newspapers circulating in Paris in 1800 had been abolished; a Press Bureau had been established, and one paper converted into a Government organ. Later on, when public opinion became restive under the appalling bloodshed of unending wars, the whole Press was practically suspended. After September 1811 political news was only published with the Government's consent, and the official bulletins were composed with an eye to the Emperor's prestige rather than the facts.

There was still one thing left. He could seek to secure his own position by indoctrinating loyalty and repressing freedom of thought: he could prove his fitness to rule by the display of an incomparable genius in the arts of war and peace; but how could he ensure the perpetuation of the Empire he had made? He could divorce the devoted Joséphine because she bore him no child; he could marry into the ancient Hapsburg house; he could bid all France rejoice with him on the birth of a son, and hail the infant King of Rome: but how could he make certain that the child should never lose the Imperial purple in which he was born? ' Our fathers had for their rallying-cry,' he said, ' " The King is dead. Long live the King ! " In these words the principal advantages of monarchy are summed up.' But there was no long chain of kings behind the Corsican adventurer and his baby son to make the succession accepted as inevitable. So Napoleon turned, as autocracy always has and always must, to invoke the sanction of a Power whose authority none but the godless could dispute. The man who had professed his sympathy with Islâm in order to smooth the path of conquest in Egypt and the East, did not underestimate the influence of religion or scruple to use it as the ultimate safeguard of his dynasty. He revived the theory of Divine Right in the spirit of a successful gambler who plays the trump-card he has held in reserve. In 1808 he published a declaration in the official newspaper to this effect: 'The first representative of the nation is the Emperor; for all authority is derived from God and the nation.' Only God, he implied, could appoint the true representative of the nation. 'To put the nation itself before the Emperor would be at once chimerical and criminal.' The new catechism for children contained the doctrine that 'to honour our Emperor and to serve him is to honour and serve God Himself'. And of the same significance was his dramatic action at the coronation. The Pope himself had been persuaded to officiate, but, when the supreme moment came, Napoleon gently repelled the Holy Father and placed the crown on his head with his own hands. He received his authority not through God's vicar, but direct from God.

VI

Absolutism was thus revived in France, and absolutism more drastic than that of the Bourbon monarchy. What was its effect on the affairs of Europe and the policy of Pitt?

By the inexorable laws of its being it intensified the forces of disruption and aggrandizement called into play by the crusading spirit of the Revolution. It was by military achievements that 'the popular general' attained the goal of his ambitions. As early as the first *coup d'État* in 1795, he cried, 'My sword is at my side, and with it I will go far!' It was no empty boast. With the sword he carved his way to the throne; but, once on the throne, for the very reason that his sword had set him there, he could not cast it from him or leave it rusting in its sheath. It must be drawn again and again, and used, as only he could use it, to dazzle the popular imagination, to rekindle the cooling ardour of his subjects, to give new proof of his divine prerogative of victory, and above all to provide work, promotion, and plunder for the soldiers on whom his power rested. Thus, as the judgement of war at Marengo confirmed his position as First Consul, so Ulm and Austerlitz set the seal of victory on his assumption of the crown. And, when his prestige began to wane, it was by war and yet more war that he strove to restore it. 'I must have battles and triumphs!' was his motto.

War was required for the preservation of despotism, and the despot was by no means personally averse to it. He recked nothing of the waste of life. 'I can use up twenty-five thousand men a day,' he said, and he bled France white and spread carnage over Europe with a light heart. Nothing gave him more personal happiness than to ride out among his troops to war, and the lust for military glory became his most deep-seated passion. With the name of the loved and discarded Joséphine he murmured on his death-bed his favourite title, 'Tête d'armée'.

Such being the nature of a military despotism and such the nature of this particular despot, there was no hope of peace in Europe. The militant ardour of the Revolution had been fostered by the oligarchs of the

Committee: it was inflamed still further by the autocrat. Worse still, its aim was extended and degraded. Once more the logic of autocracy had its way. Napoleon had become the first man in France, but the craving for power has no limits, and he was not the first man in Europe, as long as the more powerful of his brother monarchs were as planets in the European system, following their own paths, rather than satellites revolving in his orbit. Only if France dominated the other Great Powers, could the master of France be also master of the Continent. Now this involved a decisive change in the motives of the war in which France was engaged. The revolutionary crusaders desired, it is true, to extend the French frontier to the 'natural boundary' of the Alps and the Rhine. They desired, further, to create beyond those limits a defensive girdle of Republics, and to bestow on England and on Italy the gift of French institutions. The more sanguine spirits also dreamed of planting the tree of liberty in the heart of the great central monarchies, but there was as yet no notion of trying to dominate Europe for the sake of domination. That, however, was Napoleon's aim. In 1797 he already pictured the France of the future as '*la grande nation, the arbiter of Europe*'. Some years later he drew the picture on more definite lines. 'European society must be regenerated,' he said; 'a superior power must control the other Powers and compel them to live at peace with each other, and France is well situated for that purpose.' When Italy and the lesser German States lay at his feet, he conceived himself as repeating the part played by the founder of the Holy Roman Empire. 'I have succeeded not to the throne of Louis XIV but to that of Charlemagne.' From ancient Aachen

Introduction

the insignia of the Frankish Emperor were brought to Paris for his coronation, and the Pope of Rome officiated at the crowning of a Caesar as he had 1,004 years before. In 1807 Pius VII protested against the occupation of the Papal States by French troops, and Napoleon sent this message in reply: 'Tell him that I am Charlemagne, the Emperor, and must be treated as such.' But, after Austerlitz had laid Austria and Russia low (December 2, 1805) and revealed the suicidal selfishness of Prussia, his ambitions had already o'ervaulted the old-world limits of the Holy Roman Empire. A few years later he had surrounded France, not by sympathetic Republics, but by States, mostly kingdoms, and ruled by his own relations or retainers. He had made his brother Louis king of Holland and his brother Joseph king of Spain, and he had carved out from the territories of defeated Prussia a new kingdom of Westphalia for his brother Jerome. His ex-marshal, Murat, was king in Naples, and the German States had been welded into a Confederation of the Rhine under his own immediate protection. Setting out on the disastrous Russian campaign of 1812, he boasted that he was 'going to make an end of Europe'. But, if Europe meant a system of independent States, the boast had already been fulfilled.

Nor was that his only boast. The logical process had already advanced, the limits of possible power expanded. France, Europe—why not the world? He had confessed, some years before, that he was weary of old Europe, and now in 1812 he declared that in three years he would be master of the universe. It was not a new idea to him. Side by side with his designs on Europe, he had from the beginning dreamed dreams of vaster conquests. One was the restoration of the old colonial dominion of France beyond the Atlantic, and he had recaptured San Domingo, and purchased Louisiana from Spain. Only fifty years ago Canada had been a French colony, and doubtless he intended one day to recover it. South Africa and Australia would be the natural perquisites of world-mastery, and French geographers, as if in prophecy, named South Australia 'Terre Napoléon' on their map. But the dream which haunted his mind with most persistence, bewitching it with memories of Alexander and the glamour of the East, was that of wresting from England the possession of India. It so happened that recent events—the suicide of Clive, the trial of Warren Hastings, and the lofty appeals which constitute Burke's best service to his country—had awakened in the conscience of England the first uneasy thought, destined to ripen in the course of years to a deep conviction, that the position of India within the bounds of the British Commonwealth did not merely offer England a field of commerce and an opportunity of material enrichment, but laid on her the greatest moral responsibility that any people had ever borne. Of such ideas Napoleon was innocent. He spoke with frank cynicism of his intended seizure of the treasure-house of India as a robbery to be committed 'on robbers less daring than ourselves'.

Now his ambitions both in Europe and the East were confronted by one solid obstacle, the sea-power of England. He might dominate the Continent, but, as long as the British fleet could blockade its ports, cut off its commerce, or convoy hostile forces to unexpected points, his domination was imperfect and precarious. And the same ships, as long as they rode supreme, set an absolute veto on any durable conquests in the East. His career, therefore, was still young when he began to concentrate his mind on the problem of destroying British sea-power and crushing the island State. When he returned to Paris for the *coup d'État* of 1797, Barras, the Director, welcomed him as the conqueror designate of England. 'Go', he said, 'go, capture the giant corsair that infests the seas: go, punish in London outrages that have been too long unpunished.' Napoleon required no invitation. 'Let us concentrate', he wrote to Talleyrand, 'all our activity on our fleet and destroy England. That done, all Europe is at our feet.' Thenceforward England was *the* enemy, and the hope of humbling her the mainspring and final object of his policy, whatever its immediate end. This master motive is everywhere apparent, not only in such direct measures as the strengthening of the French navy, the coalition of allied fleets, the re-organization of Antwerp as a naval base 'to hold a pistol at the heart of England', and the assembly on the Channel coast of the army of invasion, but also in his dealings with foreign Powers. The easy terms, for instance, granted to Austria at the Treaty of Campo Formio (1797) were dictated by the desire of isolating England. The series of conquests, again, which began at Ulm and Austerlitz, had for its primary object the imposition on all Europe of the 'Continental System' designed to starve England into surrender by excluding her merchant ships from every port on the Continent. The same motive dominated his relations with Russia. 'I hate the English as much as you do,' exclaimed the Czar at Tilsit in 1807. 'In that case, peace is made,' Napoleon replied, and by the subsequent treaty Russia was incorporated in the

Continental system. But, when in 1810 the Czar declined to recognize its later and more unscrupulous developments, and refused to confiscate at his ally's request some six hundred neutral merchant-ships, mostly American, then lying in Russian harbours, on the ground that their cargoes were of British origin, Napoleon began at once to meditate war on a monarch whose dislike of England was weaker than his respect for neutral rights, and to plan the ill-starred adventure of 1812.

But nowhere was Napoleon aiming more directly at England than in his Eastern policy. India would not only be a rich prize in itself, but its acquisition would cut off the main current of British trade at its source and dry up the financial springs of British sea-power. A web of French intrigue was therefore spread among the Asiatic chieftains from Cape Comorin to Kabul, and a definite alliance was concluded with Tippoo, the powerful Sultan of Mysore, who was even said to have embraced Republicanism with fervour and to have quaintly added 'Citizen' to his despotic titles. Meanwhile, to get astride the direct route to India, Napoleon planned to invade Egypt, cut a canal through the isthmus of Suez, seize British trading stations on the Red Sea, and join hands in the Indian Ocean with French warships from Réunion and Île de France. 'Egypt once in possession of the French,' he declared at St. Helena, 'farewell India to the English.'

Thus, directly and indirectly, he strove to break the Power which alone persistently obstructed his path to world-dominion. From 1793 to 1815, with one year's interval of unsubstantial peace, France was at war in Europe, and England was the only State which fought against her all those years. The conflict as a whole,

Introduction xlv

indeed, was a duel to the death between those two protagonists : on the one side the British spirit of independence, with Pitt, the peace-lover, as its interpreter; on the other, the revolutionary spirit of aggrandizement, soon absorbed, intensified, and guided by the personality of Napoleon. He was himself quick to recognize the inherent singleness of the combat. 'England', he said, 'is everywhere, and the struggle is between her and me. The whole of Europe will be our instruments, sometimes serving one, sometimes the other.' To come to terms with England was to resign for ever his ambitions in Europe and beyond it; and as year by year she still defied him from across the narrow seas, his hatred of her grew. No abuse became too coarse to hurl at the piratic mistress of the ocean. 'All the ills and curses', he cried, ' which can afflict mankind come from London.' And the fate he had in store for her, if only he could break down her iron guard, is evident enough from his regretful retrospect—' England would finally have been no more than an appendage to my France.'

Only once before had England faced so great a danger, when despotism in the person of Philip of Spain had launched against her its invincible armada, to be thwarted and harried by Drake and his seamen, and scattered by the winds of heaven. In the presence of this second crisis she was bound to show the same resolute front. If the necessity of resisting the revolutionary crusade was clear to Pitt, the necessity of resisting Napoleon was clearer still. The issues were the same, but now every argument was underlined. He still fought for honour, but now the very conception of international right and public faith was openly derided; for Napoleon looked on treaties as scraps of paper to be thrown aside as soon as they had served his ends. He still fought to preserve 'the political system of Europe' from the wilful interference of a single Power, but now Napoleon had frankly envisaged his *grande nation* as the mistress of the Continent. He still fought to maintain the independence of small States, but now Belgium was annexed and Napoleon boasted, and not idly, that 'it is recognized in Europe that Italy, Holland, and Switzerland are at the disposal of France.' He still fought, lastly, in self-defence, but Napoleon's legions gathered at Boulogne were far more real a menace than the threats and taunts of the Girondin leaders.

All these issues, thus clarified and deepened as Napoleon's power grew, cannot be better summarized from first to last than they were by Pitt himself. He was once challenged to state in a sentence his motives for continuing the struggle. His answer was a single word, 'Security.'[1] Security for Europe from the aggressions of a self-appointed arbiter; security for England from the attack, which, since only by the downfall of England could he realize his full ambition, the self-appointed arbiter was sooner or later bound to make—this was Pitt's unchanging aim; and, after Pitt was dead, but owing in no small degree to his energy and courage throughout the first critical phases of the war, to the direct and confident appeal by which he roused and braced British patriotism, and to the great example he gave of it himself, this aim was eventually attained.

VII

A hundred years passed, and men believed that Caesarism had died for ever with Napoleon. To those who marked the general progress of civilization in the nineteenth

[1] p. 285.

century it seemed as if swords had indeed been beaten into ploughshares and industrial machines; as if the dawn of a perpetual peace might not be far away. The rise of democracy, the growing concentration on domestic problems, the spread of humanitarian ideas, the deepening respect for nationality, the increasing intellectual, scientific, and commercial interdependence of nations, the elaboration of the system of international use and wont, the development of arbitration as a preventive of war, and the establishment of a court to which interstate disputes could be referred—all those symptoms of a wiser and kindlier age made it almost inconceivable that any European Government of 'light and leading' could let itself be dazzled by the old Napoleonic dream, or think for a moment of renewing the wars of aggrandizement which once devastated Europe. And yet, when the century was just at its end, the theocratic monarch and the military caste, who now unhappily control the destinies of the German people, revealed to an astonished world that they not only cherished the insensate ideas of Caesarism, but had deliberately planned to put them into execution.

The terrible results need no retelling here. Enough to say that England is again involved in war against a Power that strives to dominate the world. Again she fights for honour, for the preservation of the political system and public rights of Europe, for the independence of small States, and for her own protection. Again the issues can be summed up in the single word, Security. And again, as in 1812, Russia is putting forth her massive strength to defend the idea of nationality. But the happiest point in the present situation is where the analogy breaks down. Pitt's vision is at last fulfilled, and the French people, having learnt the real lesson of the Revolution and won by gradual stages the internal liberty of France, are mustered side by side with the British people to vindicate the liberty of Europe.

But in innumerable other points the analogy between the two wars is strangely exact, from the great questions of the causes and the issues down to the very phrases on the lips of the combatants. And is it, after all, so strange? Military despotism has always pursued the same path. By the logic of its nature, the only limits it accepts to its dominion, save those imposed by the measure of its own human power and the strength of the opposition it arouses, are the limits of the known world. By a similar necessity, whenever in modern history military despotism has threatened the security of Europe, in the days of Philip II or Louis XIV or Napoleon, the sea-power of England has proved its most formidable obstacle, and it has looked on England, therefore, as its most detested foe.

It is written that on each occasion England saved herself and helped to save Europe. It is a great tradition; and she is called on to maintain it to-day more urgently than ever before. It can only be maintained by the same stubborn patriotism which made and kept it in the past—a patriotism which endures to the end just because it has the tradition behind it and knows the cause for which it stands. There is no nobler figure in the tradition, no clearer exponent of the cause, than William Pitt: and it is in the hope of renewing his appeal to the hearts and minds of his countrymen and recalling his example to their memories that the following selection of his speeches has been prepared for publication.

PRELUDE

1783-1793

I

The Fruits of the American War
February 21, 1783 [1]

THE Ministry of Lord Shelburne, in which Pitt held office for the first time, as Chancellor of the Exchequer, concluded on November 30, 1782, a provisional treaty of peace with the United States. On January 20, 1783, preliminary articles of peace were signed with France, Spain, and Holland. On February 17 the two treaties were attacked by the Opposition in the House of Commons, and a hostile amendment to the address was carried by 224 votes to 208. Four days later, resolutions were moved, affirming that the treaties must be confirmed 'in consideration of the public faith', but protesting 'that the concessions made to the adversaries of Great Britain by the said Provisional Treaty and Preliminary Articles, are greater than they were entitled to, either from the actual situation of their respective possessions or from their comparative strength'.

After Fox had supported the resolutions, Pitt replied on behalf of the Government. He reprobated a policy which threatened 'to plunge this devoted country into

---
[1] *Speeches*, vol. i, p. 50.

all the horrors of another war', and declared that the terms of peace were justified by a consideration of 'the relative strength and resources of the persons at war'. Great Britain was, he argued, too much weakened by the war to obtain better terms. It had to be confessed that 'the fabric of our naval superiority' was 'visionary and baseless'. To continue the war by sea against far stronger fleets would be to risk an irreparable disaster. And the military position was equally desperate. 'It is notorious', he said, 'to every gentleman who hears me, that new levies could scarcely be torn, on any terms, from this depopulated country.' Lastly, he informed the House that the unfunded debt amounted at that instant to no less than thirty millions.[1] On the idleness, under those circumstances, of holding out for better terms, he spoke as follows:

Could the ministers, thus surrounded with scenes of ruin, affect to dictate the terms of peace? And are these articles seriously compared with the Peace of Paris?[2] There was, indeed, a time when Great Britain might have met her enemies on other conditions; and if an imagination, warmed with the power and glory of this country, could have diverted any member of His Majesty's councils from a painful inspection of the truth, I might, I hope, without presumption, have been entitled to that indulgence. I feel, Sir, at this instant, how much I had been animated in my childhood by a recital of

[1] The amount of funded debt in 1782-3 was over two hundred millions.
[2] The Peace of Paris (1763) had closed the Seven Years' War, in which, mainly through the policy of Chatham, father of the Younger Pitt, Great Britain had won Canada, broken the French power in India, and established her command of the sea.

England's victories. I was taught, Sir, by one whose memory I shall ever revere, that at the close of a war, far different indeed from this, she had dictated the terms of peace to submissive nations. This, in which I place something more than a common interest, was the memorable era of England's glory. But that era is past: she is under the awful and mortifying necessity of employing a language that corresponds with her true condition: the visions of her power and pre-eminence are passed away.

We have acknowledged American independence—that, Sir, was a needless form: the incapacity of the noble lord who conducted our affairs,[1] the events of war, and even a vote of this House, had already granted what it was impossible to withhold.

We have ceded Florida—We have obtained Providence and the Bahama Islands.

We have ceded an extent of fishery on the coast of Newfoundland—We have established an exclusive right to the most valuable banks.

We have restored St. Lucia and given up Tobago—We have regained Grenada, Dominica, St. Kitts, Nevis, and Montserrat, and we have rescued Jamaica from her impending danger. In Africa we have ceded Goree, the grave of our countrymen; and we possess Senegambia, the best and most healthy settlement.

In Europe we have relinquished Minorca—kept up at an immense and useless expense in peace, and never tenable in war.

We have likewise permitted his most Christian Majesty[2]

---

[1] Lord North.   [2] The King of France.

to repair his harbour of Dunkirk—The humiliating clause for its destruction was inserted, Sir, after other wars than the past. But the immense expense attending its repair will still render this indulgence useless. Add to this, that Dunkirk was first an object of our jealousy when ships were constructed far inferior to their present draught. That harbour, at the commencement of the war, admitted ships of a single deck; no art or expense will enable it to receive a fleet of the line.

In the East Indies, where alone we had power to obtain this peace, we have restored what was useless to ourselves, and scarcely tenable in a continuance of the war.

But we have abandoned the unhappy loyalists[1] *to their implacable enemies*—Little, Sir, are those unhappy men befriended by such a language in this House; nor shall we give much assistance to their cause, or add stability to the reciprocal confidence of the two States, if we already impute to Congress a violence and injustice which decency forbids us to suspect. Would a continuation of the war have been justified on the single principle of assisting these unfortunate men? Or would a continuance of the war, if so justified, have procured them a more certain indemnity? Their hopes must have been rendered desperate indeed by any additional distresses of Britain—those hopes which are now revived by the timely aid of peace and reconciliation.

These are the ruinous conditions to which this country, engaged with four powerful States[2] and exhausted in all

[1] The American colonists who had retained their allegiance to the British Crown during the War of Independence.
[2] France, Spain, Holland, and the United States.

its resources, thought fit to subscribe, for the dissolution of that alliance and the immediate enjoyment of peace. Let us examine what is left, with a manly and determined courage. Let us strengthen ourselves against inveterate enemies, and reconciliate our ancient friends. The misfortunes of individuals and of kingdoms, that are laid open and examined with true wisdom, are more than half redressed; and to this great object should be directed all the virtue and abilities of this House. Let us feel our calamities—let us bear them too, like men.

Pitt proceeded to argue that, since the concessions made by Government were obviously dictated by necessity, it was not so much to censure the terms of the treaties that the resolutions had been moved as by driving the Shelburne Ministry from office to make way for an impending coalition of Fox and North. In a famous passage he denounced a union so unnatural. 'If the baneful alliance', he said, 'is not already formed, if this ill-omened marriage is not already solemnized, I know a just and lawful impediment, and, in the name of the public safety, I here forbid the banns.' He went on to disclaim for himself and the Ministry to which he belonged any share of responsibility for reducing the country to a position which rendered inevitable the acceptance of a humiliating peace. The responsibility lay entirely with Lord North.

In short, Sir, whatever appears dishonourable or inadequate in the peace on your table, is strictly chargeable to the noble lord in the blue ribbon, whose profusion of the public's money, whose notorious temerity and obstinacy in prosecuting the war, which originated in his pernicious and oppressive policy, and whose utter incapacity to fill the station he occupied, rendered peace of any description indispensable to the preservation of the State. The small part, which fell to my share in this ignominious transaction, was divided with a set of men, whom the dispassionate public must, on reflection, unite to honour. Unused as I am to the factious and jarring clamours of this day's debate, I look up to the independent part of the House, and to the public at large, if not for that impartial approbation which my conduct deserves, at least for that acquittal from blame to which my innocence entitles me. I have ever been most anxious to do my utmost for the interest of my country; it has been my sole concern to act an honest and upright part, and I am disposed to think every instance of my official department will bear a fair and honourable construction. With these intentions, I ventured forward on the public attention; and can appeal with some degree of confidence to both sides of the House, for the consistency of my political conduct. My earliest impressions were in favour of the noblest and most disinterested modes of serving the public: these impressions are still dear, and will, I hope, remain for ever dear to my heart: I will cherish them as a legacy infinitely more valuable than the greatest inheritance. On these principles alone I came into Parliament and into place; and I now take the whole House to witness, that I have not been under the necessity of contradicting one public declaration I have ever made.

I am, notwithstanding, at the disposal of this House, and with their decision, whatever it shall be, I will cheerfully comply. It is impossible to deprive me of those feelings which must always result from the sincerity of my best endeavours to fulfil with integrity every official engagement. You may take from me, Sir, the privileges and emoluments of place, but you cannot, and you shall not, take from me those habitual and warm regards for the prosperity of Great Britain which constitute the honour, the happiness, the pride of my life, and which, I trust, death alone can extinguish. And, with this consolation, the loss of power, Sir, and the loss of fortune, though I affect not to despise them, I hope I soon shall be able to forget:

*Laudo manentem; si celeres quatit
Pennas, resigno quae dedit—
——————————— probamque
Pauperiem sine dote quaero.*[1]

The first three resolutions, which contained no direct criticism of the Government, were agreed to without a division. The fourth, which condemned the concessions, was carried by 207 to 190. A vote of censure had thus been supported by a majority of 17. A few weeks later Shelburne resigned, and was succeeded by Portland, with Fox and North as his Secretaries of State.

---

[1] Horace, *Odes*, iii. 29. Pitt modestly omitted the words 'et mea Virtute me involvo'.—'If Fortune stays with me, I praise her. If she shakes her swift wings for flight, I resign the gifts she gave: (I wrap myself in my own virtue) and look for naught but honest undowered poverty.'

2

The Commercial Treaty with France
February 12, 1787[1]

THE Coalition Government was short-lived. On December 17, 1783, the India Bill was thrown out by the House of Lords, and the King proceeded to dismiss the Ministry. On the 19th he appointed Pitt First Lord of the Treasury and Chancellor of the Exchequer. The task which occupied his first nine years of power was that of restoring the strength and the prestige of England, so disastrously impaired by 'the shame and affliction' (as he called it) of the American War. His efforts could only be successful if peace were maintained for a considerable period of years. To this end, therefore, Pitt strove to break down the isolation in which Great Britain found herself at the close of the war, and by means of alliances to restore the balance of power in Europe. In pursuance of this policy he attempted to reconcile the old feud with France, and in 1786 he negotiated an Anglo-French commercial treaty, which not only promised material advantages by the establishment of a relatively free trade between the two countries, but also opened the way to a political *entente* which would provide the surest guarantee of European peace.[2]

On February 12, 1787, the House of Commons resolved itself into a committee to consider the section of the King's Speech which referred to the Commercial Treaty. Pitt, who opened the debate, devoted the first part of his speech to an exposition of the commercial aspects of the treaty. Passing to its political aspects, he questioned the existence of any fixed and eternal barrier between

---

[1] *Speeches*, vol. i, p. 344. [2] Introduction, pp. xii–xiii.

the two countries 'which must prevent them from ever forming any connexion or cherishing any species of amity'.

Considering the treaty in its political view, he should not hesitate to contend against the too-frequently advanced doctrine, that France was, and must be, the unalterable enemy of Britain. His mind revolted from this position as monstrous and impossible. To suppose that any nation could be unalterably the enemy of another, was weak and childish. It had neither its foundation in the experience of nations, nor in the history of man. It was a libel on the constitution of political societies, and supposed the existence of diabolical malice in the original frame of man.

But these absurd tenets were taken up and propagated; nay, it was carried farther; it was said, that, by this treaty, the British nation was about blindly to throw itself into the arms of this constant and uniform foe. Men reasoned as if this treaty was not only to extinguish all jealousy from our bosoms, but also completely to annihilate our means of defence; as if by the treaty we gave up so much of our army, so much of our marine; as if our commerce was to be abridged, our navigation to be lessened, our colonies to be cut off or to be rendered defenceless, and as if all the functions of the State were to be sunk in apathy. What ground was there for this train of reasoning? Did the treaty suppose that the interval of peace between the two countries would be so totally unemployed by us as to disable us from meeting France in the moment of war with our accustomed strength? Did it not much rather, by opening new sources of wealth, speak this forcible language—that the interval of peace, as it would enrich the nation, would also prove the means of enabling her to combat her enemy with more effect when the day of hostility should come ?

It did more than this. By promoting habits of friendly intercourse and of mutual benefit, while it invigorated the resources of Britain, it made it less likely that she should have occasion to call forth those resources. It certainly had at least the happy tendency to make the two nations enter into more intimate communion with one another, to enter into the same views even of taste and manners; and while they were mutually benefited by the connexion, and endeared to one another by the result of the common benefits, it gave a better chance for the preservation of harmony between them, while, so far from weakening, it strengthened their sinews for war. That we should not be taken unprepared for war was a matter totally distinct from treaty. It depended in no degree on that circumstance, but simply and totally on the watchfulness and ability of the administration for the time being. He had heard of the invariable character of the French nation and of the French Cabinet; her restless ambition and her incessant enmity and designs against Britain; and he noticed the particular instance of her interference in our late disputes, and of the result of her attack at that time. That France had, in that instant of our distress, interfered to crush us, was a truth over which he did not desire to throw even the slightest veil.

Having premised that the provisions of the treaty would neither delude us into security, nor accomplish our reduction; that, on the contrary, it would strengthen our hands, and, whilst it did not diminish our means, would throw the prospect and the necessity of war at a very great distance: friendly assurances, he added, were not always to be relied on; but, although he thought France the aggressor in most of our former wars, yet, her assurances and frankness during the present negotiation were such as, in his opinion, might be confided in. What might be the projects which wild ambition might one day dictate, was beyond his penetration; but, at present, the Court of France was governed by maxims too prudent and political, not to consult its own safety and happiness beyond the ministerial aims of impracticable conquest. Oppressed as this nation was during the last war, by the most formidable combination for its destruction, yet had France very little to boast at the end of the contest, which should induce her again to enter deliberately into hostilities against this country. In spite of our misfortunes, our resistance must be admired, and in our defeats we gave proofs of our greatness and almost inexhaustible resources, which, perhaps, success would never show us—

> *Duris ut ilex tonsa bipennibus*
> *Nigrae feraci frondis in Algido,*
> *Per damna, per caedes, ab ipso*
> *Ducit opes animumque ferro.*[1]

Indeed, whilst he recollected the whole of that dreadful

---

[1] Horace, *Odes*, iv. 4. 'Like an oak shorn by the stubborn axe in the dark leafy woods of Algidus, so, through death and disaster, it wins from the sword itself new strength and a new soul.'

controversy, he could deduce arguments from it to reconcile the present conduct of France with more equitable and more candid principles of policy than gentlemen seemed willing to attribute to our rival. When France perceived that, in that dreadful contest, when with the enormous combination of power against us it might be truly said that we were struggling for our existence, we not only saved our honour, but manifested the solid, and, he might also be tempted to say, the inexhaustible resources of the land; reflecting that, though she had gained her object in dismembering our empire, she had done it at an expense which had sunk herself in extreme embarrassment; and reflecting also, that such a combination of hostile power against us, without a single friend in Europe on our side, can never be imagined again to exist; may I not (exclaimed Mr. Pitt) be led to cherish the idea, that, seeing the durable and steady character of our strength, and the inefficacy as well as the ruin of hostility, France would eagerly wish to try the benefits of an amicable connexion with us?

It was a singular line of argument which he had heard and which he saw was also propagated out of doors, that the treaty would prove objectionable, if it should be found that, though advantageous to ourselves, it would be equally so to them. It was ridiculous to imagine that the French would consent to yield advantages without an idea of return. The treaty would be of benefit to them; but he did not hesitate to pronounce his firm opinion, even in the eyes of France, and pending the business, that though advantageous to her, it would be more so to us.

France and Britain complementary

Pitt proceeded to argue that the balance of gain would be on the side of England, because she would obtain a new market of twenty-four millions of people, and France a new market of only eight millions. He continued:

In this view, then, though France might gain, we must be, comparatively, so much more benefited, that we ought not to scruple to give her the advantages: and surely ought not to fear that this very disproportionate gain could be injurious to us in case of a future contest. It was in the nature and essence of an agreement between a manufacturing country and a country blessed with peculiar productions, that the advantages must terminate in favour of the former; but it was particularly disposed and fitted for both the connexions. Thus France was, by the peculiar dispensation of Providence, gifted, perhaps more than any other country upon earth, with what made life desirable in point of soil, climate, and natural productions. It had the most fertile vineyards and the richest harvests; the greatest luxuries of man were produced in it with little cost and with moderate labour. Britain was not thus blest by nature; but, on the contrary, it possessed, through the happy freedom of its constitution and the equal security of its laws, an energy in its enterprise and a stability in its exertions, which had gradually raised it to a state of commercial grandeur; and, not being so bountifully gifted by Heaven, it had recourse to labour and art, by which it had acquired the ability of supplying its neighbour with all the necessary embellishments of life in exchange for her natural luxuries. Thus standing with regard to each other, a friendly connexion seemed to be pointed out between them, instead of the state of unalterable enmity, which was falsely said to be their true political feeling towards one another.

At the conclusion of the speech, Pitt moved his first resolution. A motion by the Opposition, 'That the Chairman do leave the chair, &c.,' was defeated by 252 to 118; and the main question was then put and carried.

The treaty, which had been signed at Versailles on September 26, 1786, was now ratified in due course, and came into operation on May 10, 1787.

3

The Prosperity of the Nation
February 17, 1792 [1]

PITT's successful restoration of the national finances during his first nine years of government is one of his chief titles to fame.[2] The primary condition of this achievement had been the maintenance of peace, and, if only the ruinous sacrifices entailed by war could be avoided for a few more years, the recovery of national prosperity promised to be final and complete. At the beginning of 1792, Pitt was sanguine enough to believe that there was little prospect in the near future of another European conflict in which Great Britain would be involved, and he based his financial plans for the immediate future on the expectation that the peace would be still unbroken for fifteen years to come.

On February 17, the House of Commons resolved itself into Committee to consider the financial paragraphs of the King's speech, and Pitt rose to explain his Budget proposals. He dealt first with the revenue of the preceding year, and showed that it had exceeded by over half a million the average yield of the last four years: but he cautiously based his estimate of revenue for 1792, not on the high total of 1791, but on a four-years average. Nevertheless, after making a slight reduction in expenditure on the navy and the army—a proof in itself of his firm belief in a continued peace—he proposed in the coming year to reduce taxation to the extent of £200,000, certain permanent taxes being remitted which had pressed hardly on the poorer classes,

---
[1] *Speeches*, vol. ii, p. 24.
[2] Introduction, p. x.

and to allot £400,000 for the repeal of the temporary extra-duty on malt and for the reduction of the national debt. He further declared his intention of paying £200,000 in any future year into the Sinking Fund, which would thus, at the end of fifteen years, yield an annual amount of £4,000,000, the sum at which the limits of the Fund had originally been fixed. On this point he spoke as follows :

The material question which on these suppositions it is natural to ask is, When will the Sinking Fund arise to the amount of £4,000,000 per annum, which is the limit after which, according to the Act of 1786, it is no longer to accumulate, but the interest of the capital, which it thenceforth may redeem, is to be left open for the disposition of Parliament ? It will amount to that sum, on the suppositions which I have stated, in 1808, a period of about fifteen years from the present time.

I am not, indeed, presumptuous enough to suppose that, when I name fifteen years, I am not naming a period in which events may arise which human foresight cannot reach and which may baffle all our conjectures. We must not count with certainty on a continuance of our present prosperity during such an interval; but unquestionably there never was a time in the history of this country when, from the situation of Europe, we might more reasonably expect fifteen years of peace, than we may at the present moment.

Having completed his exposition of the Budget, Pitt passed to wider considerations. He showed that the increase in revenue had been accompanied by a proportionate increase in trade and industry. The growth of national prosperity had been general. 'What', he went on to inquire, 'have been the peculiar circumstances to which these efforts are to be ascribed?'

The first and most obvious answer which every man's mind will suggest to this question, is, that it arises from the natural industry and energy of the country: but what is it which has enabled that industry and energy to act with such peculiar vigour, and so far beyond the example of former periods? The improvement which has been made in the mode of carrying on almost every branch of manufacture, and the degree to which labour has been abridged, by the invention and application of machinery, have undoubtedly had a considerable share in producing such important effects. We have besides seen during these periods, more than at any former time, the effect of one circumstance which has principally tended to raise this country to its mercantile pre-eminence —I mean that peculiar degree of credit which, by a twofold operation, at once gives additional facility and extent to the transactions of our merchants at home, and enables them to obtain a proportional superiority in markets abroad. This advantage has been most conspicuous during the latter part of the period to which I have referred; and it is constantly increasing, in proportion to the prosperity which it contributes to create.

In addition to all this, the exploring and enterprising spirit of our merchants has been seen in the extension of our navigation and our fisheries, and the acquisition of new markets in different parts of the world; and undoubtedly those efforts have been not a little assisted by the additional intercourse with France in consequence of the commercial treaty; an intercourse which, though probably checked and abated by the distractions now prevailing in that kingdom, has furnished a great additional incitement to industry and exertion.

But there is still another cause, even more satisfactory than these, because it is of a still more extensive and permanent nature; that constant accumulation of capital, that continual tendency to increase, the operation of which is universally seen in a greater or less proportion, whenever it is not obstructed by some public calamity, or by some mistaken and mischievous policy, but which must be conspicuous and rapid indeed in any country which has once arrived at an advanced state of commercial prosperity. Simple and obvious as this principle is, and felt and observed as it must have been in a greater or less degree, even from the earliest periods, I doubt whether it has ever been fully developed and sufficiently explained but in the writings of an author of our own times, now unfortunately no more—I mean the author of a celebrated treatise on the Wealth of Nations—whose extensive knowledge of detail and depth of philosophical research will, I believe, furnish the best solution to every question connected with the history of commerce or with the systems of political economy. This accumulation of capital arises from the continual application of a part, at least, of the profit obtained in each year, to increase the total amount of capital to be employed in a similar manner, and with continued profit in the year following. The great mass of the property of the nation is thus constantly increasing at compound interest; the progress of which, in any considerable period, is what at first view would appear incredible. Great as have been the effects of this cause already, they must be greater in future; for its powers are augmented in proportion as they are exerted. It acts with a velocity continually accelerated, with a force continually increased:

Mobilitate viget, viresque acquirit eundo.[1]

It may indeed, as we have ourselves experienced, be checked or retarded by particular circumstances—it may for a time be interrupted, or even overpowered; but, where there is a fund of productive labour and active industry, it can never be totally extinguished. In the season of the severest calamity and distress, its operations will still counteract and diminish their effects; in the first returning interval of prosperity, it will be active to repair them. If we look to a period like the present, of continued tranquillity, the difficulty will be to imagine limits to its operation. None can be found, while there exists at home any one object of skill or industry short of its utmost possible perfection; one spot of ground in the country capable of higher cultivation and improvement; or while there remains abroad any new market that can be explored, or any existing market that can be extended. From the intercourse of commerce, it will in some measure participate in the growth of other nations, in all the possible varieties of their situations. The rude wants of countries emerging from barbarism and the artificial and increasing demands of luxury and refine-

[1] Virgil, *Aeneid*, iv. 175. 'It is nourished by movement, and gathers strength with every step.'

ment will equally open new sources of treasure and new fields of exertion, in every state of society and in the remotest quarters of the globe. It is this principle which, I believe, according to the uniform result of history and experience, maintains on the whole, in spite of the vicissitudes of fortune and the disasters of empires, a continued course of successive improvement in the general order of the world.

Such are the circumstances which appear to me to have contributed most immediately to our present prosperity. But these again are connected with others yet more important.

They are obviously and necessarily connected with the duration of peace, the continuance of which, on a secure and permanent footing, must ever be the first object of the foreign policy of this country. They are connected still more with its internal tranquillity and with the natural effects of a free but well-regulated Government.

What is it which has produced, in the last hundred years, so rapid an advance, beyond what can be traced in any other period of our history? What but that, during that time, under the mild and just government of the illustrious princes of the family now on the throne, a general calm has prevailed through the country, beyond what was ever before experienced; and we have also enjoyed, in greater purity and perfection, the benefit of those original principles of our constitution, which were ascertained and established by the memorable events that closed the century preceding? This is the great and governing cause, the operation of which has given scope to all the other circumstances which I have enumerated.

It is this union of liberty with law, which, by raising a barrier equally firm against the encroachments of power, and the violence of popular commotion, affords to property its just security, produces the exertion of genius and labour, the extent and solidity of credit, the circulation and increase of capital; which forms and upholds the national character, and sets in motion all the springs which actuate the great mass of the community through all its various descriptions.

The laborious industry of those useful and extensive classes (who will, I trust, be in a peculiar degree this day the object of the consideration of the House) the peasantry and yeomanry of the country; the skill and ingenuity of the artificer; the experiments and improvements of the wealthy proprietor of land; the bold speculations and successful adventures of the opulent merchant and enterprising manufacturer; these are all to be traced to the same source, and all derive from hence both their encouragement and their reward. On this point, therefore, let us principally fix our attention. Let us preserve this first and most essential object, and every other is in our power! . Let us remember, that the love of the constitution, though it acts as a sort of natural instinct in the hearts of Englishmen, is strengthened by reason and reflection, and every day confirmed by experience; that it is a constitution which we do not merely admire from traditional reverence, which we do not flatter from prejudice or habit, but which we cherish and value, because we know that it practically secures the tranquillity and welfare both of individuals and of the public, and provides, beyond any other frame of government which has ever existed, for the real and useful ends which form at once the only true foundation and only rational object of all political societies.

I have now nearly closed all the considerations which I think it necessary to offer to the committee. I have endeavoured to give a distinct view of the surplus arising on the comparison of the permanent income (computed on the average which I have stated) with what may be expected to be the permanent expenditure in time of peace, and I have also stated the comparison of the supply, and of the ways and means of this particular year. I have pointed out the leading and principal articles of revenue in which the augmentation has taken place, and the corresponding increase in the trade and manufactures of the country; and finally, I have attempted to trace these effects to their causes, and to explain the principles which appear to account for the striking and favourable change in our general situation. From the result of the whole, I trust I am entitled to conclude, that the scene which we are now contemplating is not the transient effect of accident, not the short-lived prosperity of a day, but the genuine and natural result of regular and permanent causes. The season of our severe trial is at an end, and we are at length relieved, not only from the dejection and gloom which, a few years since, hung over the country, but from the doubt and uncertainty which, even for a considerable time after our prospect had begun to brighten, still mingled with the hopes and expectations of the public. We may yet indeed be subject to those fluctuations which often happen in the affairs of a great nation and which it is impossible to calculate or foresee ; but as far as there can be any reliance on human speculations, we have the best ground, from the experience of the past, to look with satisfaction to the present and with confidence to the future. '*Nunc demum redit animus, cum non spem modo ac votum securitas publica, sed ipsius voti fiduciam et robur assumpserit.*'[1] This is a state not of hope only, but of attainment ; not barely the encouraging prospect of future advantage, but the solid and immediate benefit of present and actual possession.

The financial resolutions were carried without a division. But the hopes of peace, on which the full fruition of Pitt's policy depended, were not to be fulfilled.

---

[1] Tacitus, *Agricola*, 3. 'Now, at last, our spirit is reviving, since the safety of the people is no longer merely the object of our hopes and prayers, but has been itself attained with all the certainty and strength we prayed for.'

THE WAR: FIRST PHASE
1793-1797

I

French Ambitions and the Liberty of Europe
February 1, 1793 [1]

DEVELOPMENTS in France soon dimmed and finally extinguished the hopes of peace expressed by Pitt in the speeches of February 12, 1787, and February 17, 1792. They reached their culminating point in the French decree of December 15, 1792.[2] Unless the Republic were willing to withdraw from the position then taken up, war with Great Britain—to Pitt's mind at any rate—was sooner or later inevitable. Thus the execution of Louis XVI on January 21, 1793, was not the cause of the war. It was, in effect, its declaration; the flinging down, in Danton's phrase, of the gage of battle.

On February 1, the House of Commons considered the following message from the King:

'GEORGE R.

'His Majesty has given directions for laying before the House of Commons, copies of several papers which have been received from M. Chauvelin, late minister plenipotentiary from the Most Christian King, by His Majesty's Secretary of State for Foreign Affairs,[3] and of the answers

---
[1] *Speeches*, vol. ii, p. 93.
[2] See Introduction, p. xxi, and *infra*, pp. 37, 40-43, &c.
[3] Lord Grenville,

returned thereto; and likewise a copy of an Order made by His Majesty in Council, and transmitted by His Majesty's commands to the said M. Chauvelin, in consequence of the accounts of the atrocious act recently perpetrated at Paris.

'In the present situation of affairs, His Majesty thinks it indispensably necessary to make a further augmentation of his forces by sea and land; and relies on the known affection and zeal of the House of Commons to enable His Majesty to take the most effectual measures, in the present important conjuncture, for maintaining the security and rights of his own dominions; for supporting his allies; and for opposing views of aggrandizement and ambition on the part of France, which would be at all times dangerous to the general interests of Europe, but are peculiarly so, when connected with the propagation of principles, which lead to the violation of the most sacred duties and are utterly subversive of the peace and order of all civil society.

'G. R.'

The Speaker having read the message, Pitt rose.

Sir,—I shall now submit to the House some observations on the many important objects which arise out of the communication of His Majesty's message and out of the present situation of this country. And in proceeding to the consideration of that message, the attention of the House should, in the first instance, be strongly directed to that calamitous event, to that dreadful outrage against every principle of religion, of justice, and of humanity, which has created one general sentiment of indignation and abhorrence in every part of this island, and most undoubtedly has produced the same effect in every civilized country.

At the same time I am aware, that I should better consult not only my own feelings, but those of the House, if considerations of duty would permit me to draw a veil over the whole of this transaction, because it is, in fact, in itself, in all those circumstances which led to it, in all that attended it, and in all which have followed, or which are likely to follow it hereafter, so full of every subject of grief and horror, that it is painful for the mind to dwell upon it. It is a subject which, for the honour of human nature, it would be better, if possible, to dismiss from our memories, to expunge from the page of history, and to conceal it, both now and hereafter, from the observation of the world.

> *Excidat ille dies aevo, neu postera credant*
> *Secula; nos certe taceamus, et obruta multa*
> *Nocte tegi nostrae patiamur crimina gentis.*[1]

These, Sir, are the words of a great historian of France in a former period, and were applied to an occasion which has always been considered as an eternal reproach to the French nation:[2] and the atrocious acts lately perpetrated at Paris are, perhaps, the only instances that furnish any match to that dreadful and complicated scene of proscription and blood. But whatever may be our feelings on this subject, since, alas! it is not possible

---

[1] Statius, *Silvae*, v. 2. 88. 'Let that day be blotted out of Time, and let not after ages believe the story. Let us at least be silent and suffer the sins of our race to be hid and buried deep in night.'

[2] Applied by De Thou to the Massacre of St. Bartholomew.

that the present age should not be contaminated with its guilt; since it is not possible that the knowledge of it should not be conveyed by the breath of tradition to posterity, there is a duty which we are called upon to perform—to enter our solemn protestation, that, on every principle by which men of justice and honour are actuated, it is the foulest and most atrocious deed which the history of the world has yet had occasion to attest.

There is another duty immediately relating to the interest of this and of every other country. Painful as it is to dwell upon this deed, since we cannot conceal what has happened, either from the view of the present age or of posterity, let us not deprive this nation of the benefit that may be derived from reflecting on some of the dreadful effects of those principles which are entertained and propagated with so much care and industry by a neighbouring country. We see in this one instance concentrated together the effect of principles, which originally rest upon grounds that dissolve whatever has hitherto received the best sanctions of human legislation, which are contrary to every principle of law, human and divine. Presumptuously relying on their deceitful and destructive theories, they have rejected every benefit which the world has hitherto received from the effect either of reason, experience, or even of Revelation itself. The consequences of these principles have been illustrated by having been carried into effect in the single person of one whom every human being commiserates. Their consequences equally tend to shake the security of commerce, to rob the meanest individual in every country of whatever is most dear and valuable to him.

They strike directly against the authority of all regular government and the inviolable personal situation of every lawful sovereign. I do feel it, therefore, not merely a tribute due to humanity, not merely an effusion of those feelings which I possess in common with every man in this country, but I hold it to be a proper subject of reflection to fix our minds on the effect of those principles which have been thus dreadfully attested, before we proceed to consider of the measures which it becomes this country to adopt, in order to avert their contagion and to prevent their growth and progress in Europe.

However, notwithstanding that I feel strongly on this subject, I would, if possible, entreat of the House to consider even that calamitous event rather as a subject of reason and reflection than of sentiment and feeling. Sentiment is often unavailing, but reason and reflection will lead to that knowledge which is necessary to the salvation of this and of all other countries. I am persuaded the House will not feel this as a circumstance which they are to take upon themselves, but that they will feel it in the manner in which I state it, as a proof of the calamities arising out of the most abominable and detestable principles; as a proof of the absence of all morals, of all justice, of all humanity, and of every principle which does honour to human nature; and, that it furnishes the strongest demonstration of the dreadful outrage which the crimes and follies of a neighbouring nation have suggested to them. I am persuaded the House will be sensible that these principles, and the effects of them, are narrowly to be watched, that there can be no leading consideration more nearly connected with the prospect of all countries, and most of all, that there can be no consideration more deserving the attention of this House, than to crush and destroy principles which are so dangerous and destructive of every blessing this country enjoys under its free and excellent constitution.

We owe our present happiness and prosperity, which has never been equalled in the annals of mankind, to a mixture of monarchical government. We feel and know we are happy under that form of government. We consider it as our first duty to maintain and reverence the British constitution, which, for wise and just reasons of lasting and internal policy, attaches inviolability to the sacred person of the Sovereign, though, at the same time, by the responsibility it has annexed to government, by the check of a wise system of laws, and by a mixture of aristocratic and democratical power in the frame of legislation, it has equally exempted itself from the danger arising from the exercise of absolute power on the one hand, and the still more dangerous contagion of popular licentiousness on the other. The equity of our laws and the freedom of our political system have been the envy of every surrounding nation. In this country no man, in consequence of his riches or rank, is so high as to be above the reach of the laws, and no individual is so poor or inconsiderable as not to be within their protection. It is the boast of the law of England, that it affords equal security and protection to the high and the low, to the rich and the poor.

Such is the envied situation of England, which may be compared, if I may be allowed the expression, to the situation of the temperate zone on the surface of the globe, formed by the bounty of Providence for habitation and enjoyment, being equally removed from the polar frosts on the one hand and the scorching heat of the torrid zone on the other; where the vicissitude of the seasons and the variety of the climate contribute to the vigour and health of its inhabitants and to the fertility of its soil; where pestilence and famine are unknown, as also earthquakes, hurricanes, and the like, with all their dreadful consequences. Such is the situation, the fortunate situation of Britain: and what a splendid contrast does it form to the situation of that country which is exposed to all the tremendous consequences of that ungovernable, that intolerable and destroying spirit, which carries ruin and desolation wherever it goes!

Sir, this infection can have no existence in this happy land, unless it is imported, unless it is studiously and industriously brought into this country. These principles are not the natural produce of Great Britain, and it ought to be our first duty and principal concern, to take the most effectual measures in order to stop their growth and progress in this country, as well as in the other nations of Europe.

Under this impression, I wish to bring the House to the consideration of the situation in which we stand with respect to France, and with respect to the general state of the different Powers of Europe. This subject was very much discussed on the first day of the present session, and I had the good fortune to concur with a very large majority of the House in the address that was presented to His Majesty, for his most gracious speech to both houses of Parliament. Gentlemen then drew their inferences from those notorious facts which every man's observation presented to him : and those circumstances were supposed to excite every sentiment of jealousy and precaution. They induced the House to arm His Majesty and the executive Government with those powers which were indispensably necessary for effectually providing for the safety of the country. Many weeks have now elapsed since the beginning of the session, when the country appeared to be in a critical situation. Let us consider what are the circumstances now to attract our attention at the moment when the message of His Majesty calls on us for farther decision.

The papers which contain the communication between this country and France, consist of two different parts. The one comprehends the communication between this country and France, prior to the period which attracted those sentiments of jealousy I have stated. This part also contains those comments which have taken place since, and those explanations which have been entered into by His Majesty's permission, with a view, if possible, that our jealousy might be removed in consequence of some step that might be taken. The other part consists, either of what were notorious facts at the meeting of Parliament, or of those notorious facts which, though not officially communicated by His Majesty, were very generally known to the public.

The first part of these papers has never before been made public. The date of the first communication is May 12, 1792. And the communication from that period till July 8 contains the system on which His

Majesty acted between France and the other European Powers. From that period down to the meeting of Parliament, His Majesty had most scrupulously observed the strictest neutrality with respect to France.[1] He had taken no part whatever in the regulation of her internal government. He had given her no cause of complaint; and therefore the least return he might expect was, that France would be cautious to avoid every measure that could furnish any just ground of complaint to His Majesty. He might also well expect that France would have felt a proper degree of respect for the rights of himself and his allies.[2] His Majesty might most of all expect, that, in the troubled state of that country, they would not have chosen to attempt an interference with the internal government of this country, for the sole purpose of creating dissension among us, and of disturbing a scene of unexampled felicity. But fortunately for this country, they did not succeed. The express assurances contained in the papers which have been printed and are now on the table, the very compact on the part of France does distinctly and precisely apply to every one of these points.

I have no doubt but gentlemen have applied the interval in perusing these papers with sufficient attention to make it unnecessary for me to trouble them with more than the leading points. You will perceive that the very first communication is from M. Chauvelin, May 12, 1792, and contains this passage:

'Thus the King (of France) saw himself forced into a war, which was already declared against him; but,

[1] Introduction, pp. xvi, xxii.   [2] Prussia and Holland.

religiously faithful to the principles of the constitution, whatever may finally be the fate of arms in this war, France rejects all ideas of aggrandizement. She will preserve her limits, her liberty, her constitution, her inalienable right of reforming herself whenever she may think proper: she will never consent that, under any relation, foreign Powers should attempt to dictate, or even dare to nourish a hope of dictating laws to her. But this very pride, so natural and so great, is a sure pledge to all the Powers from whom she shall have received no provocation, not only of her constantly pacific dispositions, but also of the respect which the French well know how to show at all times for the laws, the customs, and all the forms of government of different nations.

'The King indeed wishes it to be known, that he would publicly and severely disavow all those of his agents at foreign courts in peace with France, who should dare to depart an instant from that respect, either by fomenting or favouring insurrections against the established order, or by interfering in any manner whatever in the interior policy of such States, under pretence of a proselytism, which, exercised in the dominions of friendly Powers, would be a real violation of the law of nations.'

This paper, therefore, contains a declaration, that whatever might be the fate of arms, France rejected all ideas of aggrandizement; she would preserve her rights, she would preserve her limits and her liberty. This declaration was made in the name of the King.

Gentlemen must remember, after the first revolution,

and after the establishment of what they called the model of a government of liberty, the King wished it to be known, that he would publicly disavow all those of his agents at foreign courts, in peace with France, who should dare to depart an instant from that respect, either by fomenting or raising insurrections, or by interfering in any manner whatever in the internal government of such States, under pretence of proselytism, which would be a real violation of the law of nations. They have therefore passed, by anticipation, that sentence on their own conduct; and whether we shall pass a different sentence, is one of the objects of this day's consideration.

In the passage I have read, two distinct principles are laid down: the one, that whatever might be the fate of arms, France renounced all ideas of aggrandizement, and declared she would confine herself within her own territories; the other, that to foment and raise insurrections in neutral States, under pretence of proselytism, was a violation of the law of nations. It is evident to all Europe, her conduct has been directly the reverse of those principles, both of which she has trampled under foot, in every instance where it was in her power. In the answer to that Note of M. Chauvelin, His Majesty expresses his concern for the war that had arisen, for the situation of His Most Christian Majesty, and for the happiness of his dominions. He also gives him a positive assurance of his readiness to fulfil, in the most exact manner, the stipulations of the Treaty of Navigation and Commerce;[1] and concludes with these words:

'Faithful to all his engagements, His Majesty will pay

[1] The Commercial Treaty of 1786.

the strictest attention to the preservation of the good understanding which so happily subsists between him and His Most Christian Majesty, expecting with confidence, that, animated with the same sentiments, His Most Christian Majesty will not fail to contribute to the same end, by causing, on his part, the rights of His Majesty and his allies to be respected, and by rigorously forbidding any step which might affect the friendship which His Majesty has ever desired to consolidate and perpetuate, for the happiness of the two Empires.'

We may also see what general assurances France thought fit to make to Great Britain, from a Note from M. Chauvelin to Lord Grenville, dated June 8, 1792; where it is said,

' The King of the French is happy to renew to the King of Great Britain the formal assurance, that everything which can interest the rights of His Britannic Majesty will continue to be the object of his most particular and most scrupulous attention.

' He hastens, at the same time, to declare to him, that the rights of all the allies of Great Britain, who shall not have provoked France by hostile measures, shall by him be no less religiously respected.

' In making, or rather renewing this declaration, the King of the French enjoys the double satisfaction of expressing the wish of a people, in whose eyes every war, which is not rendered necessary by a due attention to its defence, is essentially unjust, and of joining particularly in the wishes of His Majesty, for the tranquillity of Europe, which would never be disturbed, if France and England would unite in order to preserve it.'

Such then, Sir, is the situation in which His Majesty stands with respect to France. During the transactions of the last summer, when France was engaged in a war against the Powers of Austria and Prussia, His Majesty departed in no shape from that neutrality. His Majesty did no one act from which it could be justly inferred that he was friendly to that system. But what, let me ask the House, has been the conduct of France as to those express reiterated assurances, applied to the public concerns which I have now detailed?

These assurances went to three points: to a determination to abstain from views of aggrandizement; not to interfere with the government of neutral nations, which they admitted to be a violation of the law of nations; and to observe the rights of His Majesty and his allies. What has been the conduct of France on these three points, under the new system? She has, both by her words and actions, manifested a determination, if not checked by force, to act on principles of aggrandizement. She has completely disclaimed that maxim, 'that whatever was the fate of their arms in war, France rejected all ideas of aggrandizement.' She has made use of the first moment of success to publish a contradiction to that declaration. She has made use of the first instance of success in Savoy,[1] without even attempting the ceremony of disguise (after having professed a determination to confine herself within her ancient limits), to annex it for ever as an eighty-fourth department to the present sovereignty of France. They have by their decree announced a determination to carry on a similar opera-

[1] Introduction, p. xx.

tion in every country into which their arms can be carried, with a view, in substance, if not in name, to do the same thing in every country where they can with success.

Their decree of the 15th of December contains a fair illustration and confirmation of their principles and designs. They have by that decree expressly stated the plan on which they mean to act. Whenever they obtain a temporary success, whatever be the situation of the country into which they come, whatever may have been its antecedent conduct, whatever may be its political connexions, they have determined not to abandon the possession of it, till they have effected the utter and absolute subversion of its form of government, of every ancient, every established usage, however long they may have existed and however much they may have been revered. They will not accept, under the name of liberty, any model of government, but that which is conformable to their own opinions and ideas; and all men must learn from the mouth of their cannon the propagation of their system in every part of the world. They have regularly and boldly avowed these instructions, which they sent to the commissioners who were to carry these orders into execution. They have stated to them what this House could not believe, they have stated to them a revolutionary principle and order, for the purpose of being applied in every country in which the French arms are crowned with success. They have stated, that they would organize every country by a disorganizing principle; and afterwards, they tell you all this is done by the will of the people. Wherever our arms come, revolutions must take place, dictated by the will of the people. And then comes this plain question, what is this will of the people? It is the power of the French. They have explained what that liberty is which they wish to give to every nation; and if they will not accept of it voluntarily, they compel them. They take every opportunity to destroy every institution that is most sacred and most valuable in every nation where their armies have made their appearance; and under the name of liberty, they have resolved to make every country in substance, if not in form, a province dependent on themselves, through the despotism of Jacobin societies. This has given a more fatal blow to the liberties of mankind than any they have suffered, even from the boldest attempts of the most aspiring monarch. We see, therefore, that France has trampled under foot all laws, human and divine. She has at last avowed the most insatiable ambition and greatest contempt for the law of nations, which all independent States have hitherto professed most religiously to observe; and unless she is stopped in her career, all Europe must soon learn their ideas of justice—law of nations—models of government —and principles of liberty from the mouth of the French cannon.

I gave the first instance of their success in Savoy as a proof of their ambition and aggrandizement. I wish the House to attend to the practical effect of their system, in the situation of the Netherlands. You will find, in some of the correspondence between France and this country, this declaration on the part of France:

'She has renounced, and again renounces every conquest, and her occupation of the Low Countries shall only continue during the war and the time which may be necessary to the Belgians [1] to ensure and consolidate their liberty; after which they will be independent and happy. France will find her recompense in their felicity.'

I ask whether this can mean anything else, than that they hope to add the Netherlands, as an eighty-fourth or eighty-fifth department, to the French Republic; whether it does not mean a subjugation of the Netherlands to the absolute power of France, to a total and unequalled dependence on her? If any man entertains doubts upon the subject, let him look at the allegations of Dumouriez,[2] enforced by martial law. What was the conduct of this general, when he arrived at Brussels? Did he not assemble the inhabitants in the most public part of their city to elect the primary assemblies? How agreeable must have been his arrival in the Netherlands, by his employing threats to procure a general illumination on his entrance into Brussels! A hollow square of the French troops was drawn round the tree of liberty, to prevent the natives from pulling down the emblem of French freedom. This shows how well disposed the people were to receive the French system of liberty!

---

[1] Introduction, pp. xxi, xxiii, xxvii.

[2] French Foreign Minister and War Minister in 1792. General in command of French Army of the North, 1792-3. He was defeated by the Austrians in March 1793; attempted without success to lead his troops against the Convention; fled to the enemy; and ultimately lived as a refugee in England.

This is the manner in which their principles are carried into effect in the different countries of Europe.

I may here mention the conduct of the Convention, on the occasion of an address from the people of Mons, in which they desire that the province of Hainault might be added as an eighty-fifth department of France. The Convention referred the address to a committee, to report the form in which countries, wishing to unite with France, were to be admitted into the union. The Convention could not decide upon it, and therefore they sent it to a committee to point out the manner in which they were to make their application for that purpose, so that the receiving of them was to be a fixed and standing principle, which in its consequences, if not timely prevented, must destroy the liberties and independence of England, as well as of all Europe.

I would next proceed to their confirmed pledge, not to interfere in the government of other neutral countries. What they have done here is in countries which, under some pretence or other, they have made their enemies. I need not remind the House of the decree of the 19th of November, which is a direct attack on every Government in Europe, by encouraging the seditious of all nations to rise up against their lawful rulers, and by promising them their support and assistance. By this decree, they hold out an encouragement to insurrection and rebellion in every country in the world. They show you they mean no exception, by ordering this decree to be printed in all languages. And therefore I might ask any man of common sense, whether any nation upon earth could be out of their contemplation at the time they passed it? And whether it was not meant to extend to England, whatever might be their pretences to the contrary? It is most manifest they mean to carry their principles into every nation, without exception, subvert and destroy every government, and to plant on their ruins their sacred tree of liberty.

Some observations, to which they have affected to give the name of explanations, have been applied to this decree, and are these: 'Now to come to the three points which can alone make an object of difficulty at the Court of London, the executive council observe respecting the first, which is the decree of the 19th of November, that we have not been properly understood by the Ministry of His Britannic Majesty, when they accuse us of having given an explanation *which announces to the seditious of all nations, what are the cases in which they may previously count on the support and assistance of France.* Nothing could be more foreign than this reproach to the sentiments of the National Convention, and to the explanation we have given of them; and we did not think it was possible we should be charged with the open design of favouring the *seditious*, at the very moment when we declare that it would be *wronging the National Convention, if they were charged with the project of protecting insurrections, and with the commotions that may break out in any corner of a State, of joining the ringleaders, and of thus making the cause of a few private individuals that of the French nation.*

'We have said, and we desire to repeat it, that the decree of the 19th of November could not have any application, unless to the single case in which the GENERAL WILL of a nation clearly and unequivocally expressed, should call the French nation to its assistance and fraternity. Sedition can certainly never be construed into the GENERAL WILL. These two ideas mutually repel each other, since a sedition is not and cannot be any other than the movement of a small number against the nation at large. And this movement would cease to be seditious, provided all the members of a society should at once rise, either to reform its Government, or to change its form *in toto*, or for any other object.

'The Dutch were assuredly not seditious when they formed the generous resolution of shaking off the yoke of Spain; and when the general will of that nation called for the assistance of France, it was not reputed a crime in Henry IV, or in Elizabeth of England, to have listened to them. The knowledge of the *general will* is the only basis of the transactions of nations with each other; and we can only treat with any Government whatever on this principle, that such a Government is deemed *the organ of the general will of the nation governed.*

'Thus when by this natural interpretation, the decree of the 19th of November is reduced to what it truly implies, it will be found, that it announces nothing more than an act of the general will, and that beyond any doubt so effectually founded in right, that it was scarcely worth the trouble to express it. On this account, the executive council think that the evidence of this right might, perhaps, have been dispensed with, by the National Convention, and did not deserve to be made the object of a particular decree; but, with the interpretation that precedes it, it cannot give uneasiness to any nation whatever.'

To all this I shall only observe, that in the whole context of their language, on every occasion, they show the clearest intention to propagate their principles all over the world. Their explanations contain only an avowal and repetition of the offence. They have proscribed royalty as a crime, and will not be satisfied but with its total destruction. The dreadful sentence which they have executed on their own unfortunate monarch applies to every sovereign now existing. And lest you should not be satisfied that they mean to extend their system to this country, the conduct of the National Convention has applied itself, by repeated acts, to yourselves by name, which makes any explanation on their part unsatisfactory and unavailing. There is no society in England, however contemptible in their numbers, however desperate in their principles and questionable in their existence, who possessed treason and disloyalty, who were not cherished, justified, and applauded, and treated even with a degree of theatrical extravagance at the bar of the National Convention. You have also a list of the answers given to them at the bar. And, after all this, am I to ask you, whether England is one of the countries into which they wish to introduce a spirit of proselytism, which, exercised in the dominions of friendly Powers, they themselves admit, would be a violation of the law of nations?

On the third point it is unnecessary for me to expatiate —I mean on the violation of the rights of His Majesty, or of his allies.

To insist upon the opening of the River Scheldt,[1] is an act of itself, in which the French nation had no right

[1] Introduction, pp. xxiv–xxv.

to interfere at all, unless she was the sovereign of the Low Countries, or boldly professed herself the general arbitress of Europe. This singular circumstance was an aggravation of their case, because they were bound by the faith of solemn and recent treaties to secure to the Dutch the exclusive navigation of the Scheldt, and to have opposed the opening of that river if any other Power had attempted it. If France were the sovereign of the Low Countries, she would only succeed to the rights which were enjoyed by the House of Austria : and if she possessed the sovereignty, with all its advantage, she must also take it with all its incumbrances, of which the shutting up of the Scheldt was one. France can have no right to annul the stipulations relative to the Scheldt, unless she has also the right to set aside, equally, all the other treaties between all the Powers of Europe, and all the other rights of England, or of her allies. England will never consent that France shall arrogate the power of annulling at her pleasure, and under the pretence of a natural right of which she makes herself the only judge, the political system of Europe, established by solemn treaties, and guaranteed by the consent of all the Powers. Such a violation of rights as France has been guilty of, it would be difficult to find in the history of the world. The conduct of that nation is in the highest degree arbitrary, capricious, and founded upon no one principle of reason or justice. They declare this treaty was antiquated, and extorted by despotism, or procured by corruption. But what happened recently in the last year ? This new and enlightened nation renewed her assurances of respecting all the rights of all His Majesty's allies, without any exception, without any reservation, so that the advancement of this claim is directly contrary to their recent professions. From the Treaty of Munster down to the year 1785, the exclusive navigation of the Scheldt has been one of the established rights of Holland.

We are told it is to be said, no formal requisition has been made by Holland for the support of this country. I beg gentlemen to consider, whether ships going up the Scheldt, after a protest of the States-General,[1] was not such an act as to have justified them in calling upon this country for a contingent of men. If this House means substantial good faith to its engagements, if it retains a just sense of the solemn faith of treaties, it must show a determination to support them. Without entering too far upon this subject, let me call to their attention, for a moment, one circumstance— I mean the sudden effect and progress of French ambition and of French arms. If from that circumstance Holland had just reason to be afraid to make a formal requisition; if she had seen just reason not to do what she might have been well justified in doing, that was no reason why we should not observe our treaty. Are we to stand by as indifferent spectators, and look at France trampling upon the ancient treaties of the allies of this country? Are we to view with indifference the progress of French ambition and of French arms, by which our allies are exposed to the greatest danger? This is surely no reason for England to be inactive and slothful. If Holland has not immediately called upon us for our support and assistance, she may have been influenced by motives of

[1] The Dutch Government.

policy, and her forbearance ought not to be supposed to arise from her indifference about the River Scheldt. If Holland had not applied to England when Antwerp was taken,[1] the French might have overrun her territory. And unless we wish to stand by, and to suffer State after State to be subverted under the power of France, we must now declare our firm resolution effectually to oppose those principles of ambition and aggrandizement, which have for their object the destruction of England, of Europe, and of the world.

The next thing is, whether we see anything in these papers which furnishes an answer to the past, or gives any security for the future? What does the explanation amount to on the subject of the treaty of our allies? It refers to the possibility of negotiation at an indefinite period. She says, 'she (France) has renounced, and again renounces every conquest, and her occupation of the Low Countries shall only continue during the war, and the time which may be necessary to the Belgians to ensure and consolidate their liberty; after which, they will be independent and happy, and France will find her recompense in their felicity.' What is this but an avowal of their former declarations?

On the subject of interference with neutral nations, there are one or two explanations of the decree of the 19th of November, which has been so often discussed. We are, indeed, told it is injurious to suppose the National Convention could have intended to apply this decree to any country but where, by the public will, they have been called to give assistance and fraternity. This is in

[1] Introduction, p. xxv.

fact to advertise for treason and rebellion. Is there any man who could give credit to the reception which the English societies received in France? Though their numbers are too contemptible for the animadversion of the law, or the notice of our own Executive Government, they were considerable enough for the National Convention. They tell you they are the clear, undisputed, constituted organ of the will of the people at large. What reliance can be placed on all their explanations, after the avowal of principles to the last degree dangerous to the liberty, the constitution, the independence, and the very existence of this country?

My time and my strength would fail me, if I were to attempt to go through all those various circumstances which are connected with this subject. I shall take the liberty of reading a passage from a publication which came into my hands this morning, and I am extremely glad to have seen collected together so many instances in which the conduct of France is detected. In a Note from M. Chauvelin, dated December 27, 1792, he complains of the harsh construction which the British Ministry had put on the conduct of France, and professes the strongest friendship for Great Britain. And yet, on the 31st of December, 1792, that is in four days after, one of the members of the Executive Council, who had given these assurances to England, wrote this letter to the friends of liberty and equality in all the seaports in France:

'The Government of England is arming, and the King of Spain, encouraged by this, is preparing to attack us. These two tyrannical Powers, after persecuting the patriots in their own territories, think, no doubt, that they shall be able to influence the judgement to be pronounced on the tyrant Louis. They hope to frighten us. But no! a people who has made itself free; a people who has driven out of the bosom of France, and as far as the distant borders of the Rhine, the terrible army of the Prussians and Austrians; the people of France will not suffer laws to be dictated to them by a tyrant.

'The King and his Parliament mean to make war against us! Will the English republicans suffer it? Already these free men show their discontent and the **repugnance** which they have to bear arms against their brothers, the French. Well! we will fly to their succour; we will make a descent on the island; we will lodge there fifty thousand caps of liberty; we will plant there the sacred tree, and we will stretch out our arms to our republican brethren; *the tyranny of their Government will soon be destroyed.* Let every one of us be strongly impressed with this idea!—MONGE.'

Such is the declaration of the sentiments of the Minister of the Marine; a declaration which separates not only the King, but the King and Parliament of Great Britain from the people, who are called republicans. What faith can be put in assurances given on the part of France by M. Chauvelin, on the 27th of December, when, in four days after, we find the Minister of the Marine writing such a letter? It was to be hoped we might have seen reasons, perhaps, in consequence of friendly explanations, for not going to war. But such explanations as this communication contains have been justly rejected. I shall not detain the House longer on this subject.

I shall state now what appears to be the state of the

1793]   *The French* ultimatum   49

negotiations. I take the conduct of France to be inconsistent with the peace and liberty of Europe. They have not given us satisfaction with respect to the question in issue. It is true, what they call explanations have taken place; but their principles, and the whole manner of their conduct, are such, that no faith can be put in their declarations. Their conduct gives the lie to their public professions; and, instead of giving satisfaction on the distinct articles, on which you have a right to claim a clear and precise explanation, and showing any desire to abandon those views of conquest and aggrandizement, to return within their ancient limits, and to set barriers to the progress of their destructive arms, and to their principles still more destructive; instead of doing so, they have given—explanations I cannot call them, but an avowal of those very things you complain of. And in the last paper from M. Chauvelin, which may therefore be considered as the *ultimatum*, are these words:

'After so frank a declaration, which manifests such a sincere desire of peace, His Britannic Majesty's Ministers ought not to have any doubts with regard to the intentions of France. If her explanations appear insufficient, and if we are still obliged to hear a haughty language; if hostile preparations are continued in the English ports, after having exhausted every means to preserve peace, we will prepare for war with the sense of the justice of our cause, and of our efforts to avoid this extremity. We will fight the English, whom we esteem, with regret —but we will fight them without fear.'

This is an *ultimatum* to which you cannot accede. They have neither withdrawn their armies from the neighbouring nations, nor shown the least disposition to withdraw them. If France is really desirous of maintaining friendship and peace with England, she must show herself disposed to renounce her views of aggression and aggrandizement, and to confine herself within her own territory, without insulting other governments, without disturbing their tranquillity, without violating their rights. And unless she consent to these terms, whatever may be our wishes for peace, the final issue must be war. As to the time, as to the moment when war is to commence, if there is yet any possibility of satisfactory explanation and security for the future, it is not to the last moment precluded. But I should disguise my sentiments to the House, if I stated, that I thought it in any degree probable. This country has always been desirous of peace. We desire it still, but such as may be real and solid, and consistent with the interests and dignity of Britain, and with the general security of Europe. War, whenever it comes, will be preferable to peace without honour, without security, and which is incompatible either with the external safety or the internal happiness of this country.

I have endeavoured to comprehend as much as possible, though I am sensible I have left a great deal untouched. If any topic should afterwards arise, I trust I shall meet with the indulgence of the House in stating it. I shall now move, 'That an humble address be presented to His Majesty, to return His Majesty the thanks of this House for his most gracious message and the communication of the papers, which, by His Majesty's command, have been laid before us.

' To offer His Majesty our heartfelt condolence on the ferocious act lately perpetrated at Paris, which must be viewed by every nation in Europe as an outrage on religion, justice, and humanity, and as a striking and dreadful example of the effects of principles which lead to the violation of the most sacred duties, and are utterly subversive of the peace and order of all civil society.

' To represent to His Majesty, that it is impossible for us not to be sensible of the views of aggrandizement and ambition which, in violation of repeated and solemn professions, have been openly manifested on the part of France, and which are connected with the propagation of principles incompatible with the existence of all just and regular government; that under the present circumstances, we consider a vigorous and effectual opposition to those views as essential to the security of everything that is most dear and valuable to us as a nation, and to the future tranquillity and safety of all other countries.

' That impressed with these sentiments, we shall, with the utmost zeal and alacrity, afford His Majesty the most effectual assistance, to enable His Majesty to make a further augmentation of his forces by sea and land, and to act as circumstances may require in the present important conjuncture, for maintaining the security and honour of his crown, for supporting the just rights of his allies, and for preserving to his people the undisturbed enjoyment of the blessings, which, under the Divine Providence, they receive from the British constitution!'

The address was agreed to without a division. On the same day the French Convention declared war on Great Britain and Holland.

2

The French Declaration of War

February 12, 1793[1]

ON February 12 the following message from the King was read to the House of Commons:

'GEORGE R.

'His Majesty thinks proper to acquaint the House of Commons, that the assembly now exercising the powers of government in France have, without previous notice, directed acts of hostility to be committed against the persons and property of His Majesty's subjects, in breach of the law of nations and of the most positive stipulations of treaty; and have since, on the most groundless pretences, actually declared war against His Majesty and the United Provinces. Under the circumstances of this wanton and unprovoked aggression, His Majesty has taken the necessary steps to maintain the honour of his crown and to vindicate the rights of his people; and His Majesty relies with confidence on the firm and effectual support of the House of Commons and on the zealous exertions of a brave and loyal people, in prosecuting a just and necessary war, and in endeavouring, under the blessing of Providence, to oppose an effectual barrier to the farther progress of a system which strikes at the security and peace of all independent nations, and is pursued in open defiance of every principle of moderation, good faith, humanity, and justice.

[1] *Speeches*, vol. ii, p. 113.

'In a cause of such general concern, His Majesty has every reason to hope for the cordial co-operation of those Powers who are united with His Majesty by the ties of alliance, or who feel an interest in preventing the extension of anarchy and confusion, and in contributing to the security and tranquillity of Europe.

'G. R.'

As soon as the message was read,

Mr. Pitt rose and observed, that in proposing to the House an address in answer to His Majesty's message, he did not conceive that there could be any necessity, in the present instance, at least in one view of the subject, for troubling them much at large. Whatever difference of opinion might formerly have existed with respect to subjects on which, however, the great majority both of that House and the nation had coincided in sentiment, whatever doubts might be entertained as to the interest which this country had in the recent transactions on the continent, whatever question might be made of the satisfaction to which this country was entitled, or whatever question might be made of the mode of conduct which had been pursued by Government, which lately had not been carried so far as to produce even a division; yet when the situation in which we now stood was considered, when those circumstances which had occurred to produce an alteration in the state of affairs since the last address, were taken into the account, he could not doubt but that there would be one unanimous sentiment and voice expressed on the present occasion. The question now was not what degree of danger or insult we should find it necessary to repel, from a regard to our safety, or from a sense of honour; it was not whether we should adopt in our measures a system of promptitude and vigour, or of tameness and procrastination; whether we should sacrifice every other consideration to the continuance of an uncertain and insecure peace. When war was declared and the event no longer in our option, it remained only to be considered, whether we should prepare to meet it with a firm determination, and support His Majesty's Government with zeal and courage against every attack. War now was not only declared, but carried on at our very doors; a war which aimed at an object no less destructive than the total ruin of the freedom and independence of this country. In this situation of affairs, he would not do so much injustice to the members of that House, whatever differences of opinion might formerly have existed, as to suppose there could be any but one decision, one fixed resolution, in this so urgent necessity, in this imminent and common danger, by the ardour and firmness of their support, to testify their loyalty to their sovereign, their attachment to the constitution, and their sense of those inestimable blessings which they had so long enjoyed under its influence. Confident, however, as he was, that such would be their unanimous decision, that such would be their determined and unalterable resolution, he should not consider it as altogether useless to take a view of the situation of the country at the time of His Majesty's last message, of the circumstances which had preceded and accompanied it, and of the situation in which we now stood, in consequence of what had occurred during that interval.

When His Majesty, by his message, informed them, that in the present situation of affairs he conceived it indispensably necessary to make a farther augmentation of his forces, they had cheerfully concurred in that object, and returned in answer, what then was the feeling of the House, the expression of their affection and zeal, and their readiness to support His Majesty in those purposes, for which he had stated an augmentation of force to be necessary. They saw the justice of the alarm which was then entertained, and the propriety of affording that support which was required. He should shortly state the grounds upon which they had then given their concurrence. They considered that whatever temptations might have existed to this country from ancient enmity and rivalship—paltry motives indeed!—or whatever opportunity might have been afforded by the tumultuous and distracted state of France, or whatever sentiments might be excited by the transactions which had taken place in that nation, His Majesty had uniformly abstained from all interference in its internal government, and had maintained, with respect to it, on every occasion, the strictest and most inviolable neutrality.

Such being his conduct towards France, he had a right to expect on their part a suitable return; more especially, as this return had been expressly conditioned for by a compact, into which they entered, and by which they engaged to respect the rights of His Majesty and his allies, not to interfere in the government of any neutral country, and not to pursue any system of aggrandizement, or make any addition to their dominions, but to confine themselves, at the conclusion of the war, within their own territories. These conditions they had all grossly violated, and had adopted a system of ambitious and destructive policy, fatal to the peace and security of every government, and which in its consequences had shaken Europe itself to its foundation. Their decree of November 19, which had been so much talked of, offering fraternity and affiance to all people who wish to recover their liberty, was a decree not levelled against particular nations, but against every country where there was any form of government established; a decree not hostile to individuals, but to the human race; which was calculated everywhere to sow the seeds of rebellion and civil contention, and to spread war from one end of Europe to the other, from one end of the globe to the other. While they were bound to this country by the engagements which he had mentioned, they had showed no intention to exempt it from the consequences of this decree. Nay, a directly contrary opinion might be formed, and it might be supposed that this country was more particularly aimed at by this very decree, if we were to judge from the exultation with which they had received from different societies in England every address expressive of sedition and disloyalty, and from the eager desire which they had testified to encourage and cherish the growth of such sentiments. Not only had they showed no inclination to fulfil their engagements, but had even put it out of their own power, by taking the first opportunity to make additions to their territory in contradiction to their own express stipulations. By express resolutions for the destruction of the existing government of all invaded countries, by the means of Jacobin societies, by orders given to their generals, by the whole system adopted in this respect by the National Assembly, and by the actual connexion of the whole country of Savoy, they had marked their determination to add to the dominions of France, and to provide means, through the medium of every new conquest, to carry their principles over Europe. Their conduct was such as in every instance had militated against the dearest and most valuable interests of this country.

The next consideration was, that under all the provocations which had been sustained from France, provocations which, in ordinary times and in different circumstances, could not have failed to have been regarded as acts of hostility, and which formerly, not even a delay of twenty-four hours would have been wanting to have treated as such, by commencing an immediate war of retaliation, His Majesty's Ministers had prudently and temperately advised all the means to be previously employed of obtaining reasonable satisfaction, before recourse should be had to extremities. Means had been taken to inform their agents, even though not accredited, of the grounds of jealousy and complaint on the part of this country, and an opportunity had been afforded through them of bringing forward any circumstances of explanation or offering any terms of satisfaction. Whether the facts and explanations which these agents had brought forward were such as contained any proper satisfaction for the past, or could afford any reasonable assurance with respect to the future, every member might judge from the inspection of the papers. He had already given it as his opinion, that if there was no other alternative than either to make war or depart from our principles, rather than recede from our principles a war was preferable to a peace; because a peace, purchased upon such terms, must be uncertain, precarious, and liable to be continually interrupted by the repetition of fresh injuries and insults. War was preferable to such a peace, because it was a shorter and a surer way to that end which the House had undoubtedly in view as its ultimate object—a secure and lasting peace. What sort of peace must that be in which there was no security? Peace he regarded as desirable only so far as it was secure. If, said Mr. Pitt, you entertain a sense of the many blessings which you enjoy, if you value the continuance and safety of that commerce which is a source of so much opulence, if you wish to preserve and render permanent that high state of prosperity by which this country has for some years past been so eminently distinguished, you hazard all these advantages more, and are more likely to forfeit them, by submitting to a precarious and disgraceful peace, than by a timely and vigorous interposition of your arms. By tameness and delay you suffer that evil which might now be checked to gain ground, and which, when it becomes indispensable to oppose, may perhaps be found irresistible.

It had on former debates been alleged, that by going to war we expose our commerce. Is there, he would ask, any man so blind and irrational, who does not know that the inevitable consequence of every war must be much interruption and injury to commerce? But, because our commerce was exposed to suffer, was that a reason why we should never go to war? Was there no combination of circumstances, was there no situation in the affairs of Europe, such as to render it expedient to hazard for a time a part of our commercial interests? Was there no evil greater, and which a war might be necessary to avoid, than the partial inconvenience to which our commerce was subjected, during the continuance of hostile operations? But he begged pardon of the House for the digression into which he had been led—while he talked as if they were debating about the expediency of a war, war was actually declared: we were at this moment engaged in a war.

He now came to state what had occurred since His Majesty's last message; and to notice those grounds which had served as a pretext for the declaration of war. When His Majesty had dismissed M. Chauvelin, what were then the hopes of peace? He was by no means sanguine in such hopes, and he had stated to the House that he then saw but little probability that a war could be avoided. Such then was his sentiment, because the explanations and conduct of the French agent were such as afforded him but little room to expect any terms which this country could, either consistently with honour or a regard to its safety, accept. Still, however, the last moment had been kept open to receive any satisfactory explanation which might be offered. But what, it might be asked, was to be the mode of receiving such explanation? When His Majesty had dismissed M. Chauvelin, as, by the melancholy catastrophe of the French monarch, the only character in which he had ever been acknowledged at the British Court had entirely ceased, eight days had been allowed him for his departure, and if during that period he had sent any more satisfactory explanation, still it would have been received. Had any disposition been testified to comply with the requisitions of Lord Grenville, still an opportunity was afforded of intimating this disposition. Thus had our Government pursued to the last a conciliatory system, and left every opening for accommodation, had the French been disposed to embrace it. M. Chauvelin, however, instantly quitted the country, without making any proposition. Another agent had succeeded (M. Maret) who, on his arrival in this country, had notified himself as the *chargé-d'affaires* on the part of the French Republic, but had never, during his residence in the kingdom, afforded the smallest communication.

What was the next event which had succeeded? An embargo was laid on all the vessels and persons of His Majesty's subjects who were then in France. This embargo was to be considered not only as a symptom, but as an act, of hostility. It certainly had taken place without any notice being given, contrary to treaty, and against all the laws of nations. Here perhaps it might be said, that on account of their stopping certain ships loaded with corn for France, the Government of Great Britain might be under the same charge; to this point he should come presently. He believed if Government were chargeable with anything, it might rather be, that they were even too slow in asserting the honour and vindicating the rights of this country. If he thought that His Majesty's Ministers wanted any justification, it would be for their forbearance and not for their promptitude, since to the last moment they had testified a disposition to receive terms of accommodation, and left open the means of explanation. Notwithstanding this violent and outrageous act, such was the disposition to peace in His Majesty's Ministers, that the channels of communication, even after this period, were not shut. A most singular circumstance happened, which was the arrival of intelligence from His Majesty's Minister at The Hague[1] on the very day when the embargo became known here, that he had received an intimation from General Dumouriez, that the general wished an interview, in order to see if it were yet possible to adjust the differences between the two countries and to promote a general pacification. Instead of treating the embargo as an act of hostility, and forbearing from any communication, even after this aggression, His Majesty's Ministers, on the same day on which the embargo was made known to them, gave instructions to the ambassador at The Hague, to enter into a communication with General Dumouriez. And they did this with great satisfaction, on several accounts: first, because it might be done without committing the King's dignity; for the general of an army might, even in the very midst of war, without any recognition of his authority, open any negotiation of peace. But this sort of communication was desirable also, because, if successful, it would be attended with the most immediate effects, as its tendency was immediately to stop the progress of war, in the most practical,

[1] Lord Auckland.

and perhaps, in the only practical way. No time was therefore lost in authorizing the King's Minister at The Hague to proceed in the pursuit of so desirable an object, if it could be done in a safe and honourable mode, but not otherwise. But before the answer of Government could reach the ambassador, or any means be adopted for carrying the object proposed into execution, war was declared, on the part of the French, against this country. If then we were to debate at all, we were to debate whether or not we were to repel those principles, which not only were inimical to this, and to every other Government, but which had been followed up in acts of hostility to this country. We were to debate whether or not we were to resist an aggression which had already been commenced. He would, however, refer the House, not to observations of reasoning, but to the grounds which had been assigned by the assembly themselves in their declaration of war. But first, he must again revert for a moment to the embargo. He then stated, that a detention of ships, if no ground of hostility had been given, was, in the first place, contrary to the law of nations. In the second place, there was an actual treaty between the two countries, providing for this very circumstance: and this treaty (if not set aside by our breach of it, which he should come to presently) expressly said that, in case of a rupture, time shall be given for the removal of persons and effects.[1]

He should now proceed to the declaration itself. It began with declaring, 'That the King of England has not ceased, especially since the revolution of August 10, 1792, to give proofs of his being evil-disposed towards

[1] The Commercial Treaty of 1786: Article II.

French nation, and of his attachment to the coalition crowned heads.' Notwithstanding the assertion that his Majesty had not ceased to show his evil dispositions towards the French nation, they had not attempted to show any acts of hostility previous to August 10; nor in support of the charge of his attachment to the coalition of crowned heads had they been able to allege any fact, except his supposed accession to the treaty between the Emperor of Germany and the King of Prussia.[1] This treaty had already, this evening, been the subject of conversation: it had then been mentioned, which he should now repeat, that the fact, thus alleged, was false, and entirely destitute of foundation; and that no accession to any such treaty had ever taken place on the part of His Majesty. And not only had he entered into no such treaty, but no step had been taken, and no engagement formed on the part of our Government, to interfere in the internal affairs of France, or attempt to dictate to them any form of constitution. He declared that the whole of the interference of Great Britain had been (in consequence of French aggressions) with the general view of seeing whether it was possible, either by our own exertions, or in concert with any other Powers, to repress this French system of aggrandizement and aggression, with the view of seeing whether we could

[1] Treaty of alliance between Leopold II of Austria (='Emperor' or 'Holy Roman Emperor', wrongly entitled 'Emperor of Germany') and Frederick William II of Prussia, resulting in the Declaration of Pillnitz, August 27, 1791, in which the monarchs declared their intention of re-establishing the position of the French King by force and invited the other sovereigns of Europe to assist them. Introduction p. xviii).

not re-establish the blessings of peace, whether we could not, either separately, or jointly with other Powers, provide for the security of our own country and the general security of Europe.

The next charge brought by the National Assembly was, 'That, at the period aforesaid, he ordered his ambassador at Paris to withdraw, because he would not acknowledge the provisional Executive Council, created by the legislative assembly.' It was hardly necessary for him to discuss a subject with which all were already so well acquainted. After the horrors of August 10, which were paralleled but not eclipsed by those of September 2, and the suspension of the French monarch, to whom alone the ambassador had been sent, it certainly became proper to recall him. He could not remain to treat with any government to whom he was not accredited; and the propriety of his being recalled would appear still more evident, when it was considered that it was probable that the banditti who had seized upon the government would not long retain their power; and, in fact, in the course of a month, they had been obliged to yield to the interest of a different party, but of a description similar to their own. It was also to be remarked, that this circumstance of recalling the ambassador had never till now been complained of as an act of hostility. When a government was overturned, it became a fair question how long an interval should intervene till ⟨the new⟩ government should be acknowledged. And, especially if that change of government was accompanied with all the circumstances of tumult and distraction, it certainly became a matter of extreme hardship that a war should be the consequence to the nation which should refuse to acknowledge it in the first instance. The force of this reasoning became increased in the particular application, when it was considered, that France had not yet established any constitution of its own; that all, hitherto, was merely provisional and temporary; and that, however the present republican system might be confirmed by force or change of opinion, a little before, the voice of the nation, as far as its wish could be collected, had expressed itself in favour of a monarchy.

They proceeded to state, as farther grounds of their declaration of war, 'That the Cabinet of St. James's has ceased, since the same period (August 10), to correspond with the French ambassador at London, on pretext of the suspension of the heretofore King of the French. That, since the opening of the National Convention, it has refused to resume the usual correspondence between the two States, and to acknowledge the powers of this Convention. That it has refused to acknowledge the ambassador of the French Republic, although provided with letters of credit in its name.' M. Chauvelin had been received at this Court as ambassador of the King, and in no other capacity or character. From the period of the suspension of the King, he, for some months, ceased to hold any communication with the Government here, or to act in any capacity; nor was it till the month of December that he had received his letter of credence to act here as the ambassador of the French Republic. With respect to the charge of not having acknowledged the Convention, he confessed it to be true. When these letters of credence had been tendered, they were refused;

but it was to be considered whether it would have been proper to have recognized them, after the repeated instances of offence, for which no compensation had been made, and of which, indeed, every fresh act presented not only a repetition, but an aggravation. Indeed, it would have been impossible at that period, without showing a deviation from principle and a tameness of disposition, to have recognized their authority, or accepted of the person who presented himself in the character of their ambassador. At that very moment, it was to be recollected, they were embarked in the unjust and inhuman process which had terminated in the murder of their King—an event which had everywhere excited sentiments of the utmost horror and indignation! Would it have been becoming in our Government first to have acknowledged them at such a moment, when the power they had assumed was thus cruelly and unjustly exercised against that very authority which they usurped? But, whatever might be the feelings of abhorrence and indignation which their conduct on this occasion could not fail to excite, he should by no means hold out these feelings as a ground for hostility, nor should he ever wish to propose a war of vengeance. The catastrophe of the French monarch they ought all to feel deeply; and consistently with that impression, be led more firmly to resist those principles from which an event of so black and atrocious a nature had proceeded; principles which, if not opposed, might be expected in their progress to lead to the commission of similar crimes; but, notwithstanding Government had been obliged to decline all communication which tended to acknowledge the authority of the Convention, still, as he had said before, they had left open the means of accommodation; nor could that line of conduct which they had pursued be stated as affording any ground of hostility.

He should now consider, collectively, some of the subsequent grounds which they had stated in their declaration, which were expressed in the following articles:

'That the Court of St. James's has attempted to impede the different purchases of corn, arms, and other commodities ordered in England, either by French citizens or the agents of the Republic.

'That it has caused to be stopped several boats and ships loaded with grain for France, contrary to the Treaty of 1786,[1] while exportation to other foreign countries was free.

'That in order still more effectually to obstruct the commercial operations of the Republic in England, it obtained an Act of Parliament prohibiting the circulation of *assignats*.[2]

'That in violation of the fourth article of the Treaty of 1786,[3] it obtained another Act, in the month of January

[1] The Commercial Treaty of 1786: see *supra*, p. 8.

[2] See *infra*, p. 130, note 1.

[3] Article IV of the Commercial Treaty: 'The subjects and inhabitants of the respective dominions of the two sovereigns shall have liberty, freely and securely, without licence or passport, general or special, by land or sea, or any other way, to enter into the kingdoms, dominions, provinces, countries, islands, cities, villages, towns, walled or unwalled, fortified or unfortified, ports, or territories whatsoever, of either sovereign, situated in Europe, and to return from thence, to remain there, or to pass through the same and therein to

last, which subjects all French citizens, residing in, or coming into England, to forms the most inquisitorial, vexatious, and dangerous.[1]

'That at the same time, and contrary to the first article of the Peace of 1783,[2] it granted protection and pecuniary aid not only to the emigrants, but even to the chiefs of the rebels, who have already fought against France; that it has maintained with them a daily correspondence, evidently directed against the French Revolution: that it has also received the chiefs of the rebels of the French West India colonies.'[3]

All these had been stated as provocations; but what sort of provocations? What, he would ask, was a provocation? That we had, indeed, taken measures, which, if

---

buy and purchase, as they please, all things necessary for their subsistence and use, and they shall mutually be treated with all kindness and favour. Provided, however, that, in all these matters, they behave and conduct themselves conformably to the laws and statutes, and live with each other in a friendly and peaceable manner, and promote reciprocal concord by maintaining a mutual good understanding.'

[1] The Alien Bill, passed December 31, 1792, provided for official supervision of all alien immigrants.

[2] Article I of the Peace of Versailles: 'The high contracting parties shall give the greatest attention to the maintaining between themselves and their said dominions and subjects this reciprocal friendship and intercourse, without permitting thereafter, on either part, any kind of hostilities to be committed ... and they shall carefully avoid, for the future, everything which might prejudice the union happily re-established ... without giving any assistance or protection, directly or indirectly, to those who would do any injury to either of the high contracting parties.'

[3] See *infra*, pp. 126–7.

considered by themselves, and not as connected with the situation of affairs in which they were adopted, might perhaps be considered in the light of provocations, he would allow; but if these measures were justified by the necessity of circumstances, if they were called for by a regard to our own safety and interests, they could only be viewed as temperate and moderate precautions. And in this light, these grounds, assigned in the declaration, could only be regarded as frivolous and unfounded pretences. With respect to the charge of having stopped supplies of grain and other commodities, intended for France, what could be more ridiculous than such a pretext? When there was reason to apprehend that France intended an attack upon the allies of this country and against the country itself, upon which, at the same time, it depended for the stores and ammunitions necessary for carrying on hostilities, was it natural to suppose that they should furnish, from their own bosom, supplies to be turned against themselves and their allies? Could they be such children in understanding, could they be such traitors in principle, as to furnish to their enemies the means of hostility and the instruments of offence? What was the situation of France with respect to this country? Had they not given sufficient cause for jealousy of their hostile intentions? By their decree of November 19, they had declared war against all governments. They had possessed themselves of Flanders, and were there endeavouring to establish, by force, what they styled a system of freedom, while they actually menaced Holland with an invasion.

Another ground which they had stated in their

declaration as an act of hostility on the part of our Government was, that they had not suffered *assignats* to be circulated in this country. Truly, they had reason to be offended that we would not receive what was worth nothing; and that, by exercising an Act which came completely within our own sovereignty with respect to the circulation of any foreign paper currency, we thus avoided a gigantic system of swindling! If such, indeed, were the pretences which they brought forward as grounds for a declaration of war, it was matter of wonder that, instead of a sheet of paper, they did not occupy a volume, and proved that their ingenuity had been exhausted before their modesty had been at all affected.

Of much the same nature was that other pretext, with respect to the passing of the Alien Bill; a Bill absolutely necessary for the safety of the country, as it shielded us from the artifice of the seditious, perhaps the dagger of the assassin. This Bill they had held out as an infringement of the Treaty of Commerce. It could be no infringement of their treaty, as in the treaty itself it was expressly declared, that nothing was to be considered as an infringement, unless, first, proper explanations had taken place. Secondly, it was not to be expected that any treaty could supersede the propriety of adopting new measures in a new situation of affairs. Such was the case, when an inundation of foreigners had poured into this country under circumstances entirely different from those which were provided for by the treaty. But who were those who complained of the severity of the regulations adopted by the Alien Bill in this country? The very persons who, during the late transactions in their own country, had adopted restrictions of police ten times more severe, but of which our Government, however much its subjects might be affected, had never made the smallest complaint.

The next ground, assigned in the declaration, was the armament which had taken place in this country.

'That in the same spirit, without any provocation, and when all the maritime Powers are at peace with England, the Cabinet of St. James's has ordered a considerable naval armament, and an augmentation of the land forces.

'That this armament was ordered at a moment when the English Minister was bitterly persecuting those who supported the principles of the French Revolution in England, and was employing all possible means, both in Parliament and out of it, to cover the French Republic with ignominy, and to draw upon it the execration of the English nation and of all Europe.'

And under what circumstances had the armament complained of taken place? At the period when the French, by their conduct with regard to the Treaty of the Scheldt, showed their intention to disregard the obligation of all treaties, when they had begun to propagate principles of universal war, and to discover views of unbounded conquest. Was it to be wondered at that, at such a time, we should think it necessary to take measures of precaution, and to oppose, with determination, the progress of principles, not only of so mischievous a tendency, but which, in their immediate consequences, threatened to be so fatal to ourselves and our allies? Indeed they now seemed rather to despair of these principles being so generally adopted and attended with such striking and immediate success as they had at first fondly imagined. How little progress these principles had made in this country they might be sufficiently convinced by that spirit, which had displayed itself, of attachment to the constitution, and those expressions of a firm determination to support it, which had appeared from every quarter. If, indeed, they mean to attack us, because we do not like French principles, then would this indeed be that sort of war which had so often been alleged and deprecated on the other side of the House —a war against opinions. If they mean to attack us because we love our constitution, then indeed it would be a war of extirpation; for not till the spirit of Englishmen was exterminated, would their attachment to the constitution be destroyed, and their generous efforts be slackened in its defence.

The next articles of complaint on the part of the French were,

'That the object of this armament, intended against France, was not even disguised in the English Parliament.

'That although the provisional Executive Council of France has employed every measure for preserving peace and fraternity with the English nation, and has replied to calumnies and violations of treaties only by remonstrances, founded on the principles of justice, and expressed with the dignity of free men; the English Minister has persevered in his system of malevolence and hostility, continued the armaments, and sent a squadron to the Scheldt to disturb the operations of the French in Belgium.

'That, on the news of the execution of Louis, he carried his outrages to the French Republic to such a length, as to order the ambassador of France to quit the British territory within eight days.

'That the King of England has manifested his attachment to the cause of that traitor, and his design of supporting it, by different hostile resolutions adopted in his Council, both by nominating generals of his land army, and by applying to Parliament for a considerable addition of land and sea forces, and putting ships of war in commission.'

They clearly showed their enmity to that constitution, by taking every opportunity to separate the King of England from the nation, and by addressing the people as distinct from the Government. Upon the point of their fraternity he did not wish to say much : he had no desire for their affection. To the people they offered fraternity, while they would rob them of that constitution by which they are protected, and deprive them of the numerous blessings which they enjoy under its influence. In this case, their fraternal embraces resembled those of certain animals who embrace only to destroy.

Another ground which they had assigned was the grief which had been expressed in the British Court at the fate of their unhappy monarch. Of all the reasons he ever heard for making war against another country, that of the French upon this occasion was the most extraordinary. They said they would make war on us, first, because we loved our own constitution ; secondly because we detested their proceedings ; and lastly, because we presumed to grieve at the death of their murdered King. Thus would they even destroy those principles of justice and those sentiments of compassion, which led us to reprobate their crimes and to be afflicted at their cruelties. Thus would they deprive us of that last resource of humanity—to mourn over the misfortunes and sufferings of the victims of their injustice. If such was the case, it might be asked, in the emphatic words of the Roman writer, *Quin gemitus Populo Romano liber erit?*[1] They would not only endeavour to destroy our political existence, and to deprive us of the privileges which we enjoyed under our excellent constitution, but they would eradicate our feelings as men; they would make crimes of those sympathies which were excited by the distresses of our common nature; they would repress our sighs and restrain our tears. Thus, except the specific fact, which was alleged as a ground of their declaration of war, namely, the accession of His Majesty to the treaty between Austria and Prussia, which had turned out to be entirely false and unfounded, or the augmentation of our armament, a measure of precaution indispensably requisite for the safety of the country and the protection of its allies, all the others were merely unjust, unfounded, absurd, and frivolous pretexts—pretexts which never could have been brought to justify a measure of which they were not previously strongly desirous, and which showed that, instead of waiting for provocation, they only sought a pretence of aggression. The death of Louis, though it only affected the individual, was

---

[1] 'How shall the Roman people not be free—at least to groan?' The text of the *Speeches* (vol. ii, p. 129) gives 'quis'. The passage is probably an adaptation of Cicero, *Philippics* ii. 26.

aimed against all sovereignty, and showed their determination to carry into execution that intention, which they had so often professed, of exterminating all monarchy. As a consequence of that monstrous system of inconsistency which they pursued, even while they professed their desire to maintain a good understanding with this country, the Minister of the Marine had written a letter to the seaport towns, ordering them to fit out privateers: for what purpose but the projected view of making depredations on our commerce? While they affected to complain of our armament, they had passed a decree to fit out fifty sail of the line—an armament which, however, it was to be observed, existed only in the decree.

He feared that, by this long detail, he had wearied the patience of the House, and occupied more of their time than he at first intended. The pretexts, which he had been led to examine, alleged as grounds for the declaration of war, were of a nature that required no refutation. They were such as every man could see through; and in many of his remarks he doubted not he had been anticipated by that contempt with which the House would naturally regard the weak reasoning, but wicked policy, of these pretexts.

He now came to his conclusion. We, said Mr. Pitt, have, in every instance, observed the strictest neutrality with respect to the French: we have pushed, to its utmost extent, the system of temperance and moderation: we have held out the means of accommodation: we have waited till the last moment for satisfactory explanation. These means of accommodation have been slighted and abused, and all along there has appeared no disposition to give any satisfactory explanation. They have now, at last, come to an actual aggression, by seizing our vessels in their very ports, without any provocation given on our part. Without any preparations having been adopted but those of necessary precaution, they have declared, and are now waging, war. Such is the conduct which they have pursued; such is the situation in which we stand. It now remains to be seen whether, under Providence, the efforts of a free, brave, loyal, and happy people, aided by their allies, will not be successful in checking the progress of a system, the principles of which, if not opposed, threaten the most fatal consequences to the tranquillity of this country, the security of its allies, the good order of every European Government, and the happiness of the whole of the human race!

Pitt then proceeded to move the following address in answer to His Majesty's message:

' That an humble address be presented to His Majesty, to return His Majesty the thanks of this House for his most gracious message, informing us, that the assembly, now exercising the powers of government in France, have, without previous notice, directed acts of hostility to be committed against the persons and property of His Majesty's subjects, in breach of the law of nations and of the most positive stipulations of treaty; and have since, on the most groundless pretences, actually declared war against His Majesty and the United Provinces: to assure His Majesty that, under the circumstances of this wanton and unprovoked aggression, we most gratefully acknowledge His Majesty's care and vigilance in taking the necessary steps for maintaining the honour of his crown and vindicating the rights of his people : that His Majesty may rely on the firm and effectual support of the representatives of a brave and loyal people in the prosecution of a just and necessary war, and in endeavouring, under the blessing of Providence, to oppose an effectual barrier to the farther progress of a system which strikes at the security and peace of all independent nations, and is pursued in open defiance of every principle of moderation, good faith, humanity, and justice.

'That, in a cause of such general concern, it must afford us great satisfaction to learn that His Majesty has every reason to hope for the cordial co-operation of those Powers who are united with His Majesty by the ties of alliance, or who feel an interest in preventing the extension of anarchy and confusion, and in contributing to the security and tranquillity of Europe.

'That we are persuaded, that whatever His Majesty's faithful subjects must consider as most dear and sacred, the stability of our happy constitution, the security and honour of His Majesty's crown, and the preservation of our laws, our liberty, and our religion, are all involved in the issue of the present contest; and that our zeal and exertions shall be proportioned to the importance of the conjuncture and to the magnitude and value of the objects for which we have to contend.'

An amendment, moved by Fox, was negatived, and the address agreed to without a division.

3

War Finance

March 11, 1793[1]

THE House of Commons having resolved itself into Committee of Supply, Pitt rose and explained his financial proposals.

It is impossible, in the present situation of affairs, not to look to the means of providing for those exigencies which must arise, and of prosecuting the struggle in which we are engaged, with the utmost vigour. I have accordingly taken the earliest opportunity which was afforded me, of laying before you the expenses of the present year, and the means and aids by which they are to be supplied: but before I proceed to this enumeration, I must first mention the leading object which has governed my mind upon this occasion, namely, the recollection of the unanimous opinion, with respect to the present struggle, which the House have carried to the throne and published to the world—that they regarded it as a struggle for whatever was most dear and sacred, for the security of the throne and the preservation of the constitution; and that they were prepared to prosecute it with the greatest exertion and a zeal proportioned to the importance of the objects of contest. Fortified with these considerations, I am prepared for that task which my duty on the present occasion requires me to undertake. What, in the first place, is to be looked to, is the vigorous and effectual prosecution of this war,

[1] *Speeches*, vol. ii, p. 132.

in which we have everything at stake; and it is by such a prosecution of the war, that we shall best consult true prudence and rational economy. I do not wish to conceal from the House and from the public, that large preparations must be made and considerable expenses incurred. Economy to me seems in our present situation to consist, not in limiting the extent of these expenses, but in controlling their application. In this point of view, I rely upon this House for a liberal supply, adequate to the exigency and importance of the crisis.

There is another point which I wish to inculcate; that whatever degree of exertion we may regard as necessary, or may be disposed to make, the public ought not in any respect to be deluded and flattered—they ought to be made sensible of the full extent to which they may be liable to be called upon to defray the expenses of the war. I will omit nothing on my part to bring forward annually the whole accounts. But, though in calculating the expenses of a war, much may be done by estimate, a great deal must still depend on contingency. Unforeseen occurrences will continually arise, which will render additional expenses necessary. Taking then these occurrences into view, it is proper to allow considerable latitude for the expenses that may be incurred. It is part of my plan to allow a considerable sum for these extraordinary emergencies, so as to make a full provision for every part of the expense.

But there is another object to be attended to. Whatever degree of exertion may be made in the present contest, which involves the dearest and most sacred objects, still we must not allow ourselves to neglect what likewise involves in it the permanent interests of ourselves and our posterity. I not only mean still to employ the annual million for the reduction of the national debt, but likewise the sum of £200,000 which was last year understood to be set apart for that purpose, so as to provide, even during the continuance of the war, for the lessening of the debt by compound interest. I likewise mean to avoid another evil which has taken place in all former wars—the accumulation of an unfunded debt. I therefore intend to bring the unfunded debt every year to a distinct account. In conformity with this principle, I shall propose the payment of the navy debt, in order to reduce it to the establishment mentioned by the committee in their report last year.

I shall now proceed in the usual way to state, first, the total amount of the supply, and the total amount of the ways and means, distinguishing the excesses of the services and of the resources.

Navy

25,000 seamen, including marines	£1,300,000	0	0
20,000 ditto	1,040,000	0	0
Ordinary	£669,205	5	10
Extraordinary	387,710	0	0
	1,056,915	5	10
Excess of Navy Debt beyond the estimate of the Committee	575,000	0	0
	£3,971,915	5	10

Expenditure

ARMY

Army . .	£2,573,187	18 0
Hanoverians . .	455,851	14 8
Militia . . .	939,519	15 7
	£3,968,559	8 3

ORDNANCE

Ordinary, Extraordinaries	£502,686	13 5
Additional estimate .	281,079	18 8
	£783,766	12 1
Cobb at Lyme . .	9,802	4 0
	793,568	16 1
	£8,734,043	10 2
Miscellaneous services . . .	175,844	11 2½

DEFICIENCY OF GRANTS

Arising from interest on Exchequer Bills		
Lottery	£222,325	2 4
Deficiency of ways and means . .		
Deficiency of land and malt . .	350,000	0 0
To be made annually to the Sinking Fund	200,000	0 0

With regard to the first article, the total amount of the expense of the navy, for which there have been already voted 45,000 seamen, I would by no means have it understood that these are the whole number which may be necessary to be employed. These sums, however, constitute the whole of the supply in the ordinary mode of the estimate; to which is to be added such a sum as the committee may think proper to allow for the latitude of unforeseen and unavoidable expense. I have before mentioned the extraordinary charges which may be expected to occur. I have just now stated the possibility of some exceeding with regard to seamen. If the situation of this country lead us, as I hope it will, to take an efficient part along with our numerous allies, in carrying on offensive operations against the enemy, a considerable increase of expense in our military establishment will be necessary. Hitherto, we have hired none but the Hanoverian troops; but, in this case, we may have occasion to employ a considerable body of other foreign troops, in order to press on all sides the common enemy. Some additional expense will be incurred by domestic encampments. An increase will also accrue in the sum allowed to the loyalists, some of whom have been sent to Canada.[1] A loss may perhaps accrue in the lottery, on account of certain regulations which it has been found necessary to make. It is, therefore, my opinion, that a considerable sum should be set apart to enable His Majesty to provide for the unexpected occurrences of a war, and defray its exigencies as they arise. So many are the contingencies of a war, that, whatever sum may be voted for this purpose, I will not pledge myself for its sufficiency. In other wars, let it be recollected

[1] Compensation was paid by the British Government to the American Loyalists, many of whom settled in Canada and were known as the 'United Empire Loyalists'.

that, after the sums allotted for them had been expended, very considerable debts were brought forward to be defrayed at a future period. After endeavouring to take everything into the account, and to calculate as exactly as I can, I will not pretend to state the precise sum; but I would not propose less than that a million and a half should be given to His Majesty with a view to contingencies. The mode of giving it, I would suggest to be by Exchequer Bills upon a vote of credit; but as I do not wish the number of Exchequer Bills in circulation to be increased, I would likewise propose to pay off a million and a half of those which are now in circulation. The total of these sums amount to £11,182,213 3s. 8½d.

I now come to state the means with which we are furnished, and to suggest the aids which may yet be wanting to defray this expense.

Land Tax £2,000,000
Malt Tax 750,000
Surplus of Consolidated Fund on January 5,
   1793 435,696
Surplus of Consolidated Fund on April 5,
   1794, viz.:
Expected Surplus on April 5, 1793 £274,000
 Expected surplus of the four quarters to April 5, 1794, estimated on the four years' average, after deducting £220,000 for duties to be appropriated to pay the interest of money to be borrowed 2,185,000

Imprest monies to be repaid . 250,000
Money to be paid by the East
India Company . . . 500,000
                                                3,209,000
Money from the Commissioners for
the National Debt, including
the annual contribution of
£200,000   1,650,000
Continuation of temporary taxes .   255,000
                                         £8,299,696

That part of the statement, which relates to the surplus of the consolidated fund on January 5 last, I trust will afford much satisfaction. Gentlemen will recollect that the expenses of 1792 were to be defrayed by the amount of the revenue to April 5, 1793; but it happens that the expenses were not only defrayed on January 5, 1793, but a surplus actually remained; consequently the produce of the quarter ending on April 5, is applicable to the exigencies of the present year. Of the produce of this quarter, £435,000 have been already voted. Supposing it to be as favourable as it has been in former years, £274,000 will remain of this quarter, in addition to the £435,000 of which the nation will have to avail itself. Still, however, I mean to carry on the year from April 5, 1793, to April 5, 1794. However sanguine in my own expectations of the flourishing state of the revenue, I have always wished to be moderate in my calculations; I have therefore, upon former occasions, as at present, taken it upon the average of the four last years. It is my intention to continue those temporary taxes which were imposed upon occasion of the Spanish armament,[1] and which expire at different periods. They had been found to be attended with no particular inconvenience to the country, and would consequently be submitted to with less reluctance than any fresh imposts. These amount to £255,000, which sum I should henceforth propose to consider as part of the supply.

The aid which I have now to suggest is, what often has been looked upon as entirely chimerical and has been treated, at best, as precarious and uncertain; namely, the assistance to the finances of this country to be derived from those of India. This assistance my right honourable friend [2] pledged himself for, when he could neither foresee the war which threatened the opulence of India, nor the present war which could render its resources desirable to this country. I am now happy to state that the fulfilment of his promise has arrived, notwithstanding the difficulties which seemed to bar its accomplishment; and that, in 1794, a sum of not less than £500,000 from the finances of India will be applicable to the expenses of this country. My right honourable friend has not only stated his propositions on this subject distinctly, article by article, but published them to the world; and thus taken every method to invite discussion and challenge contradiction. The political and commercial arrangements of India are not yet before the House; nor has any plan, with respect

[1] In 1790 Pitt mobilized the navy at a cost of £2,821,000 in support of the British claim against Spain to the possession of Nootka Sound, a harbour in what is now Vancouver Island.

[2] Dundas.

to them, been definitely settled : but, whatever may be the plan adopted, I trust it will be one attended with no less advantage than that proposed by my right honourable friend ; so that, in any case, I may with confidence promise the benefit which it has been stated will result from the assistance of India. The whole make a total of £6,649,000, so that there remains £4,500,000 to be provided for by other resources. Of this sum, there is £1,650,000 in the hands of the commissioners of the national debt, which they would readily subscribe ; and for the rest there will be wanting a loan of £2,900,000.

I have not made any proposals concerning the terms of the loan, because I considered it, first, as my duty to submit this statement to the public, in order to avoid anything which might have the appearance of deception. A sum of £240,000 will be wanting to pay the interest of this loan : for which purpose I mean to devote the taxes imposed upon occasion of the Spanish armament. These taxes were of two kinds, some of them temporary, and others perpetual. Of these, the additional tax on bills and the game duty amounted to £85,000. The tax of one penny per gallon on all British spirits, which surely was, in itself, a matter of proper regulation, produced a sum of £112,000. Another of these was the addition of 10 per cent. upon all assessed taxes, which amounted to about £90,000 ; making, upon the whole, a sum of £287,000. According to the present price of stocks, and recent events are not likely to diminish their value, I will now lay before the committee a general statement of the whole subject, in one connected point of view :

General Statement

Amount of supply . £11,182,213
Do. of ways and means 8,299,696
———— £2,882,517
Add, money from commissioners 1,650,000
———— £4,532,517 say £4,500,000

£4,500,000 at 75 per cent. is equal to . £6,000,000

£6,000,000 at 3 per cent. is equal to . £180,000
To which add an additional 1 per cent.   60,000
———— £240,000

10 per cent. on assessed taxes . £90,000 ⎫ temporary
British spirits . . . . 112,000 ⎬ taxes to be
                                              ⎭ continued.

Bills and receipts . . . 68,000
Game duty 17,000
———— £287,000

This, I believe, is nearly the statement which I meant to submit to the committee. You will have perceived that I have stated a large and ample provision, in point of expense, with a view to an extended scale of operations. You will also perceive that I have made a large provision for the extraordinary and unforeseen occurrences which may arise during the war; while, at the same time, I have attended to the object of keeping down the unfunded debt, and applying the annual surplus to the extinction of the funded debt. The committee will at least see that I have not neglected, however painful, to do my duty; that I have prepared, decidedly, to meet events, and to let them know the extent of the operations with which the present and future state of the war may be attended : and though I should deem it presumptuous to speculate much about the events of a war which must always be accompanied with some degree of suspense and uncertainty, I do not think it useless to suggest some observations with respect to the war in which we are engaged. The excess of the permanent revenue, if kept up, is no less than £900,000 above the peace establishment; which, even if destroyed by war, will leave the country in possession of all its ordinary revenue. This £900,000 I have not taken into my reasoning. I have taken care not to found any calculation upon it; because I was desirous to leave it as a security against those accidents and contingencies to which every war is liable. Nothing, certainly, is so difficult, as to calculate, with any degree of certainty, upon the events of a war; yet, if the same good fortune, which has attended us in the outset, shall continue to accompany us, we have everything to hope, and little reason to dread that our commerce will meet with much interruption; in which case, our revenue could not suffer. At the same time, it has been my object to prepare you for sinister events, and to make provision against every calamity that can possibly occur. The committee will see, from the statements which I have submitted to them, that even if the struggle in which we are engaged should last beyond the present year, we shall be able to carry it on during the next without any additional burden.

I am not desirous to draw a sanguine picture. I was

careful to state none of these encouragements to a war in any of the previous discussions. I considered that we ought then to determine solely on the merits of the case; and that, if we considered a war as necessary, we were bound to meet it, even to its utmost extent. There is no part which we ought not to be prepared to sacrifice for the preservation of the whole. This is a war in which, not merely adopting empty professions, but speaking the language of our hearts and fulfilling the impressions of our duty, we are ready to sacrifice our lives and fortunes for the safety of the country, the security of Europe, and in the cause of justice, humanity, and religion. I will not do such injustice to any one as to suppose, that, in such a cause, they are not ready to go the greatest length, and to make every sacrifice that may be required. I will here barely touch upon the contrast which the present situation of the country offers to the flourishing state during the last session with regard to revenue. That contrast no man feels more severely than I do. No man can more deeply regret any interruption to the prosperous state of the revenue, the object of my most anxious attention and my most favourite wishes; but if they consider the situation of the neighbouring and hostile State with respect to revenue, they have no reason to despond. Instead of giving way to feelings of useless regret upon that occasion, I trust you are influenced by far different sentiments.

Many are the motives which have induced us to enter into the war. I have heard of wars of honour; and such, too, have been deemed wars of prudence and policy. On the present occasion, whatever can raise the feelings, or animate the exertions of a people, concur to prompt us to the contest. The contempt which the French have shown for a neutrality, on our part most strictly observed; the violations of their solemn and plighted faith; their presumptuous attempts to interfere in the government of this country, and to arm our subjects against ourselves; to vilify a monarch, the object of our gratitude, reverence, and affection; and to separate the Court from the people, by representing them as influenced by different motives, and acting from different interests. After provocation so wanton, so often repeated, and so highly aggravated, does not this become, on our part, a war of honour; a war necessary to assert the spirit of the nation, and the dignity of the British name? I have heard of wars undertaken for the general security of Europe; was it ever so threatened as by the progress of the French arms, and the system of ambition and aggrandizement which they have discovered? I have heard of wars for the defence of the Protestant religion: our enemies in this instance are equally the enemies of all religion—of Lutheranism, of Calvinism; and desirous to propagate, everywhere, by the force of their arms, that system of infidelity which they avow in their principles. I have heard of wars undertaken in defence of the lawful succession; but now we fight in defence of our hereditary monarchy. We are at war with those who would destroy the whole fabric of our constitution. When I look at these things, they afford me encouragement and consolation; and support me in discharging the painful task to which I am now called by my duty. The retrospect to that flourishing state in which we were placed previous to this war, ought to teach us to know the value of the present order of things; and to resist the malignant and envious attempts of those who would deprive us of that happiness which they despair themselves to attain. We ought to remember, that that very prosperous situation at the present crisis supplies us with the exertions, and furnishes us with the means, which our exigencies demand. In such a cause as that in which we are now engaged, I trust that our exertions will terminate only with our lives. On this ground I have brought forward the resolutions which I am now to propose; and on this ground I now trust for your support.

The financial resolutions were agreed to.

4

On a Motion for Peace

June 17, 1793 [1]

GREAT BRITAIN was too ill prepared for war to take a large part in the opening campaign. Pitt's vigorous naval policy had made possible the mobilization of 90 ships of the line, but the regular army in this country amounted to less than 15,000 men. A naval squadron was at once dispatched to protect the Dutch coast and inlets, but only a few thousand men could be sent to assist the Dutch on land. In February 1793 the French army invaded Holland and captured Breda: but the Dutch and British troops, supported by the fleet, prevented the enemy crossing the Hollandsch Diep. The

[1] *Speeches*, vol. ii, p. 157.

French were soon compelled to fall back by the advance of the main Austrian army, and on March 18 they were decisively defeated by it at Neerwinden, and retreated into France. The allies then moved against the frontier fortresses, and in June the Austrians and the British began the siege of Valenciennes. A Prussian army, meanwhile, was threatening the Republic on the Rhine.

Such was the military position when Fox[1] moved in the House of Commons that an address should be presented to the King, requesting him to take the earliest measures for procuring peace with France. Pitt opposed the motion in the following speech.

After what has been already so ably urged, I do not, in the present stage of the debate, conceive it necessary to speak to the merits of the question. The almost unanimous call of the House shows, that on that point they have already sufficiently made up their minds. But something has been alleged on the general grounds on which the motion is brought forward, and particular allusions have been made to me, which I cannot allow to pass over in silence. The motion has been introduced by the honourable gentleman on the eve of the conclusion of the session, no doubt as a solemn expression of the sentiments entertained by him on the present state of affairs, and I should be sorry that my opinion on the present occasion should be at all equivocal. I do not then hesitate to declare that this motion is in itself the most impolitic and preposterous which could possibly be adopted, the most contradictory to those general principles which at all times ought to regulate our conduct, and the most unsuitable to those particular circum-

---

[1] For Fox's attitude to the war, see Introduction, pp. xxvii–xxviii.

stances in which we are now placed. Such is my opinion of the nature of this motion, which points out to us a line of conduct we can by no means pursue, namely, to make peace upon terms which, even if within our reach, we ought not to accept, but which, in fact, is only calculated to amuse and delude the people, by holding out to them a possibility of peace, when, in reality, peace is impossible, and thus serving to create groundless discontents and dissatisfaction with the present situation of affairs.

Are we, I would ask, in pursuance of this motion, to be content merely with the French relinquishing those conquests which they have unjustly made, without either obtaining reparations for the injuries they have already done us, or security against their future repetition? There might, indeed, be situations in which we might be compelled to adopt such a conduct. Against necessity there is no possibility of contending. But, indeed, it would be rather strange if we should do that at the beginning of a most successful war, which could only be advisable at the conclusion of a most disastrous one. It would be a principle somewhat new, if, when unjustly attacked and forced into a war we should think proper to cease from all hostilities, as soon as the enemy should be unwilling to support their attack and go on with the contest. Has such been the case in any of the most favourite periods of the history of this country, to which the honourable gentleman is so fond of alluding? Where can he find any such principle in any of those wars which this country has carried on in support of its independence? And if so, what is there in the peculiar situation of the French, the disturbers of the peace of Europe, and the unprovoked aggressors of this country, that should require any other measure to be dealt to them, than what we have been accustomed on former occasions to afford to our enemies? With a prospect of success so great as we have in the present moment, are we to grant them an impunity for all those designs which they have so unjustly formed and attempted to carry into execution? Would this tend in any degree to remedy the temporary inconvenience to this country, which the honourable gentleman has stated as resulting from the war, but which, in reality, is produced by collateral causes? In no case would the conduct here pointed out be expedient. But of all cases, where we ought not to stop merely because the enemy stops, ⟨the clearest⟩ is that where we have suffered an injury without having either obtained reparation or security.

This I will illustrate by what is at present our situation. And first I will ask, what was the state of this country with respect to France, previous to the declaration of war on her part? We then contended, first, That she had broken a treaty with our allies, which we were bound to support: secondly, That she had engaged in schemes of ambition and aggrandizement, inconsistent with the interests of this country, and the general security of Europe: thirdly, That she had entertained principles hostile to all governments, and more particularly to our own. In consequence of all these circumstances, you then declared in addresses to His Majesty that if proper satisfaction was not obtained, a war must be the consequence. But while this was in agitation, they had themselves declared war, and been guilty of a sudden and unprovoked aggression upon this country. Is then that aggression, the climax of all their injuries, to induce you to abandon those reasonable views of satisfaction which before you entertained ? The necessity of security against those three points, their disregard of treaties, their projects of ambition, and their dangerous principles, certainly becomes greater, inasmuch as their injuries are increased by the aggression. The argument for satisfaction, instead of being diminished, derives greater strength from this last circumstance. Indeed if we were foiled, we might then be induced to abandon those views with which we had set out, to submit to the hardship of our fate, and to receive such terms as necessity might dictate. But those terms which the motion prescribed are not such as are to be aimed at in the first instance, but such as are only to be submitted to in the last extremity. The question then is, whether we shall now court calamity, whether we shall, after a most successful commencement, voluntarily submit to all the most direful consequences of failure and defeat ? At present we have both right and interest on our side. Shall we abandon both ? Shall we, with the means of doing ourselves justice, pass by the most repeated and aggravated injuries, and grant peace to those whose unprovoked aggression alone compelled us to arm in our own defence ? The question resolves itself into this ; shall we, from a view of the present situation of the belligerent Powers, risk more by vigorously persisting in the war till we have obtained its objects, or by abandoning it without either reparation or security ? I shall only put the question, and leave it to you to decide.

Allow me only to subjoin a few remarks with reference to some points urged by the honourable gentleman who made the motion. We thought it necessary in the first instance, upon being attacked, to enter vigorously into the war. Did we not see the evils which we might expect to encounter in carrying it on? Were we insensible of those calamities with which every war is attended? Have these evils and calamities turned out to be greater than at first were expected and foreseen? On this point I shall not refer you to the inflamed exaggerations of the honourable gentleman, who predicted from the war, even in its commencement, every possible calamity, such as the most alarming discontents at home, the total stagnation of commerce and interruption of public prosperity; and who represented that its infallible consequence must be not to check the schemes and repulse the progress of the enemy, but, on the contrary, to unite their views and concentrate their vigour. No—however justified I might be in taking this statement, I shall refer you only to the more moderate apprehensions of those who, though convinced of the necessity of the war, were not insensible to its dreadful consequences. These apprehensions happily have been disappointed, and the very reverse of those calamities, which there was but too much reason to dread, has taken place. The war has been attended, even in its outset, with the most brilliant, rapid, and unexpected success. The views of the enemy have experienced a most effectual check, and every circumstance concurs to favour the hope of our being able completely to accomplish every object of the war. Is there anything, then, in this situation, to induce us to abandon our views of reparation and security? Are we to give up our claims of satisfaction, merely because we have been beyond example successful in repelling an unjust attack? To urge this point would indeed be wasting the time of the House.

The only question that remains is, at what period, and from what situation of affairs, we are to obtain that reparation and security which we desire. How long are we to wait for these objects? Are we to place them upon circumstances which may never happen, and thus pursue them without any possibility of attaining our end, which may be the case if we look to the establishment of any particular government in France? The answer to these questions, like the degree of security and reparation to be obtained, depends upon circumstances of comparison. I declare, that on the part of this Government there was no intention, if the country had not been attacked, to interfere in the internal affairs of France. This was clearly proved by the system of neutrality, on our part, so strictly observed. But having been attacked, I affirm, that there is nothing, either in the addresses to His Majesty or the declarations of his servants, which pledges us not to take advantage of any interference in the internal affairs of France that may be necessary. I, for my own part, repeat, that I have given no such pledge. I do not say that if, without any interference, sufficient security and reparation could be had for this country, I would not, in that case, be of opinion that we ought to abstain from all interference, and allow their Government to remain even upon its present footing. But I consider the question of obtaining these, while the same principle that now prevails continues to actuate their Government, to be extremely difficult, if not impossible. I should certainly think, that the best security we could obtain, would be in the end of that wild ungoverned system, from which have resulted those injuries against which it is necessary to guard. There are, however, degrees and proportions of security which may be obtained and with which we ought to rest satisfied; these must depend upon the circumstances that shall afterwards arise, and cannot be ascertained by any previous definition. But when you have seen yourselves and all Europe attacked—when you have seen a system established, violating all treaties, disregarding all obligations, and, under the name of the rights of man, uniting the principles of usurpation abroad, tyranny and confusion at home—you will judge, whether you ought to sit down without some security against the consequences of such a system being again brought into action. And this security, it appears to me, can only be obtained in one of three modes—first, That these principles shall no longer predominate; or secondly, That those, who are now engaged in them, shall be taught that they are impracticable, and convinced of their own want of power to carry them into execution; or thirdly, That the issue of the present war shall be such as, by weakening their power of attack, shall strengthen your power of resistance. Without these, you may indeed have an armed truce, a temporary suspension of hostilities; but no permanent peace; no solid security to guard you against the repetition of injury and the renewal of attack. If on these points we have made up our minds, if we are determined to prosecute the war till we shall obtain proper satisfaction, and at least be able to provide some security for the continuance of peace, the present motion can only tend to fetter the operations of war, to delude our subjects, to gratify the factious, to inflame the discontented, to discourage our allies, to strengthen our enemies.

What could be the effect of any negotiation for peace in the present moment? It is not merely to the character of Marat,[1] with whom we would have to treat, that I object; it is not to the horror of those crimes which have stained their legislators, crimes in every stage rising above another in point of enormity; but I object to the consequences of that character, to the effect of those crimes. They are such as render negotiation useless, and must entirely deprive of stability any peace which could be concluded in such circumstances. Where is our security for the performance of a treaty where we have neither the good faith of a nation, nor the responsibility of a monarch? The moment that the mob of Paris becomes under the influence of a new leader, mature deliberations are reversed, the most solemn engagements are retracted, our free will is altogether controlled by force. In every one of the stages of their repeated revolutions we have said, ' Now we have seen the worst, the measure of iniquity is complete, we shall no longer be shocked or astonished by the contemplation of added crimes and increasing enormities.' The next mail gave us reason to reproach ourselves with our credulity, and, by presenting us with fresh crimes and enormities still more dreadful, excited impressions of new astonishment

---

[1] The notorious Terrorist: one of the chief instigators of the 'September Massacres'. (See Introduction, p. xx.)

and accumulated horror. All the crimes which disgrace history have occurred in one country, in a space so short, and with circumstances so highly aggravated, as outrun thought and exceed imagination. Should we treat with Marat, before we had finished the negotiation he might again have descended to the dregs of the people from whom he sprung, and have given place to a still more desperate villain. A band of leaders had swayed the mob in constant succession, all resembling in guilt, but each striving to improve upon the crime of his predecessor, and swell the black catalogue with new modes and higher gradations of wickedness—

> *Aetas parentum peior avis tulit*
> *Nos nequiores, mox daturos*
> *Progeniem vitiosiorem.*[1]

No treaty can exist on their good faith independent of the terms of peace. Could they be bound by engagements more solemn than those to which they had pledged themselves in return for our neutrality? What new engagements can be more binding, or from what part of the character of the leaders, or what change in the principles of action, can we expect greater good faith, or stricter attention to engagements, than were exhibited by their predecessors? To make a treaty with them would only be to afford them an opportunity of breaking it off before it was finished, or violating it in its very commencement.

But if the motion can answer no good purpose, can it answer no bad one? Might it not serve to encourage

[1] Horace, *Odes*, iii. 6. 'Our parents' age, itself more wicked than their fathers', bore us yet more degenerate, soon to bring forth in our turn a progeny more evil still.'

the French? What the honourable gentleman reserved as the last part of his argument, seemed particularly to have this tendency, the conclusion which he drew of the necessity of a peace from the situation of the country. If we are really come to that period of distress and embarrassment, that peace upon such terms is necessary, we must indeed submit to the decrees of Providence with the resignation with which we would submit to the sacrifice of our independence. If the period of our ruin is come, we must prepare to meet the fate which we cannot avert: we cannot meet it in any shape more dreadful than that which is proposed by the motion of the honourable gentleman. But our situation is not yet so desperate. With respect to the embarrassment of credit and the consequent interruption of commerce, I may safely say, that none have watched it more carefully than myself, none can have felt it more anxiously. The honourable gentleman states the means of relief, which have been adopted by the legislature, as, in his opinion, a proof of the extent of the calamity. For my part, I have formed a very different conclusion. The effect of the relief held out by the legislature, even before it was experienced, was completely to restore confidence and vigour to commerce—a proof that the embarrassed state of credit was only temporary, and, in a great measure, accidental. It clearly was not the effect of the war in which this country was engaged, but was influenced by the state of the Continent, where the war had previously subsisted, and where it had taken away the market for our commodities. This embarrassment then could only be ascribed to that cause which had produced so many other calamities—that destroying spirit on the Continent, which devours not only the fruits, but the seeds of industry, which overturns the very altar of society, and lets loose upon the world all the horrors of anarchy and desolation!

The question then is, whether we shall persevere in those exertions, by which we may at least remove this inconvenience, while, in co-operation with our allies, we strive to remove its cause—a cause which, if not checked, might have led to distress and ruin. The present motion, by magnifying the inconvenience which we have sustained into a calamity, is calculated to give a false impression, and give to what at most could only be the object of apprehension at home all the mischievous consequences of a real distress abroad. It is calculated to discourage our allies, and inspire our enemies with confidence.

Having thus given my opinion as a member of Parliament, there are some allusions which have been made to myself, as a member of the Cabinet, which I am called upon to notice. I have only to say, that if ever that honourable gentleman should be a member of the Cabinet, I trust that he will be better informed of the proceedings of the councils of other nations, than at present he seems to be with what every man would desire to have some acquaintance with, those of his own. He stated, that he brought forward his motion with a view of giving support to certain opinions; which he understood to be entertained in the Cabinet respecting the war. If he brought forward his motion from any motive of personal kindness to me, I have only to request that he will withdraw it. Not having lately been much in the habit of reading newspapers, I could not easily conceive to whom the honourable gentleman alluded. Indeed, there is no proposition which I could deem so impolitic to be brought forward by any of His Majesty's servants as the present motion. If there is any difference in opinion between me and the other members of the Cabinet, I can only assure him, that I am the most determined to oppose the grounds and principles upon which that motion is founded. The question is, whether, in conjunction with our allies, with whom our own prosperity is so intimately connected, and with those prospects of success which our situation affords, we shall persevere vigorously to oppose those destructive principles with which, even though baffled at present, we may expect to contend to the latest hours of our lives : and on this issue I allow it to rest. I have spoken at much greater length than at first I intended ; but on this subject, whenever it occurs, I find it impossible to keep those bounds which I had prescribed to myself, prompted as I am to enlarge by the dearest feelings and principles of my heart, affection and gratitude to my sovereign, and that duty which I owe as a member of the community.

Fox's motion was defeated by 187 to 47.

5
The Jacobin Government of France
January 21, 1794 [1]

BY midsummer, 1793, the allied forces of the First Coalition reached the limit of their success. At the end of July, Valenciennes had fallen to the Austro-British

[1] *Speeches*, vol. i, p. 166.

army, and Mainz to the Prussians. Then the tide turned. Reinforced by new levies and brilliantly reorganized by Carnot, the French armies resumed the offensive. In October the Austrians were defeated at Wattignies and retreated into Belgium. A little later they were also driven out of northern Alsace. The Prussians meanwhile remained inactive, and the efforts of the British forces were directed to minor objects. Our army in Flanders was drawn off to besiege Dunkirk, and an expedition was dispatched to the Mediterranean to hold Toulon for the French Royalists. The attack on Dunkirk miscarried; and in December, largely owing to the skilful management of the Republican artillery by the young Buonaparte, the British were forced to evacuate Toulon. By the end of the year France was free from alien invaders.

The case for an immediate peace, pressed continuously by Fox and his followers, seemed strengthened by the failure of the Coalition; but, while the soldiers of the Republic on the frontiers were winning the respect of their opponents in the field, the conduct of their political leaders in Paris was outraging humanity and demonstrating that the peace of Europe was an idle dream as long as they controlled the fortunes of France.[1]

Such, at any rate, was Pitt's conviction; and in the King's Speech at the opening of the Session in 1794, the following paragraph was inserted:

'Although I cannot but regret the necessary continuance of the war, I should ill consult the essential interests of my people, if I was desirous of peace on any grounds but such as may provide for their permanent safety, and for the independence and security of Europe. The attainment of these ends is still obstructed by the prevalence of a system in France, equally incompatible with the happiness of that country, and with the tranquillity of all other nations.'

[1] For the horrors of the Jacobin régime, see Introduction, p. xx.

In the debate on the address, Fox moved, as an amendment, 'To recommend to His Majesty to treat, as speedily as possible, for a peace with France upon safe and advantageous terms, without any reference to the nature or form of the government that might exist in that country.'

Pitt opened his reply by reminding the House of the sentiments with which they had entered on the war.

It had been the opinion of the majority of that House, and of the great body of the nation, that it was undertaken upon grounds strictly defensive; and that the nation were equally compelled to engage in it by the obligations of duty and the urgency of necessity. An honourable gentleman had asked—Would not we have engaged in the war, even if France had not previously declared against us? To this he would answer, what he had last session asserted, That if we did not receive satisfaction for past injuries and security with respect to the future, most certainly we would.

He then reviewed the attitude of the Government to the question of peace during the last year, and declared that their determination to continue the war had been strengthened by the progressive degradation in character of the men who had so rapidly succeeded one another in the control of the affairs of France. The process had culminated in the establishment of the revolutionary Government on May 21—'a new Government, more dreadful in its character and more fatal in its effects than any which preceded it'.

My noble friend[1] began (he continued) by stating that one of the leading features of this Government was the abolition of religion. It will scarcely be maintained that

[1] Lord Clifden, who moved the address.

this step could tend only to affect opinions, and have no influence upon the conduct of a nation. The extinction of religious sentiment was only intended to pave the way for the introduction of fresh crimes, and entirely to break asunder those bands of society which had been already loosened. It was intended only to familiarize the mind with guilt, and, by removing the obstacle of fear, to relieve it from the restraints of conscience. Infidelity, as my noble friend remarked, was only meant to go hand in hand with insurrection. A second measure of this revolutionary Government was the destruction of property, a precedent which tended not less to destroy all ideas of justice, than the former to extinguish all sentiments of piety. Not less detestable was their conduct in their mode of inflicting punishments—a mode which took away from the accused all privilege of defence, and from their trials even the appearance of legal forms. All these crimes, however, they contrived to convert into sources of revenue. From the pillage of the churches, from the destruction of property, from the confiscation of the effects of those who were condemned, they derived the means for conducting their military operations. They pushed every resource to its utmost extent; as for instance, the unbounded circulation of *assignats*, and the imposition of a forced loan. What can be expected from a system acting upon such principles, and supported by such resources? Resources so desperate afford in themselves the most certain symptoms and indications of the approaching decay of that system with which they are connected. If then such be the system, if such the means of its support, and if France in consequence has, during these few months, experienced a degree of distress the greatest perhaps ever known in that country during the same space of time, what prospect can there be of either stability or permanence to the present order of things? Can it be supposed to rest on that something approaching to instinct—that spirit of enthusiasm which has been so highly extolled by the gentlemen on the other side? What can we think of the probability of the duration of a system which has sent as many suspected persons to the prison or scaffold, as it has sent recruits to the field?

But it has been urged, that the French have distinguished themselves in the field; nor will it be denied that, independently of any other circumstance, the spirit of a people called forth by the impulse which acts so strongly in such a situation, may have the effect to make them brave in the moment of action. But their efforts are merely the result of a system of restraint and oppression, the most terrible and gigantic, that has, perhaps, ever existed. They are compelled into the field by the terror of the guillotine—they are supported there only by those resources which their desperate situation affords; and in these circumstances, what can be the dependence on the steadiness of their operations, or what rational prospect can there be of the permanence of their exertions? On this ground, the more monstrous and terrible the system has become, the greater is the probability that it will be speedily overthrown. From the nature of the mind of man, and the necessary progress of human affairs, it is impossible that such a system can be of long duration; and surely no event can be looked for more desirable than a destruction of that system, which at present exists to the misery of France and the terror of Europe.

As to the question of the honourable gentleman, whether I am never to make peace with the Jacobins, it is extremely difficult to answer, and it would be neither prudent nor rational in me to give him any definitive reply in the present moment. It is a question, the solution of which must depend upon a combination of events. As circumstances may vary, a different line of conduct must necessarily be pursued; nor would it be proper to bind up my discretion to act with a regard to those contingencies that may arise, by pledging myself at present to one set of measures. In the present circumstances, I have no hesitation to declare, that I would rather choose to persevere in the war, even amidst the worst disasters, and should deem such a conduct much more safe and honourable, than to conclude a peace with the ruling powers in France on their present system. The question of pursuing the war must, in every instance, depend upon the convenience with which it can be carried on to ourselves; and of that you must be best qualified to judge. On this great and interesting crisis, I have no hesitation to state, that I should think myself deficient in point of candour, if I did not most unequivocally declare, that the moment will never come, when I shall not think any alternative preferable to that of making peace with France, upon the system of its present rulers.

After pointing out that the amendment moved by Fox would, if carried, suggest to our allies 'that they are no longer to consider us as eager in the cause, or acting upon the principles with which we embarked on war along with them ', Pitt explained his views on the restoration of the French monarchy.

The honourable gentleman has inaccurately stated, that I attach the same degree of importance to the restoration of monarchy in France, as to the destruction of the present system. This is by no means the case: I attach importance to the restoration of monarchy, from an opinion that, in the present state of France, some settled form should take place, in which the greater part of the people may be disposed to concur. The ancient government I consider as affording the best materials upon which they could work, in introducing any change into the fabric of their constitution. Besides, as I have thought it incumbent, in any interference which I proposed in the internal affairs of that country, to consult chiefly the happiness of the people, monarchy appeared to me the system most friendly to their true interests. In another respect, the honourable gentleman has misrepresented me, by stating the restitution of monarchy as an event which must necessarily be preceded by the conquest of France. I consider monarchy only as the standard under which the people of France might be united, the more especially as it is that form of government which my noble friend has proved to be most agreeable to the wishes of two-thirds of the inhabitants. But it has been said, that even the re-establishment of royalty would afford us no additional security for the permanence of peace, and that the French would still be equally formidable to this country. It is, however, surely a wild and extravagant assertion, that the monarchy of France, stripped as it would then be of much of its power, and diminished in its revenues, should be as formidable as a system which has proved itself to be more dangerous than monarchy ever was, in the plenitude of its power and the height of its greatness.

But there is one part of the argument of my noble friend to which I must particularly call your attention, and which, independently of every other consideration, precludes even the possibility of our treating with France in the present moment. A decree has been passed by the Convention, forbidding to treat with any enemy till they shall have evacuated the territories of the Republic; and on the 13th of April it was again decreed that those persons should be punished with death who should propose to treat with any Power which should not have previously acknowledged the independence of the French nation, and the unity and indivisibility of the Republic, founded upon liberty and equality. Thus, by any proposal to treat, we should not only incur the disgrace of the most abject humiliation, but absolutely put ourselves at their mercy, and subject ourselves to the necessity of receiving any terms which they might be disposed to dictate. Are you then to withdraw your armies, to deprive yourself of the co-operation of your allies, to forgo all your acquisitions, to give up Condé, Quesnoi, Tobago, Fort Louis, all the factories in the East Indies? Are you to abandon all these acquisitions, the rewards of your past labours, and the pledges of your future success? Should you consent to do all this, should you even hasten to send an ambassador to treat with the Convention (and the right honourable gentleman[1] I believe on a former occasion volunteered himself for that service), you not only must acknowledge the unity and indivisibility of the French Republic, but you must do so in their own way. You must acknowledge it as founded on liberty and equality. You must subscribe to the whole of their code, and by this act sanction the deposition of their sovereign and the annihilation of their legislature.

It may be said, that they would not insist upon all this to its full extent; but of this I can have but little confidence, when I compare their past declarations and their conduct. To whatever pitch of extravagance they may have reached in what they have said, they have always outstript it by what they have done. The absurdity of their expressions has in every instance been surpassed by the outrages of their conduct; nor can we have any hopes of more moderation from any change of parties. In all revolutions that have hitherto taken place, the first recommendation to favour has been hostility to England. The most violent party have always predominated. The leading feature in their character at present is a spirit of military enterprise, exerted not for the purposes of ambition, but everywhere spreading, in its progress, terror and desolation. We are called in the present age to witness the political and moral phenomenon of a mighty and civilized people, formed into an artificial horde of banditti, throwing off all the restraints which have influenced men in social life, displaying a savage valour directed by a sanguinary spirit, forming rapine and destruction into a system, and perverting to their

[1] Fox.

detestable purposes, all the talents and ingenuity which they derived from their advanced stage of civilization, all the refinements of art, and the discoveries of science. We behold them uniting the utmost savageness and ferocity of design with consummate contrivance and skill in execution, and seemingly engaged in no less than a conspiracy to exterminate from the face of the earth all honour, humanity, justice, and religion. In this state, can there be any question but to resist, where resistance alone can be effectual, till such time as, by the blessing of Providence upon our endeavours, we shall have secured the independence of this country and the general interests of Europe?

The amendment was negatived by 277 to 59, and the address was then agreed to.

6
On a Motion for a Separate Peace with France
March 6, 1794 [1]

One of the chief difficulties with which Pitt had to contend was the unpopularity of Britain's allies.[2] Because he was acting in co-operation with the despotic sovereigns of Prussia and Austria—Prussia who had already joined with Russia in the second partition of Poland, and Austria who was preparing to take her share in the third partition —the Opposition derided his claim to be defending the liberties and the international rights of Europe: and

[1] *Parliamentary History*, vol. xxx, p. 1483.
[2] Introduction, pp. xxiii, xxviii.

when the tide turned against the Coalition, they declared that the time had come for Great Britain to break with her allies and make a separate peace with France. Thus, on March 6, 1794, Whitbread moved an address to the King, deploring that 'His Majesty should have been advised to make a " common cause " with Powers whose objects are unavowed and undefined, but from whose conduct his faithful Commons have too much ground to dread that they carry on war for the purpose of dictating in the internal affairs of other countries ', and entreating His Majesty ' to extricate himself from engagements which oppose such difficulties to His Majesty's concluding a separate peace '. In opposition to this motion, Pitt spoke as follows :

Sir, the question which has been now brought forward comes within a very narrow compass. If the House or the country conceived the present contest to be what it is represented to be ; if they conceived it to have originated from a league of despots for the purpose of crushing the rising liberties of a neighbouring State ; if they considered it as a contest into which we had unnecessarily entered, and in which no interest of our own was involved, they might then be of opinion that the present motion ought to be adopted. But if the House and the country continue to think that the war was originally undertaken to repel aggression, and to secure our dearest and most important interests, and that in such circumstances we had the happiness to find allies in some Powers already engaged in the same contest, and likewise to find others who were disposed to concur with us for the same purpose, will they not then be of opinion, that instead of seeking to abandon our present alliances, we ought rather to do everything in our power to cement and confirm them? The arguments, upon which the motion has been supported, have been derived from particular parts of the conduct of some of our allies, or from general objections, which apply equally to all confederacies; but while such are the arguments upon which it rests, what are the effects which it is calculated to produce? It tends to discourage our allies, and impress them with the idea that they can no longer depend upon our co-operation, while it holds out a signal to the enemy that we are prepared to receive such a peace as they may be disposed to give us. The motion is no less than a motion for peace, and that upon any terms.

A great part of the speech of the right hon. gentleman who spoke last was taken up in proving that the objections, which are urged against war in general, apply to the present war. This surely was not necessary. So much do the objections against war in general apply to every particular war, that they ought, no doubt, to be allowed the greatest influence, whenever there is any option between war and peace. But in every case where it is necessary to undertake a war in support of the interests or independence of a country, these objections are supposed to vanish.

Pitt then briefly discussed the prospects of the war. Returning to the question at issue, he continued:

If the war in which we are engaged is just, is there anything in the system of our alliances inconsistent with sound policy? Complaints have been made of detached parts of the conduct of our allies; some of them previous to the war, and others during the war, but all of them independent of the cause in which we are engaged. With respect to La Fayette,[1] I have only to say that his fate was never at the disposal of this country. The situation of Poland has often been brought forward, but I have never hesitated to express my disapprobation of the treatment of that country. But the question is whether we should allow one act of injustice to deprive us of the assistance of those Powers in resisting a system of intolerable injustice, not merely existing in France, but attempted to be introduced into every other country?

It has been asked, what are the views of our allies with respect to the future government of France? Do they mean to restore the former absolute monarchy? I have no reason to impute to them any such intention; but this I know, that this country is engaged in the contest, only so far as relates to her own defence. But it has been urged that even should the combined Powers succeed, there may be danger from their subsequent divisions. This is an objection which must equally apply to all confederations; but it is surely no reason why Great Britain, the soul and cement of the confederacy, should at present withdraw her assistance and co-operation from the other Powers.

The motion was rejected by 138 to 26.

[1] See *infra*, p. 151, note 1.

7

The Folly of a Premature Peace

December 30, 1794 [1]

THE outlook had been gloomy in January; it was still gloomier in December. Early in the year, the Austrians and Prussians had been driven back to the Rhine, and by the autumn Coblentz and the whole of the left bank of the river had been occupied by the French. On October 21, the results of the year's campaigns were announced in the Convention in these terms: 'Eight pitched battles gained, 116 towns and 230 forts taken, 90,000 prisoners and 3,800 cannons captured.' Meanwhile Belgium was evacuated by the allies, and in December the French armies, taking advantage of the severe frost, overran Holland. The Stadtholder prepared for flight, and the States-General opened negotiations for peace.

It was already clear, before the year ended, that the First Coalition, by which Pitt had hoped to crush the ambitions of revolutionary France, was breaking down. Prussia and Austria were more concerned in sharing with Russia the spoils of Poland than in carrying out their joint obligations in the west. In the second half of 1794 the Poles made their last desperate effort to recover their independence, but in November the rising was suppressed, and the three Powers sat down to arrange the final partition of the country.

While the events of the year had thus darkened the prospects of the war, they had also made a peace in accordance with the principles he had laid down more impracticable than ever. The spring and early summer of 1794 were the bloodiest period of the Terror, and,

[1] *Speeches*, vol. ii, p. 236.

though the reaction, marked by the execution of Robespierre in July, had begun, there was as yet no guarantee that the more sober elements in the Republican ranks would be strong enough to prevent a general relapse into anarchy and massacre.

Meanwhile, at Westminster, the attacks on Pitt for declining to consider terms of peace persisted. As in January, so in December, an amendment was moved to the address at the beginning of the session, advising the King to negotiate for peace; but the mover on this occasion was Wilberforce, not Fox, and it was in reply not to his old political opponent, but to one who had been an intimate personal friend, that Pitt rose once more to vindicate the policy of continuing the war.

I should not have so much endeavoured, Sir, to have engaged your attention at the present moment, had not a sudden indisposition seized me, which I was apprehensive might, at a later hour, have incapacitated me from entering fully into the discussion of a question, upon which I must be supposed to feel most anxious to deliver my sentiments.

I am aware, that there are some gentlemen with whom the original opinions, which they have expressed on the war, prevent me from entertaining any hopes of concurrence. But there are other gentlemen, who, having supported the war at its commencement, have been led, by the disastrous events of the campaign, to change their former sentiments and to withdraw their former support. It is with these gentlemen that I shall consider myself more immediately at issue. And, Sir, I must first make some remarks on the arguments which they have drawn from the words of the address. To this address they say that they cannot give their assent, because it pledges them *never* to make peace with the *Republican* Government of France. I do not consider that it does so pledge them. It says only, that with a Government, such as the present Government of France, we cannot treat on terms that can be deemed secure.[1] And, Sir, where does there exist this imperious necessity to sue for peace? Are we sunk down and depressed to such an absence of hope and to such a want of resources? If we were indeed so calamitously situated, if we were indeed so devoid of hope and so deprived of resources, if the continuance of the war produced so intolerable a pressure, then, perhaps, we might consent to a change of system. I am ready to confess, that I can conceive an imaginary case of a peace being made with the Government of France, even in its republican form; but I will fairly say also, that I have no idea of any peace being secure, unless France return to the monarchical system. That there may, however, be intermediate changes that may give the probability of a peace with that country, even should it continue a republic, I am ready to allow, though I certainly think that the monarchical form of constitution is best for all the countries of Europe, and most calculated to ensure to each of them general and individual happiness. Considering myself, therefore, as I said

---

[1] The address contained a reference to peace negotiations in the following terms: 'No established Government or independent State can, under the present circumstances, derive real security from such negotiations. On our part, they could not be attempted without sacrificing both our honour and safety to an enemy, whose chief animosity is avowedly directed against these kingdoms.'

before, principally at issue with those who now, for the first time, dissent from the prosecution of the war, I am content to deliver my sentiments before I hear the arguments of some gentlemen, who will probably enter into a more full discussion than the subject has yet received.

Sir, the reasons that have induced gentlemen to dissent from the prosecution of the war, seem to have possessed a considerable influence on the manner in which they speak of the justice and necessity of the war at its commencement; and their language is now fainter and feebler than I had reason to expect. Contending, as these gentlemen and I did, with the new and monstrous systems of cruelty, anarchy, and impiety, against those whose principles trampled upon civilized society, religion, and law—contending, I say, with such a system, I could not have entertained the slightest expectation, that from them would have proceeded such an amendment.

It has pleased inscrutable Providence that this power of France should triumph over everything that has been opposed to it! But let us not therefore fall without making any efforts to resist it; let us not sink without measuring its strength. If anything could make me agree to retire from the contest, it would be the consciousness of not being able to continue it. I would at least have no cause to reproach myself on the retrospect. I would not yield till I could exclaim,

——Potuit quae plurima virtus
Esse, fuit: toto certatum est corpore regni.[1]

[1] Virgil, *Aeneid*, xi. 312-13. 'All that valour could be, has been ours : we have fought with the whole body of our kingdom.'

If, Sir, I have expressed myself with more emotion than is consistent with the propriety of debate, the particular situation in which I stand, opposing and contesting the opinions of those with whom I have been, on all occasions, in almost all points fortunate enough to agree, will, I trust, excuse the warmth of my feelings.

The arguments used by my honourable friend, in support of his amendment, may be divided into two classes : the impolicy of continuing the war, and the insecurity of peace. One of the arguments which he uses in support of the impolicy of continuing the war, is grounded on the recent changes that have taken place in France. My right honourable friend's speech was a sufficient answer to that argument. The change that has taken place in France is only the change of an attachment to a name, and not to a substance. Those who have succeeded to the government since the fall of Robespierre, have succeeded to the same sort of government. They adopt the same revolutionary system ; and, though they have made a more moderate use of their power than Robespierre, yet they differ from him only about as much as Robespierre did from Brissot,[1] who incited the war against this country. The present Government, therefore, deserves no more the name of moderation than that established by Brissot and his followers, who committed the unprovoked aggression against Great Britain. The system of the present governors has its root in the same unqualified rights of man, the same

[1] Brissot, the Girondist leader, advocated war in 1792 as a means of overthrowing the monarchy (Introduction, pp. xix-xx). He was guillotined on October 31, 1793.

principles of liberty and equality—principles by which they flatter the people with the possession of the theoretical rights of man, all of which they vitiate and violate in practice. The mild principles of our Government are a standing reproach to theirs, which are as intolerant as the rankest popish bigotry. Their pride and ambition lead them not so much to conquer, as to carry desolation and destruction into all the Governments of Europe. Have we any right, therefore, to suppose that victory and triumph can produce so great a change in their detestable principles, or that success is such a corrective of all those vicious qualities that pervade their principles and their practice?

Do the gentlemen who now desert the war expect that a peace can be obtained of such a nature as has been so well described by my honourable friend?[1] Do they hope for a free and useful commerce? Do they expect that the armies on both sides will be disbanded, and the fleets be called home? Do they mean to put an end to the Traitorous Correspondence Act?[2] I believe not. I can easily suppose that those gentlemen who have, in an early part of the evening, so decidedly given their opinion with respect to the late trials, and who have supposed all the persons in this country to be so pure as not even to be infected by contact with Jacobin principles, would foresee no danger from a French alliance, and would look forward with satisfaction to the

[1] Canning.
[2] An Act passed in 1793 to stop the treasonable communications which had been passing between the enemy in France and certain Jacobin Clubs in England.

consequences of such a measure. But such is not the case with my honourable friends, who even, in such an event, talked of the necessity of additional precautions, in order to guard the dignity of the crown and preserve the tranquillity of the country.

What then would be the rational prospect of advantage to this country from a peace with an enraged enemy, in which there could exist no confidence on either side, but which must necessarily give rise to a state of jealousy, suspicion, and constant armament? How long would this state of trouble or repose last? How will you come to the contest when it is renewed? If you disband your armies, if you diminish your force, you will then put an end to that machine which, under the first two years of a war, can barely be said to have been raised to a point high enough to try the strength of the country. Disband your force, and see if the same means and the same period can raise it again to the same point. You will then be opposed in another war with a diminished military power to an enemy, who may have found it as difficult to disband his armies as you would find it difficult to collect fresh forces. They will again be prepared to start with the same gigantic resources, deriving fresh confidence from the disposition which you had shown to peace, and new vigour from the interval which had been afforded to hostilities.

But will that be all? What assistance can you expect from the continental Powers, if you dissolve the confederacy? And can you expect to assemble such a confederacy again? Suppose the enemy made an attack upon Holland, Prussia, Austria, Spain, and the States of

Italy, on all or any of these; on what grounds, I would ask, could you rouse the spirit, or raise the vigour of this country again, when, from a sense of your inferiority, you have before given up the contest at a period when the confederacy was at its height? On the event of this night's debate may depend what shall be your future situation with respect to your allies. If you do not now proclaim your weakness, if you do not renounce your prospects, you have still great hopes from the alliance of Europe. Prussia, Austria, Spain, and the States of Italy are yet in such a situation that their assistance may be looked to in carrying on the contest.

The honourable gentlemen who supported the amendment, disclaimed the language of fear; they said they knew what Great Britain could do, if once it was roused. What then is to be inferred from all their former professions? Is this a business in which, after all, we were not serious? Is this cause, which has been admitted to involve not only the most important interests of Great Britain, but the safety of Europe and the order of society, not considered to be of such a nature as requires all the energies of the country? What then is the greater necessity to which they looked? What the occasion on which they deemed that they could more worthily employ their efforts? If we should dissolve the powerful confederacy with which we are now united, could we hope again to bring it back at our summons? And shall we not, in the case of a fresh rupture, be exposed alone to the fury of France, without the smallest prospect of assistance from any other quarter? Besides, I think I shall show you that you are desired to relinquish the conflict at a time when all the national and artificial resources of your enemy are verging to a rapid dissolution.

I must now take notice of a speculation which has been indulged—that if you withdraw, France will return to some more moderate system of government. I ask whether we ought to put ourselves in such a situation of hazard, which, if decided against us, would involve us in much greater calamities than we have yet experienced, and would reduce us to a situation in which we should be without means and without resources?

When it is said, therefore, that a peace will have the effect to overthrow the Government of France, the proposition is by no means clear; the probability is much greater, that the persons now at the head of the Government will, in order to continue their own power, (and in France, it is to be recollected, that the continuance of their power is connected with that of their lives, so that, in addition to the incentives of ambition, they have the all-powerful motive of self-preservation), be induced to continue the same system of measures that now prevails. Obliged as they would be to recall a numerous army from the frontiers, will the troops of whom it was composed, after having tasted the sweets of plunder and the licence of the field, be contented to return to the peaceful occupations of industry? Will they not, in order to amuse their daring spirit, and divert from themselves the effects of their turbulence, be compelled to find them some employment? And what is the employment to which they will most naturally direct their first attention? They will employ them to crush all the remains of courage, loyalty, and piety that are yet to be found in France, and extinguish all that gallant and unhappy party from whose co-operation we may promise ourselves, at any future period, to derive advantage. What else can be expected from those Moderates, who, though assuming that appellation, have, in succeeding to the party of Robespierre, only established themselves on a new throne of terror? Thus the peace, which is in the present instance proposed as the means of safety, will ultimately only operate to ensure the work of destruction.

This being my feeling, my objection to asking for peace is, that peace, under the present circumstances, is not desirable, unless you can show that the pressure is greater than, as I shall prove to you from a comparative view of the situation and resources of the two countries, it is.

But this is but a small part of my objections to the measure. My next objection is, that my honourable friend has not told us what sort of peace we are to have: unless, therefore, they state this, I say that they would reduce us to a gratuitous loss of honour and an unnecessary despair. On the kind of peace we might obtain, I will ask my honourable friend, whether he will say that we ought to leave the Austrian Netherlands in the possession of the French?—He will not say so.

I have heard it stated in passing, that the ground of war has been done away by the Dutch negotiation for peace. However paradoxical it may appear, I assert that the safety of Holland, even if she do make peace, depends on our being at war; for if both countries were at peace, then France would be left without restraint. Who that looks to the proceedings of the Convention, does not see that it is their policy, on every occasion, to keep up their arrogant and menacing system, and to hold a high tone of superiority with respect to all other nations ? By these means they have contrived to cherish that spirit of enthusiasm among the people, which has enabled them to make such extraordinary exertions, and on which they depend for the continuance of their power. But who, I would ask, will say that France will make peace on terms, I will not make use of the word moderation, but of concession, when you make peace from a confession of her superiority ? And this naturally leads me to an assertion made use of by me during the last session (an assertion not accurately alluded to by an honourable baronet [1]), relative to the decree of the National Convention of April 13, which states that the preliminary of peace must be a recognition of the unity and indivisibility of the Republic on terms of equality ;—a decree which has neither been repealed nor modified, and which, if you make peace during its existence, would sign the dissolution of your Parliaments and of your present system of civil society.

Again, I say that, if this were only an ordinary war, and if after two years you had gained the West India islands as an indemnification, and had been convinced of the strength of your own resources and that the means of the enemy were decaying, would you consent to make concessions in order to obtain peace ? You received the West India colonies into your protection ; [2] will you then

[1] Sir Richard Hill.

[2] The settlers of Hayti and other French islands in the West Indies refused to acknowledge the Revolutionary Government, declared

give them back a system, under which they can have no protection? I say we cannot do this without being convinced that the further continuance of the war could only produce misfortune, misery, and ruin. Will you add something more terrific to the colonies than all the horrors of that miserable trade which has peopled those miserable colonies?

Before, too, you made such a surrender, there is another question to be considered: no less than whether you would afford to the French an unresisted opportunity of working upon the unfortunate system that now prevails in that country, and introducing their government of anarchy, the horrors of which are even more dreadful than those of slavery. To those who have in common deplored the miseries of the unfortunate negroes, it must appear astonishing that any proposition likely to be attended with such consequences could ever enter into the mind of my honourable friend.[1] Besides, it is impossible to ascertain what a widespread circle of calamity the adoption of this proposition may produce. If once the principles of Jacobinism should obtain a footing in the French West India islands, could we hope that our own would be safe from the contagion? If it has been found scarcely possible to shut out the infection of these principles from the well-tempered and variously blended

their separation from France, and on the outbreak of war invoked the protection of Great Britain. By the autumn of 1794, the British had taken possession of all the French islands except Guadeloupe.

[1] Wilberforce, who had devoted his life to the abolition of the Slave Trade and, a few years previously, had won Pitt's whole-hearted adherence to the cause.

orders of society which subsist in this country, where a principle of subordination runs through all the ranks of society, and all are united by a reciprocity of connexion and interest, what may be expected to be their effects operating upon the deplorable system pervading that quarter ? It would be giving up your own colonies speedily to be devoted to all the horrors of anarchy and devastation.

Such would be the *status quo*. That the *status quo* would probably not be accepted, I have before argued. Will the country, therefore, consign itself, if not to the language, at least to the posture, of supplication ?

With respect to our situation, I have not heard it so fully stated as it is my intention to do. Of the last campaign I shall not be suspected of a wish to conceal the disasters, to deny the defeats, or to disallow the bad effects of the wounds inflicted on the two great military Powers of Europe. But can I forget what the energies and perseverance of Britons have effected in former wars ? Or that constancy for a point of honour in greater difficulties has at length produced the object at which it aimed ?

Will any man say, that the bare event of military disasters, and territories taken, is a fair way of weighing the resources of the belligerent Powers ? No, not in any wars, and least of all in this, as far as it relates to this country. All wars depend now on the finances of the nations engaged in them. This observation particularly applies to the present war. The balance of territorial acquisitions and pecuniary resources is in our favour ; and I am not afraid to assert, that, putting together what has been lost in territory and what has been spent in money, yet with a view to resources, what has been lost by France is more in point of permanent value and present means than the losses of all the allies composed together.

What, let me ask, are the resources of France? They exist by means as extraordinary as the events they have brought about; their pecuniary expenses are beyond anything ever known; and, supported by requisition of person, life, and property, they depend entirely upon terror. Everything that weakens that system, weakens their means; and as the adoption of moderation saps it on one side, so the perseverance in attack cannot but pull it down on the other. Take every part of it, one by one, view their expenditure, and then see, whether terror is not the instrument by which they have raised their extraordinary supplies, and obtained all their unexampled successes.

Let us enter into a view of the actual expenditure of France. This expenditure, since the Revolution, has amounted to the enormous sum of four hundred and eighty millions, spent since the commencement of the war. Three hundred and twenty millions have been the price of the efforts that have enabled them to wrest from the allies those territories which are now in their possession. What your expenses have been during the same period, I need not state. I ask now, whether it is likely that France will see you exhausted first? I think not. But it may be said that what the French have spent proves what they can spend. To this I reply, have they been enabled to bear this expenditure, by the increase of their revenue, or by any of the ordinary means of France? No: but by the creation of an unlimited paper credit. I desire gentlemen to look at all the debates of the National Convention, and they will find that all the deputies agree in this point—that they cannot increase the emission of the paper-money without ruin, and that the miseries arising from this system aggravate all the calamities of the country. Many persons at first imagined that *assignats*[1] must have stopped early in 1793. The fact undoubtedly was, that, previously to that period, it was thought the emission was greater than France could bear, and that no further creation could take place without producing a depreciation in the value of *assignats*, and an immoderate increase in the price of provisions. The whole circulating medium of France at the highest was 90 millions sterling. In August 1793, *assignats* existed to the amount of 130 millions; commerce was then declining; agriculture was discouraged; population checked. A forced loan of 40 millions was adopted on the idea, that to the amount of 130 millions they could not maintain *assignats* in circulation. As early as May or June, *assignats* had lost nearly half their value. A louis in specie soon afterwards produced 144 livres. Then it was that the system of terror commenced, and that

---

[1] The *assignats* were inconvertible paper-notes first issued in November 1789 on the security of the confiscated Church lands. After the sale of the lands, *assignats* were still issued from time to time to enable the Revolutionary Government to tide over financial crises, and they became a regular paper currency. Their value naturally depreciated, and by 1796 they had become practically worthless.

a system of credit was begun, which had its foundation in fear.

It may be asked, could any man have imagined that such a plan would have been resorted to ? That it was resorted to—that it succeeded, has been proved. Let us look to the principles of it. There was a law which compelled every man to take at par, that which was worth only one-sixth of the sum for which it was taken : a law for the *maximum* of the price of all commodities : a law by which no person was permitted to renounce his occupation, under the penalty of twenty years' imprisonment. But you will tell me, that this proves how unlimited the powers and resources of the French are. My reply is, that such a system could neither be undertaken nor succeed but by means which could not last. I will not detain you by detail, but merely mention the other means of terror : the constant activity of the guillotine ; the ferocious despotism of the deputies on missions. In addition to all the other engines of torture, Cambon,[1] the mouth of the Convention in matters of finance, tells us, that, in every district, there were revolutionary committees to watch the execution of the decrees of the Convention, and to enable the Convention to seize the spoil of the people. The pay of these committees amounted annually to 26 millions sterling. I say this standing army of revolutionary committees is a means adequate to produce so mighty an end.

Let us add now a new creation of *assignats* of 130

[1] Cambon was the chief financial adviser of the successive Revolutionary Governments from 1791 to 1795, when he withdrew from political life.

millions, which increased the total to 260 millions. Will any man say, that though the system of terror is done away, the effects can remain? When the system of terror was at an end, the *maximum* ceased to be observed: *assignats* were then converted into money, and hence the discount became enormous. The fall of Robespierre took place in July; three months afterwards, the discount was three-fourths per cent. or 75 on the 100. I have even the authority of Tallien[1] for saying that the French cannot maintain their *assignats*, without contracting their expenses and diminishing their forces. And it should be recollected this has been their only resource. Is it then too much to say, their resources are nearly at an end? It is this unlimited power which the French Convention have assumed to purchase or to seize all property, as suited their purposes, that accounts for the stupendous scale of operations which they have been enabled to pursue. This circumstance completely solves the phenomenon, which otherwise would appear so inexplicable, and is adequate to all those miraculous effects which have attended the progress of the French Revolution, and which seemed to baffle all reasoning, as much as they have exceeded all human expectation. In all these circumstances we have sufficient inducements to carry on the war, if not with the certainty of faith, yet at least with the confidence of expectation—a war, the immediate termination of which must be attended with certain evil,

---

[1] Tallien, the prominent Terrorist: elected President of the Convention on March 24, 1794: aware of Robespierre's intention to get rid of him, he opened the attack which led to Robespierre's execution.

and the prosecution of which, under the present circumstances, is at least not without great probable hope.

If we look to the situation of France, they are now attempting to have recourse to a milder and more moderate system—a system which will only deprive them of those prodigious energies, which they have hitherto exerted with such astonishing effect. But they no longer indeed possess the same means, and cannot therefore be expected to display the same exertions. Will it be possible for them all at once to restore the farmer to the occupations of agriculture, and the merchant to the pursuits of commerce, and to replace, in an instant, the devastations of war and plunder, by the arts of peace, and the exertions of industry? It will require years of tranquillity to restore them to the enjoyment of those ordinary resources which they possessed previous to the commencement of the present destructive war—resources which they can no longer employ. For even could it be supposed that Robespierre were raised from the dead, they would no longer be qualified to display the same energies which, under his administration, were called forth by the influence of a system of terror; the means by which these exertions have been supplied are now exhausted. Where can they possibly resort for fresh supplies? Can it be supposed, that when the forced loan failed at the time it was attempted, it can again be tried and succeed in a time much more unfavourable to it, when the system of terror is almost dissolved?

The question then is—Have we, under the present circumstances, the prospect of being able to bring as great a force into the field, as will require from the

French the same degree of exertion which has been necessary in the former campaigns? Even let it be supposed that Holland should fall, and that circumstances should be such that we can no longer look for assistance from the court of Berlin, yet I see no reason to believe that, in the next campaign, we cannot increase the British forces on the Continent to an amount that shall nearly supply the deficiency of Prussian troops and act with more effect. Other Powers look with attention and anxiety on this night's debate. If you afford to those Powers the means of making large exertions, you will oblige France to make efforts to which she is now unequal. If you act with spirit, I see no reason why the Powers of Italy and Spain may not make a diversion, and thereby accomplish the important purpose I have before stated—a purpose, in the accomplishment of which, the happiness, almost the existence of Europe, entirely rests.

The amendment was rejected by 246 to 73, and the address agreed to.

8

The War Policy of the Government reviewed and defended

May 10, 1796 [1]

DURING 1795 the development of the war in Europe had gone continuously against Great Britain. In January the French conquest of Holland was complete: the Stadtholder fled to England, and General Pichegru occupied Amsterdam. In May, the Batavian Republic, as the Dutch under the domination of France now named

[1] *Speeches*, vol. ii, p. 397.

their State, declared war on England. Meanwhile, the French consolidated their position in Belgium; in October it was formally annexed and divided into nine new departments of France.[1]

The recovery of the Netherlands was rendered impossible for the present by the defection of Prussia from the Coalition. Having obtained her share in the final partition of Poland, she readily came to terms with France, and a treaty of peace was signed at Basle on April 5. By secret articles France undertook, if she finally secured the Rhine frontier, to assist Prussia to compensations on the right bank at the expense of the Empire; and the Hohenzollern at Berlin now devoted himself to the traditional policy of undermining the Hapsburg at Vienna by combating the influence of Austria in the independent German States, and tempting them to join with Prussia in subservience to France.

British troops, in the meantime, had been finally withdrawn from the Netherlands, and the only action taken on the Continent was the joint expedition with the Royalist *émigrés* to Quiberon, which proved a humiliating fiasco.

Only on and across the sea had any success been won. On the 'Glorious First of June' Howe defeated the French off Ushant, but the victory was marred by the escape of the greater part of the French fleet. In the West Indies, Martinique, St. Lucia, and Guadeloupe were captured: and, as a security against a French attack on the Dutch colonies in the Far East, a British force occupied the Cape of Good Hope. In the Mediterranean, Corsica was seized. But neither on the Atlantic nor in the Mediterranean was British sea-power effectively supreme. At the close of the year a French squadron was able to cross the ocean and recover Guadeloupe, while the Toulon fleet remained unbroken and rendered easier Buonaparte's attack on Italy.

[1] 'Belgium' was not created till 1830, but it is generally used as a convenient term for the Austrian Netherlands, Liège, and Luxemburg.

Early in 1796 the attack began. Between April 12 and 25, Buonaparte had beaten the Austrians and Piedmontese in five battles. On April 28 the King of Sardinia ceded Savoy and Nice to France, and allowed Buonaparte to occupy certain strategic fortresses in Piedmont. Within another fortnight he had crushed the Austrians at Lodi and driven them from Lombardy.

But, while the British outlook in the war grew steadily darker, the prospects of a peace with honour and security seemed steadily to brighten. The reaction of the Moderates against the Terror had proved solid and lasting. The Convention recovered its old authority: most of the leading Terrorists were executed or exiled, and the influence of the decimated Girondins was restored. In the autumn of 1795 the new régime was threatened from the other extreme by a royalist insurrection in Paris; but the Convention employed the services of Buonaparte in their defence, and the Republic was saved by his artillery. A new constitution was drawn up, and came into force in November. A legislature of two chambers was established; its decrees were to be executed by ministers named and supervised by a Directory of five, who thus became the supreme executive authority.

At first this machinery worked well. It seemed as if at last France had obtained a reputable and a settled Government, as if at last the obstacle in the way of peace, which Pitt had regarded as insuperable, had been broken down. Before the end of 1795, therefore, Pitt had decided to come to terms with the Directory, if terms could be obtained which did not jeopardize the honour and the safety of these islands. On December 8 a message from the King was read in the House of Commons, informing the House 'that the crisis, which was depending at the commencement of the session, had led to such an order of things in France as would induce His Majesty to meet any disposition to negotiation on the part of the enemy with an earnest desire to give it the full and speediest effect, and to conclude a treaty of peace, whenever it could be effected on just and suitable terms for himself and his allies'. In the debate next day Pitt was assailed for inconsistency in confessing his readiness to treat with a republican government, but he pointed out in his reply [1] that he had declined to treat for peace with the previous governments, not because they were republican, but because, if peace were made with them, there was no 'reasonable expectation of security for its continuance'. 'He did not deny that he had admitted, nay contended, that monarchy was desirable for that country, and for the general interest of mankind; but the idea that he had at any time made the restoration of monarchy a *sine qua non* was so entirely beyond all he had ever uttered upon the subject that he should not argue it.'

But, while it was possible for Pitt to treat with the Directory, he could not sue for peace on any terms, and, though the general public in France was as anxious for peace as the general public in England, the terms demanded by the Directory might prove unacceptable. And so it turned out. Early in 1796, Pitt's informal overtures at Basle were met by the demand that France should not only retain all she had acquired in Europe, but should have restored to her all that Great Britain had acquired elsewhere. On that basis, clearly, no peace could be concluded, and the negotiations broke down.

Disappointment was keen, and the assault on Pitt in Parliament was renewed with increased force. On May 10—the day of Buonaparte's victory at Lodi—Fox delivered a brilliant attack on the whole war-policy of the Government since 1792, and at the close of his speech he moved a long address to the King, deploring a policy which had brought about an unnecessary war,

[1] Speech of December 9, 1795. (*Speeches*, vol. ii, p. 342.)

and conducted it in a disastrous manner, and finally declaring that 'our only hopes rest on His Majesty's royal wisdom and unquestioned affection for his people, that he will be graciously pleased to adopt maxims of policy more suited to the circumstances of the times than those by which his ministers appear to have been governed, and to direct his servants to take measures which, by differing essentially, as well in their tendency as in the principle upon which they are founded, from those which have hitherto marked their conduct, may give this country some reasonable hope, at no very distant period, of the establishment of peace suitable to the interests of Great Britain, and likely to preserve the tranquillity of Europe'.

When the motion had been read, Pitt at once rose:

It is far from being my intention, Sir, unnecessarily to detain the attention of the House, by expatiating at any great length on the various topics introduced into the very long and elaborate speech which you have now heard pronounced. The right honourable gentleman who delivered it, thought proper to lay considerable stress on the authority of a celebrated orator of antiquity,[1] who established it as a maxim, that, from a retrospect of past errors, we should rectify our conduct for the future; and that if they were errors of incapacity only that had occasioned our misfortunes, and not an absence of zeal, strength, and resources to maintain our cause and secure our defence, instead of such a disappointment being a cause of despair, it should, on the contrary, invigorate our exertions and reanimate our hopes. That such a retrospect may, in most cases, be wise and salutary, is a proposition which will hardly be denied. It is

[1] Demosthenes.

evident that our appeal to experience is the best guard to future conduct, and that it may be necessary to probe the nature of the misfortune, in order to apply a suitable remedy. But in a question so momentous and interesting to the country as undoubtedly the present question must be, if it can be deemed expedient to run out into a long retrospective view of past calamities, surely it must be far more so to point out the mode by which their fatal effects may be averted, and by proving the origin of the evils complained of, to judge of the nature and efficacy of the remedies to be applied. Whatever, therefore, our present situation may be, it certainly cannot be wise to fix our attention solely on what is past, but rather to look to what still can and remains to be done. This is more naturally the subject that should be proposed to the discussion of a deliberative assembly. Whatever may have been the origin of the contest in which we are engaged, when all the circumstances attending it are duly considered, it has had the effect of uniting all candid and impartial men, in acknowledging the undisputed justice of our cause and the unjust and wanton aggression on the part of the enemy. Such having been, and still, I presume to say, being the more general opinion, prudence then must tell us to dismiss all retrospective views of the subject and to direct the whole of our attention to what our actual situation requires we should do. The right honourable gentleman must have consumed much time in preparing the retrospect he has just taken of our past disasters; and he has consumed much of his time in detailing it to the House; but instead of lavishing away what was so precious on evils which, according to him, admit of no remedy or change, would it not be more becoming him, as a friend to his country and an enlightened member of this House, to attend to what new circumstances may produce, and to trace out the line of conduct which in the present state of things it would be prudent to pursue?

In the close of his speech the right honourable gentleman alluded to his former professions respecting the prosecution of the war. According to these professions, he and every gentleman who thought with him, declared, that should the enemy reject overtures of peace, or appear reluctant to enter into negotiation, when proposed, then he and every man in the country would unite in advising the adoption of the most vigorous measures; and that not only such conduct on the part of the enemy would unite every Englishman in the cause, but that while it united England, it must divide France, who would be indignant against whatever government or governors should dare to reject what was the sincere wish of the majority of its inhabitants. Instead, therefore, of expatiating on the exhausted state of the financial resources of the country and running into an historical detail of all our past calamities, a subject which almost engrossed the right honourable gentleman's speech, I must beg leave to remind him of those his former professions, and invite him to make good the pledge he has so often given to this House and to the country, and not to inflame the arrogance and unjust pretensions of the enemy, by an exaggerated statement of our past misfortunes or of our present inability to retrieve them by a spirited and vigorous prosecution of the war. His feelings as an

Englishman and his duty as a member of Parliament must assuredly induce the right honourable gentleman to exert his abilities in suggesting the most effectual means of ensuring our success in the contest, especially since he heard the late arrogant and ambitious professions of the enemy. All retrospective views I therefore for the present must regard as useless, and think it far more wise and urgent to provide for the success of future exertions; not that I decline entering into the retrospect to which I am challenged, which I am ready to do with the indulgence of the House, but because I feel it of more serious importance to call your attention, not to the retrospect alone, but rather to the actual state of things, which the right honourable gentleman has entirely omitted.

And, first, let me observe, that, while I endeavour to follow the right honourable gentleman through his very long detail of facts and events, I shall follow him as they bear on a particular conclusion which he wishes to draw from them, but which the country does not call for, and which it will not admit. What is the conclusion to which he wishes to lead us? Does it not go to record a confession and retraction of our past errors, an avowal that, instead of a just and necessary war, to which we were compelled by an unprovoked aggression, we are embarked in a contest in which we wantonly and unjustly engaged, while our defence is evidently such as our dearest interests call for, and which a regard to justice, and to every moral principle, legitimates and sanctifies? Can, then, this House adopt a motion which directly contradicts its recorded opinions, and which tends to force on it new councils; or, in other words, to oblige it to rescind all the resolutions it has come to since the commencement of the war? The right honourable gentleman has, in rich and glowing colouring, depicted our exhausted resources, the want of vigour in our measures, and the inattention of ministers to seize on the more favourable opportunities for making peace. He also assumes, that the sole cause of the war was the restoration of monarchy in France; and that this cause afterwards shifted into various other complexions. All these charges, however, as well as the unjustness of the war, he establishes only by presumption.

The right honourable gentleman then goes back to 1792, when he says the first opportunity was offered of our procuring peace to Europe, but of which ministers did not avail themselves. He also refers to a speech made by me on the opening of the Budget of that year,[1] which he describes as having been uttered in a tone of great satisfaction, triumph, and exultation. It is true, indeed, that I felt much satisfaction in exhibiting to the country the high degree of prosperity to which it had then reached—not less satisfaction, I am sure, than the honourable gentleman seems to feel in giving the melancholy picture that his motion has now drawn of its present reduced situation; and I felt the more vivid satisfaction in viewing that prosperity, as it enabled us to prepare for, and enter into, a contest of a nature altogether unprecedented. Now, however, when that prosperity is over, the honourable gentleman dwells on it rather rapturously, though it seemed little to affect him at the time it was enjoyed.

[1] See *supra*, pp. 15-23.

But not only are ministers accused of having neglected the opportunities of making peace, but when they have attempted overtures of that nature, they are charged with insincerity, or with holding forth something in the shape and make of these overtures that must create suspicions of their sincerity in the enemy, or provoke their disgust. What can countenance such an accusation, I am sadly at a loss to discover: for at the periods alluded to, every motive of public duty, every consideration of personal ease, must have induced me to exert the best of my endeavours to promote a peace by which alone I could be enabled to effect the favourite objects I had in view, of redeeming the public debt and the 4 per cents., as alluded to by the honourable gentleman. No stronger proofs could be given of the sincerity of Government to promote and ensure peace than was then given by His Majesty's ministers; and if they were disappointed, the fault is not with them, but their conduct must be understood and justified by the imperious necessity which in 1793 compelled them to resist an unprovoked aggression. As to the accusations urged against us of not offering our mediation, or even refusing it when solicited, they are equally of little weight. Are ministers to be blamed for what it would be hazardous in them to attempt, and would it not be hazardous to propose a mediation where both parties were not ready to agree? To have erected ourselves into arbiters, could only expose us to difficulties and disputes, if we were determined, as we ought to be, to enforce that mediation on the parties who refused to admit it. And what is the great use which the honourable gentleman seems to be so eager to derive from that peace, if so procured? Is it fit that we should go to war in order to prevent the partition of Poland? In general policy, I am ready to confess that this partition is unjust; but it does not go, as is said, to overturn the balance of power in Europe, for which the right honourable gentleman, as it suits his argument, expresses greater or less solicitude; for that country being nearly divided equally between three great Powers, it can little contribute to the undue aggrandizement of either. But how strange did it seem in that right honourable gentleman, who inveighed so strongly against the partition of Poland, to censure ministers for their endeavours to prevent the partition of Turkey, when it was the establishment of the principle, that this country could not interfere to prevent the partition of Turkey, precluded the possibility of any interference with respect to Poland!

As to the latter transactions that have occurred between this country and France, they are too recent in the memory of the House to require that I should call their attention to them. The resolutions to which we have come on this subject are too sacred and too solemn, the opinion too settled and too deeply formed, to be lightly reversed. We cannot, surely, forget the first cause of complaint, allowed to be well founded, and the famous decree of the 19th of November, which was an insult and an outrage on all civilized nations. Seditious men, delegated from this country, with treason in their mouths and rebellion in their hearts, were received, welcomed, and caressed by the Legislature of France. That Government, without waiting until it had even established itself, declared hostilities against all the old established systems : without having scarcely an existence in itself, it had the presumption to promise to interpose to the destruction of all the existing governments in the world. All governments alike fell under its vengeance; the old forms were contemned and reprobated; those which had stood the test of experience, whether monarchy, aristocracy, or mixed democracy, were all to be destroyed. They declared that they would join the rebellious subjects of any State to overturn their Government. And what was the explanation received from M. Chauvelin on these subjects of complaint? Did it amount to any more than that the French would not intermeddle with the form of government in other countries, unless it appeared that the majority of the people required it to be changed? As to their declaration against aggrandizement, without stopping to argue a point that is so extremely clear, I will only refer the House to their whole conduct towards Belgium. They declared that they would never interfere in the government of Belgium, after it had consolidated its liberties—a strange way of declining interference when a form of constitution was forced upon it, bearing the name, but not the stamp of liberty, and compelling the Belgians to consolidate and preserve it. With respect to another cause of war, viz. the opening of the Scheldt, their explanations regarding that circumstance and their intentions upon Holland were equally unsatisfactory; their ultimatum was, that they would give no further satisfaction; and their refusing a fair explanation made them the aggressors in reality, if not in form. Still, however, the channel of negotiation was not cut off by this country. As long as the King of France retained a shadow of power, M. Chauvelin continued to be received in an official capacity; and even after the cruel catastrophe of that unfortunate monarch, His Majesty's minister at The Hague did not refuse to communicate with General Dumouriez, when he expressed a wish to hold a conference with him relative to some proposals of peace. When all these opportunities had been offered and neglected, they declared war, and left us no choice, in form or in substance, but reduced us to the necessity of repelling an unjust aggression. In every point of view, they therefore were evidently the aggressors, even according to the right honourable gentleman's own principles, and we certainly took every precaution, that it was either fit or possible to do, to avoid it.

I cannot help wishing to recall the attention of the House to the general conclusion of what I have stated, for upon that rests all I have to say on the first part of the right honourable gentleman's propositions. If the House had been hurried by passion into the war, if it had been hurried by the false opinion of others or by any unjust pretensions of its own, would it go to the enemy to atone for its misconduct, and accede to such conditions as the enemy might offer? Could it happen that a war not ordinarily just and necessary, when applied to every moral principle, should in form be so untrue that, after three years' standing, it should be found all illusion? If the House cannot acknowledge these things, much less can I believe, admitting all the depreciated statements of our resources to be true, and founded to such an extent as to make us submit almost to any humiliation, that last of all we should submit to the pride and ambition of an enemy, whose hypocrisy, injustice, tyranny, and oppression we have so repeatedly witnessed, reprobated, and deplored : and yet that was what the right honourable gentleman proposed. He proposed that we should bow down before the enemy, with the cord about our necks, when we have not felt the self-reproach of doing wrong ; to renounce and abjure our recorded professions, and receive a sentence of condemnation, as severe as undeserved. This I contend would be to renounce the character of Britons. Even if, by the adverse fortune of war, we should be driven to sue for peace, I hope we shall never be mean enough to acknowledge ourselves guilty of a falsehood and injustice, in order to obtain it.

The right honourable gentleman's next accusation against ministers is, that they have been guilty of a radical error, in not acknowledging the French Republic. It is said this has been the bar to all treaty, this has prevented every overture in subsequent situations. I admit that it has so happened, that we have never acknowledged the Republic, and I admit also, that no application nor overture for peace, on the part of this country, has been made till lately. I admit, that after the siege of Valenciennes,[1] I did say it was not then advisable to make conditions, and I admit also, that when we struggled under disadvantages, I was equally averse ; whence the right honourable gentleman infers, ' that if you will not treat for peace when you are successful, nor treat for it when you are unfortunate, there must be some secret

[1] See *supra*, pp. 92, 103.

cause which induces us to believe you are, not disposed to treat at all.' Is it reasonable, I ask, when a just hope is entertained of increasing our advantages, to risk the opportunity which those advantages would secure of making better terms; or is it reasonable when we experience great and deplorable misfortunes, to entertain a just apprehension of obtaining a permanent and honourable peace, on fair and permanent conditions? These are the principles on which I have acted, and they are raised upon the fair grounds of human action. If success enough were gained to force the enemy to relinquish a part of their possessions, and we might not yet hope to be wholly relieved from similar dangers, except by a repetition of similar efforts and similar success, was it inconsistent for a lover of his country to push those efforts further upon the reasonable expectation of securing a more permanent and honourable peace? And, on the other hand, when we experienced the sad reverse of fortune, when the spirit of our allies was broken, our troops discomfited, our territories wrested from us, and all our hopes disconcerted and overthrown, did it argue a want of reason or a want of prudence not to yield to the temporary pressure? The same situations to a well-tempered mind would always dictate the same mode of conduct. In carrying on the war, we have met with misfortunes, God knows, severe and bitter! Exclusive of positive acquisitions, however, have we gained nothing by the change which has taken place in France? If we had made peace, as the right honourable gentleman says we ought to have done, in 1793, we should have made it before France had lost her trade; before she had exhausted her capital; before her foreign possessions were captured, and her navy destroyed. This is my answer to every part of the right honourable gentleman's speech relative to making peace at those early periods.

But a discussion is once more introduced as to the object of the war. Ministers have repeatedly and distinctly stated the object, but it is a custom on the other side of the House, to take unguarded and warm expressions of individuals in favour of the war, for declarations of ministers. Thus, many things which fell from that great man (Mr. Burke [1]) have since been stated as the solemn declaration of Government, though it is known that, to a certain extent, there is a difference between ministers and that gentleman upon this subject. But then it is to be taken as clear, that ministers are not only anxious for the restoration of monarchy in France, but the old monarchy with all its abuses. That ministers wished to treat with a Government in which Jacobin principles should not prevail; that they wished for a Government from which they could hope for security, and that they thought a monarchy the most likely form of government to afford to them these advantages, is most undoubtedly true; but that ministers ever had an idea of continuing the war for the purpose of re-establishing the old Government of France, with all its abuses, I solemnly deny.

If, for the reasons I have before stated, it would not have been prudent to have made a peace in the early stage of our contest, surely it would not have been

[1] For Burke's opinions, see Introduction, pp. xvi, xxxii.

advisable when the enemy were inflated with success. The fate of the campaign of 1794 turned against us upon as narrow a point as I believe ever occurred. We were unfortunate, but the blame did not rest here. That campaign led to the conquest of Holland, and to the consternation which immediately extended itself among the people of Germany and England. What, however, was the conduct of ministers at that period? If they had given way to the alarm, they would have been censurable indeed: instead of doing so, they immediately sent out expeditions to capture the Dutch settlements, which we may now either restore to the Stadtholder, if he should be restored, or else we may retain them ourselves. If, instead of that line of conduct, His Majesty's ministers had then acknowledged the French Republic, does the right honourable gentleman, does the House, suppose that the terms we should then have obtained would have been better than those we can now expect?

Then, it was asked, why did not the Administration negotiate for peace before the confederacy was weakened by the defection of Spain and Prussia, because, of course, better terms might have been obtained when the allies were all united, than could be expected after they became divided? It undoubtedly would have been a most advantageous thing, if we could have prevailed upon the Kings of Spain and Prussia to have continued the war until the enemy were brought to terms, but that not having been the case, we at least had the advantage of the assistance of those Powers, while they remained in the confederacy. Before any blame can attach upon ministers upon this ground, it will be necessary to show that, prior to the defection of Prussia and Spain, terms were proposed to us, which we rejected. Whether these two Powers have gained much from the peace they have made, is not a question very difficult to be answered. Whether Spain was really in that state that she could not have maintained another campaign, without running the risk of utter destruction, is a point upon which I do not choose to give an opinion; but with respect to Prussia, she certainly enjoys the inactivity of peace, but she has all the preparation and expense of war.

The right honourable gentleman again adverts to the form of government which he says it was the intention of ministers to establish in France, and alludes particularly to the affair at Toulon; and from that subject the honourable gentleman makes a rapid transition to the case of M. de la Fayette.[1] With respect to what might be the treatment of that unfortunate gentleman, the Cabinet of Great Britain had no share in it, nor did ministers think themselves warranted in interfering with the allies upon the subject. With regard to Mr. Lameth,[2] the right honourable gentleman certainly did ministers justice, when he said they could feel no antipathy to that person; and they certainly did feel great reluctance in ordering him to quit the kingdom: but as to the motive which induced them to take that step, they did not conceive it to be a proper subject of discussion. The

[1] La Fayette quarrelled with the Jacobins in 1792, was declared a traitor, and fled to Liège. He was seized by the allies and imprisoned first in Prussia and then in Austria till 1797.
[2] M. Lameth, who had served in the French army under La Fayette, was condemned for treason in 1792 and fled the country.

Act of Parliament had vested discretion in the Executive Government, and they must be left to the exercise of it.

The right honourable gentleman has also alluded to the situation of the emigrants, and asserted, that if Government were of opinion that there was no prospect of making an attack with success upon France, it was the height of cruelty to have employed them. This, however, was not the case; there were at different times well-grounded expectations of success against that country, and surely it cannot be considered as cruelty to have furnished the emigrants with the means of attempting to regain their properties and their honours.

The right honourable gentleman has also thought proper, in his speech, to dwell at considerable length on the state of the enemy's finances. He is willing to admit that their finances are, as he says I have stated them to be, in the very gulf of bankruptcy, in their last agonies. But then the right honourable gentleman proceeds to ask me, whether, notwithstanding this financial bankruptcy, they have not prosecuted their military operations with increased vigour and success? Whether, notwithstanding these their last agonies, they may not make such dreadful struggles as may bring their adversaries to the grave? I will not now detain the House by contrasting the finances of this country with those of the enemy; I will not now dwell on the impossibility of a nation carrying on a vigorous war, in which it is annually expending one-third of its capital; but I will tell the right honourable gentleman that the derangement of the French armies at the latter end of the last campaign, the exhausted state of their magazines and stores, and their ultimate retreat before the allied troops, furnish a convincing proof that the rapid decline of their finances begins to affect in the greatest degree their military operations. How far their recent successes, on the side of Italy, deserve credit to the extent stated by the right honourable gentleman, I shall not take upon me to say: I have no intelligence on the subject, and therefore shall offer no opinion to the House.

The next topic which I have to consider, is the argument drawn from the question of our sincerity in the message delivered to the French minister at Basle on the 8th of March[1]; and a great variety of observations have been suggested and urged upon that point. One inference drawn by the right honourable gentleman arises from the circumstance of this message having been communicated four months after His Majesty's speech, and three months after the declaration made to Parliament, that His Majesty was ready to meet and give effect to any disposition manifested on the part of the enemy for the conclusion of a general peace. In the first place it must be remembered, that neither the Speech from the Throne nor the declaration expressed any intention in the British Government to be the first in making proposals for opening a negotiation. The fair construction went no farther than to invite the enemy to make the first advances, if they were so disposed, and to show that no obstacle would be opposed on our part to the capacity of the Government they had chosen to negotiate terms with this country. Gentlemen, therefore, have no right to feel in any degree disappointed at the delay of the

[1] See *supra*, p. 137.

communication, since, in being the first to make any overtures of peace, His Majesty's ministers went beyond any pledge they had given, or any expectation that ought to be entertained.

It has further been objected, that those proposals must be insincere, because it did not appear that on this occasion we had acted in concert with our allies. A sufficient answer to this may be given by the peculiar circumstances of affairs, the lateness of the season, and those communications being cut off by which we and our allies were before enabled to maintain a ready intercourse. Had this ceremony been complied with, the delay which it would have occasioned must unavoidably have been greater than that of which gentlemen think themselves warranted to complain. They are, however, as much mistaken in their facts as they are in their inferences, for this step was not taken without previous communication with our allies, and we acted in concert with them, though they were not formally made parties to the proposal; a ceremony which in my opinion would be wholly superfluous.

Another proof, it should seem, of our insincerity is that, in the message alluded to, we did not recognize the Republic. It is truly generous in the right honourable gentleman, generous towards them at least, to find out an objection for the French which they themselves did not discover. We had the answer of the Directory to our note, and they took not the least notice of the Republic not having been recognized. If that had been a necessary and indispensable form, without which they considered themselves insulted, their natural conduct

would have been to give no answer at all. On this point
of recognition, however, the right honourable gentleman
is always extremely tender, and has it very much at
heart. He holds up the example of America to us, as
if it was an instance that had any application to the
present question. The right honourable gentleman also
boldly contends, that if we had paid the French Government this mark of respect and confidence, it would have
induced them in return to propose more moderate terms.
I am, however, very far from expecting any such effect;
for, in fact, the Government of France never seemed to
think of it. I do not consider the omission as an act of
hostility, and they must be aware, that the proposal to
treat in itself implied a recognition, without which it
was impossible that a treaty should be concluded.

To show the consistency of the arguments on this
subject, I shall take the liberty of recalling the attention
of the House to those antecedent periods, when the
gentleman on the opposite side of the House, in defending
the French Government, held up to our imitation the
wise and temperate conduct of the Court of Denmark,
which maintained a beneficial neutrality with France,
and with which the latter showed itself capable of maintaining the necessary relations of amity and peace. It is
indeed true that France has in a great measure respected
the neutrality of Denmark, and observed with it the
relations of peace, at least, if not of amity. What, however, destroys the right honourable gentleman's argument
at once is, that this wise, peaceable, neutral, and amicable
Court of Denmark had not recognized the French Republic
till the present year. So that, in fact, Denmark did **not**

consider the French Government as one that it ought to acknowledge, till the form which it assumed rendered it in some degree equally admissible in the eyes of the other Powers of Europe.

Another argument of insincerity is that we did not propose terms to the enemy, while we called upon them for theirs. This I conceive to be that which we had no right to do. The application did not come from the enemy, it was made on our part, and it would have been ridiculous to propose any particular terms to them, till we were previously informed whether they were willing to treat at all. It has also been alleged, that we must have been insincere, because when we employed the minister at Basle to make this application, we did not at the same time give him the power to negotiate. It was extraordinary indeed that an observation of this kind should be urged by any person who professed the slightest acquaintance with diplomatic proceedings. I would ask the right honourable gentleman whether it was ever known that the person employed to sound the disposition of a belligerent party was also considered as' the proper minister for discussing all the relative interests, and concluding a treaty ? The House must remember on former occasions, when the right honourable gentleman was so warm in the recommendation of a peace with France, whatever might be its Government, that, apprehensive of an adherence to that etiquette, which might prevent us from being the first to make overtures, he advised us to make recourse to expedients, and sound the disposition of the enemy, through the medium of neutral Powers. As soon as France adopted a form of government, from which an expectation of stability was to be drawn, His Majesty's ministers readily waived all etiquette, and would not let such forms stand in the way of the permanent object of the peace and tranquillity of Europe, and they made direct proposals to the enemy. Had they, however, adopted the expedient proposed to them, and employed a neutral Power to make their communications, was it to be expected that we should appoint that neutral Power our minister plenipotentiary to manage our interests, as well as those of our allies? The gentleman through whom the communications were made at Basle, is one perfectly qualified from his talents, his zeal, and his integrity, to conduct any negotiation; but whatever may be his character, it would be the height of imprudence, or rather folly, to entrust the management of a negotiation of such uncommon moment to the discretion of an individual, and at such a distance.

The motives which induced His Majesty's ministers not to employ the same minister who had made the advances, as the negotiator of a peace, are not confined to what I have hitherto stated; it was also necessary in order to show our allies that we did not go beyond the line of that arrangement which was concerted with them, and that, true to our engagements, we had no separate object, and would not proceed a step without their concurrence. We wished to avoid anything which could excite the slightest suspicion that we were disposed to a separate negotiation, which was what France would wish, and what was her uniform aim during the present contest. This was a policy which in some instances was too successful with some of our allies, and which enabled her to enforce on them successively more harsh and unequal conditions. It was with a view to the same open dealing that it was thought proper to publish to the different courts of Europe the message and the answer, that the world might judge of the moderation of the allies and the arrogance of the enemy.

There was one ground of sincerity which I believe the right honourable gentleman did not state; but which the Directory rested upon principally in their answer. This was the proposal for holding a general congress. How this could support the charge of insincerity, I am at a loss to conceive. The British Government pointed out the mode of pacification. This the enemy thought proper to decline and to reproach, but did not attempt to substitute any other mode by which the object was likely to be obtained. So far from projecting anything which could even justly be an object of suspicion, ministers had preferred that of a congress, which was the only mode in which wars were concluded in all cases wherein allies were concerned, ever since the Peace of Munster, the two last treaties only excepted. This charge of insincerity was represented by the right honourable gentleman as the probable cause of the exorbitant terms demanded by the enemy: 'They are high in their demands', says the right honourable gentleman, 'because they know you are not in earnest; whereas, were they confident in your sincerity, they would be moderate and candid.' In my humble apprehension, the extravagance of their terms leads to an opposite conclusion, and proves that the plea of insincerity is with them only a pretence. If they really thought His Majesty's ministers insincere, their policy would have been to make just and moderate demands, which, if rejected, would exhibit openly and in the face of the world that want of candour and that appetite for war, which the right honourable gentleman joins in so unjustly attributing to us. But having, in fact, no disposition for peace, and led away by false and aspiring notions of aggrandizement, the Government of France offered us such terms as they knew could not possibly be complied with. Did they know the spirit, temper, and character of this country, when they presumed to make such arrogant proposals? These proposals I will leave to the silent sense impressed by them in the breast of every Englishman. I am, thank God! addressing myself to Britons, who are acquainted with the presumption of the enemy, and who, conscious of their resources, impelled by their native spirit, and valuing the national character, will prefer the chances and alternatives of war to such unjust, unequal, and humiliating conditions.

The plea of the French Directory, that their constitution did not permit them to accept of any terms which should diminish the extent of country annexed by conquest to the territories of the Republic, the right honourable gentleman himself very fairly condemns; because, if persevered in, it must be an eternal obstacle to the conclusion of any peace. That the interests of foreign nations should yield to those laws which another country should think proper to prescribe to itself, is a fallacy, a monster in politics, that never before was heard of. Whether their military successes are likely to enable them to preserve a constitution so framed, I will not now inquire, but of this I am certain, that the fortune of war must be tried before the nations of Europe will submit to such pretences.

On a fair examination, however, will it appear that the right honourable gentleman is right in observing that this allegation could be no more than a pretext? If so, is it not singular that the right honourable gentleman, who seems so shocked at this pretext of the law of the French constitution, should direct none of his censure against the legislators or Government of that nation, but vent all his indignation on the British ministers, for deferring their proposals for peace till the enemy had formed such a constitution as rendered peace impracticable? I will not now recount all those arguments which, on former occasions, I have so frequently submitted to the House, nor the motives which induced me to decline all proposals for peace, till some form of government was established, which had a chance of being stable and permanent. Surely, however, it is too great a task imposed upon me to be able to foresee, amongst the innumerable and varying constitutional projects of the French, the precise system on which they would fix at last. Much less could I foresee that they would have adopted a constitution which even the right honourable gentleman himself would be induced to condemn. But, having so condemned it, he should in justice have transferred his censures to those by whom it was framed; instead of which, all the thunder of the right honourable gentleman's eloquence is spent at home upon the innocent, while the guilty at a distance are not disturbed even by the report.

However the spirit of this country may be roused

and its indignation excited by the exorbitant conditions proposed to it by the enemy, yet even these extravagant pretensions should not induce us to act under the influence of passion. I could easily have anticipated that unanimity of sentiment with which such degrading proposals have been rejected by every man in this country, but our resentment or our scorn must not for a moment suffer us to lose sight of our moderation and our temper. We have long been in the habit of waiting for the return of reason in our deluded enemy, and whenever they shall descend from those aspiring and inadmissible projects which they seem to have formed and are proceeding to act upon, we shall still be ready to treat with them upon fair and honourable terms. We are particularly interested in urging them to the acceptance of such a constitution as may be best suited to their character and situation, but we must take care that their constitution shall not operate injuriously to ourselves. We do not shut the door against negotiation whenever it can be fairly entered upon, but the enemy, so far from meeting us, say plainly they cannot listen to any terms, but such as in honour we cannot accept. The terms of peace which the right honourable gentleman pointed at, and which, after all, he considers as very disadvantageous, are, that the French may retain their conquests in Europe, and that we should keep our acquisitions in the colonies. What, however, is the proposal of the Directory? No less than this: that everything should be restored to them, and they in return are to give up nothing. It is also urged by the honourable gentleman, that we were to blame in so abruptly breaking off the negotiation, and communicating the result to the world, together with the observations made upon it. To this I will answer, that the terms proposed by the enemy cut short all further treaty; and as to the communication of the result, it will have, at least, the important consequence of dividing the opinions of France and uniting those of England.

The motion was rejected by 207 to 45.

9
The Defence of England against Invasion
October 18, 1796[1]

TRIUMPHANT on land, their fleets still practically intact, the Directory had defiantly rejected peace: and it was now openly declared at Paris that the Republic would shortly take the offensive against England and attempt an invasion of the country. At the opening of the autumn session of 1796 the King's Speech referred to the enemy's 'intention of attempting a descent on these kingdoms'. On October 18, the House of Commons having resolved itself into Committee to consider this part of the Speech, Pitt spoke as follows:

After the unanimous vote which the House gave upon the first day of the session, and their general concurrence in that part of the address which respects a foreign invasion, it would be doing injustice to the feelings which were then expressed, were I to make any apology for calling their attention to the subject on the present occasion. I shall not detain them, therefore, a single

[1] *Speeches*, vol. ii, p. 430.

moment in showing the propriety of laying before them at so early a period the measures which I mean this day to propose. It is equally our duty and our interest, by every means in our power and by every exertion of which we are capable, if possible, in the language of the address, to preclude the attempt, and at the same time to take such measures of defence as shall cause the invasion, if it should be attempted, to issue in the confusion and ruin of the enemy.

I shall not at present go much at large into the detail of preparations, but merely suggest a general outline of defence, which, if it should be approved of by the Committee, may be particularly discussed when the Bills are afterwards brought in upon the resolutions. The general considerations are few and obvious. The natural defence of this kingdom, in case of invasion, is certainly its naval force. This presents a formidable barrier, in whatever point the enemy may direct their attack. In this department, however, little now remains to be done, our fleet at this moment being more respectable and more formidable than ever it was at any other period in the history of the country. But strong and powerful even as it at present is, it is capable of considerable increase, could an additional supply of seamen, or even landsmen, who in a very short time might be trained to an adequate knowledge of the naval service, be procured. For this purpose I would suggest a levy upon the different parishes throughout the kingdom—an expedient precisely similar to that which was practised with so much success nearly two years ago. This levy, however, I would not confine as a mode of supply for the sea service. It is certainly of the highest importance, both for the internal defence of the country and the security of our foreign possessions, that all the old regiments should be complete. But every one must be sensible that, from the numbers in those regiments who have fallen a sacrifice to sickness and the fortune of war, a more expeditious method must be adopted for their completion than the ordinary mode of recruiting supplies in order that the country may be able to avail itself of this arm of strength. I would propose, therefore, in the first place, a levy of 15,000 men from the different parishes for the sea service and for recruiting the regiments of the line. The Committee, however, must be sensible when a plan of invasion is in agitation—a scheme, which almost at another time would not have been conceived, and an attempt, which, by any other enemy than that with whom we have now to contend, might have been justly deemed impracticable—that a more enlarged and a more expensive plan of prevention and of defence is necessary.

In digesting this plan there are two considerations of which we ought not to lose sight. The first is the means (which must not be altogether new) of calling together a land force, sufficiently strong to frustrate the attempt, keeping our naval force entirely out of view; and secondly, to adopt such measures in raising this force as shall not materially interfere with the industry, the agriculture, and the commerce of the country. It will be for the House to decide upon the degree to which the former consideration ought to be permitted to interfere with the latter. A primary object will be to raise, and gradually to train, such a force as may in a short time be fit for service. Of all the modes of attaining this object, there is none so expeditious, so effectual, and attended with so little expense, as that of raising a supplemental levy of militia, to be grafted upon the present establishment. I should propose that this supplement shall consist of 60,000 men, not to be immediately called out, but to be enrolled, officered, and gradually trained, so as to be fit for service at a time of danger. The best mode of training them without withdrawing too many at one time from their regular pursuits, will be to embody one-sixth part in regular succession, each to be trained for twenty days, in the course of which they may become tolerable proficients in the military exercise. With respect to the mode of conducting the levy, the returns that have been lately made from the different counties show the present levies to be extremely disproportioned, and that the clause in the Act which provides against this abuse has never been executed. Accordingly we find that in some counties the proportion is one out of seven, and in others one out of three. It will be expedient, therefore, to regulate the future levy, not by the proportions now existing, but by a general estimate of the inhabitants who are able to bear arms.

The next consideration which merits attention is the manner in which the troops are to be furnished, which I think ought to be generally from all parts of the kingdom, and that an obligation be imposed upon those who are balloted, either to serve in person, or to provide a substitute; and the better to preserve the general proportion, that this substitute be provided either from the parish in which the person balloted resides, or from a parish immediately adjoining. It will be proper also to remove the present exemption from those who have more than one child, on the express condition that they shall not be called upon to serve out of the parish in which they live. The mode of training only one-sixth part of the whole, twenty days in succession, as it will only withdraw 10,000 at a time from their usual occupations, consequently will not much infringe upon the general order of the community. Of course they must be provided with some sort of uniform, but it will be of the coarsest kind, and such as may be purchased at a small expense. A sufficient number of arms will also be in readiness for supplying each man in the moment of danger.

Another measure which I would suggest to the Committee, is to provide a considerable force of irregular cavalry. The regular cavalry on the present establishment is certainly by no means inconsiderable, and the yeomanry cavalry, which from their numbers are sufficiently respectable, we have found to be highly useful in securing the quiet and maintaining the internal tranquillity of the country. But with a view to repelling an invasion, the more that this species of force is extended, the greater advantage is likely to accrue from it, as an invading enemy, who must be destitute of horses, can have no means to meet it upon equal terms. Besides, it is a species of force which may be provided in a mode that will be attended with almost no expense to the public and with little hardship to individuals. In order to calculate the extent to which these irregular cavalry may be raised, it is necessary to estimate the number of horses which are kept for pleasure throughout the kingdom, and by raising the levy in this proportion we shall have the satisfaction to think that it will fall upon those only who have a considerable stake to defend. By the produce of the tax, which is as good a criterion as any of the number of horses kept for pleasure, we find that in Scotland, England, and Wales they amount to about two hundred thousand, one hundred and twenty thousand of which belong to persons who keep only one horse of the kind, the rest to persons, some of whom keep ten, and various other proportions. It certainly would not be a very severe regulation when compared with the object meant to be accomplished, to require one-tenth of these horses for the public service. I would therefore propose that every person who keeps ten horses, shall be obliged to furnish one horse and a horseman to serve in a corps of cavalry; that every person who keeps more than ten horses, and a number falling short of twenty, after furnishing a horse and horseman, for the first ten, shall subscribe a proportionate sum for the rest, which shall be applied to defray the general expense; that those who keep twenty shall furnish two, three of thirty, and so on, and that those who keep fewer than ten shall form themselves into a class, when it shall be decided by ballot who at the common expense shall furnish the horse and the horseman. These troops thus raised will be provided with uniform and accoutrements, formed into corps, and put under proper officers. And surely when the means are compared with the object to be attained and the expense to which individuals will be subjected, with the security of the property which they possess, no one will complain that that end or that security is purchased at too dear a price.

There is still another resource which, though it may not appear so serious as those which have been already mentioned, ought not to be neglected. Upon the supposition of an invasion, it would certainly be of no small importance to form bodies of men who, from their dexterity in using firearms, might be highly useful in harassing the operations of the enemy. The employment of such men for the purpose of defending the country, and harassing the enemy in case of an invasion, must be attended with the most serious and important consequences. Gentlemen will naturally guess that I am now alluding to that description of men called gamekeepers, and to others of the same class. I do most certainly allude to them, for there are many whose personal services would be of the utmost advantage. But I also, and more particularly, allude to those instances where gentlemen are gamekeepers for their own amusement, where they are gamekeepers merely for the satisfaction of being so, not gamekeepers of necessity but of choice. In such cases there can be no hardship in obliging those gentlemen, if we cannot have their personal services, at least to find a substitute who may be as well calculated to defend the country as themselves. I do therefore propose that those persons, who shall have taken out licences to shoot game or deputations for gamekeepers, shall, within a certain period, be at liberty to return the same if they think proper; but if after that period they shall continue their licences or deputations for gamekeepers, then they shall be obliged to find substitutes. I observe gentlemen smiling at the idea of raising a force by such means, but that smile will be converted into surprise, when they hear that the number of persons who have taken out those licences are no fewer than 7,000. Such a plan cannot be considered as a means of internal defence likely to be approved of by every person in the country.

I have stated to the Committee the general outline of the Bill. I shall defer saying much more on the subject; it will be more satisfactory to speak particularly when the resolution is reported to the House, than to enter into any further detail at this moment. The number of cavalry which I propose to raise in the manner I have mentioned will be 20,000; but with respect to whether there must not be some other additional mode adopted, it is impossible to say exactly, from not being able to ascertain with certainty how many persons it may be necessary to exempt, on account of their being in orders, or for other reasons. Thus have I pointed out the means by which I propose to raise 15,000 men, to be divided between the sea and the land service; to raise the supplemental levy of 60,000 for the militia, of which one-sixth part is to be forthwith called out to exercise; to raise 20,000 men by means of persons taking out licences to shoot game and keep gamekeepers, or on such other persons as may hereafter be deemed necessary. If the propositions I have mentioned should be approved, I should wish the resolutions to be printed, and immediately to introduce the Bill, to carry it on to a committee, and to fill up the blanks, and then to allow an interval of a week for its discussion. I mention this in order that more time should not be taken up than is absolutely necessary for the due examination of the principles of the Bill; since, gentlemen, you cannot but recollect, when you are once satisfied, and have determined upon the propriety of any particular measure, every day, every hour of delay, is attended with additional danger.

I shall now move that the chairman be directed to report to the House, 'That it is the opinion of the Committee, that a Bill should be brought in for raising a certain number of men in the several counties of England, and the several counties, burghs, and stewartries of Scotland, for the service of His Majesty.'

Pitt has generally been criticized by modern writers for adopting a jejune and piecemeal military policy, instead of enrolling, as France had done, the whole manhood of the nation and facing the enemy on equal terms on the Continent. At the time, criticism was based on constitutional rather than military grounds. The Opposition attacked his measures, especially the compulsory levy, as oppressive and unprecedented. In his reply, Pitt met these criticisms by reminding the House that unprecedented circumstances required unprecedented measures. 'Why', Fox exclaimed, 'did you not call for these measures upon former occasions?' 'Are we, then, gravely deliberating', replied Pitt, 'upon a great and important subject, and are we to be told that in certain given circumstances no precautions are to be taken because at a former period such measures were not required? May not the means, which were judged adequate in a particular situation, be found insufficient when circumstances alter or when danger is increased?'

Pitt went on to emphasize the unwisdom of relying too blindly on the strength and wealth of the country.

'Prosperity', he said, 'is deceitful and dangerous, if it lead to a false security.' And he pointed out that they were engaged in no ordinary war against an enemy who allowed no ordinary considerations to stand in the way of his ambitions. He continued:

He [1] demonstrated by his actions that he was in reality sensible that the present was not like other wars, undertaken to maintain a point of national honour, or to defend a disputed interest; to support an ally that was attacked, or to guard remote or doubtful dangers; but that it was the first war in which a great and free people, in the prosecution of their commerce and the enjoyment of their prosperity, were called upon for a time to defend the sources from which they flowed, and, in compliance with the good faith which was due to their allies, and urged by a sense of common danger, found themselves compelled to oppose unprovoked aggression, and resist principles hostile to the government and constitution of these kingdoms and to every regular Government in Europe. Why did not the right honourable gentleman follow up his principles, by opposing likewise the measures which were proposed to meet this danger, but because he believed that the situation of affairs is such as to require these precautions; and because he must know that a false security could alone present the smallest chance of success in the attempt which has been threatened; because also he knew that such was the character of the enemy with whom we had to contend, that they were not so liable to be deterred by the desperate nature of

[1] Fox.

the enterprise, or by a consideration of the number of persons whom its ruin might devote to destruction?

Finally, Pitt repudiated the idea that his recourse to a compulsory levy was due to any lack of confidence in the patriotism of the people.

The right honourable gentleman [1] says, you relied on the firmness and attachment of the people two years ago; and is it less now that you have recourse to extraordinary precautions? The attachment and loyalty of the people of this country, I trust, has experienced no diminution. It lives, and is cherished by that constitution which, notwithstanding the assertions of the right honourable gentleman, still remains entire. Under the protection and support which it derives from the Acts passed by the last Parliament, the constitution inspires the steady affection of the people, and is still felt to be worth defending with every drop of our blood. The voice of the country proclaims that it continues to deserve and to receive their support. Fortified by laws in perfect unison with its principles and with its practice, and fitted to the emergencies by which they were occasioned, it still possesses that just esteem and admiration of the people which will induce them faithfully to defend it against the designs of domestic foes and the attempts of their foreign enemies.

Pitt's resolution was agreed to.

[1] Fox.

10

Belgium: the Price of Peace

December 30, 1796 [1]

NEITHER the repulse of his overtures in the spring nor the French threats of invasion deterred Pitt from continning his efforts for peace as long as a possibility of succeeding still existed. And the events of the summer inclined him to hope that the Directory would now prove more complaisant. The advance of two French armies against Austria had been checked by the strategy of the Archduke Charles, the only first-rate general in the ranks of the allies; in September, Jourdan was defeated near Würzburg, and withdrew across the Rhine; in October, Moreau retreated with difficulty into Alsace. These reverses could be considered as a makeweight against Buonaparte's Italian triumphs, and Pitt reopened negotiations. Through the neutral offices of Denmark he ascertained that a British envoy would be received at Paris; Lord Malmesbury was at once dispatched, and on October 20 he began his conversations with Delacroix, the French Foreign Minister.

He soon found that the backs of the Directory were as stiff as ever. He was instructed to offer to compensate France by a proportionate surrender to her of British acquisitions oversea if France, on her part, would restore the conquests which she had made in Europe at the expense of Great Britain's ally, Austria. Her other gains on the Continent she might retain. If the Directory had been willing to abandon their hold on Belgium [2] and Italy, or even on Belgium alone, it is probable that Pitt would have consented to almost any sacrifice in order to obtain the peace he so earnestly desired. But, after some

[1] *Speeches*, vol. iii, p. 33.   [2] See p. 135, note 1.

beating about the bush, it was made perfectly clear that there would be no peace if the surrender by either party of Belgium was its price. France had incorporated the Austrian Netherlands, Liège, and Luxemburg by a law of October 1, 1795. Delacroix now declared that no terms could be accepted which involved the infringement of any law of the Republic. Grenville, on his part, informed Malmesbury that the restoration of Belgium was a *sine qua non*. No compromise on this point being possible, the Directory abruptly closed the negotiations. They demanded on December 19 that the British envoy should either agree at once to abandon Belgium or leave Paris within twenty-four hours.

On December 30 the House of Commons was informed of the failure of the negotiations by a royal message. The message having been read, Pitt addressed the House.

Having expressed his 'deep and poignant regret' at the failure of the negotiations, and described their course in detail up to the point at which the principle of compensation was accepted as a basis, Pitt continued :

I need not argue again that a basis of compensation is reasonable—that I am entitled to assume as admitted—but to what enormous extent it was retracted, I am now to state. During that period of adverse fortune which has since by the valour and glory of the gallant Imperial army so remarkably been retrieved, considerable possessions belonging to Austria[1] and other States were added to the acquisitions of the enemy. On the other hand, the success of our brave troops, retarded indeed in particular quarters by some untoward circumstances, though not obstructed, had added to our distant possessions, and

[1] e. g. Belgium, Lombardy, &c.

extended, by colonial acquisitions, the sources of our commerce, our wealth, and our prosperity, to a degree unparalleled even in the annals of this country. Feeling the pressure which the war, no doubt, gave to our commerce, but feeling too that it neither affected the sources of our commerce, nor would ultimately retard the full tide of our prosperity, I was convinced that the temporary embarrassments which occurred were less the effect of a real distress than of an accidental derangement arising from our increasing capital and extended commerce. In looking round, you discovered no symptom of radical decay, no proof of consuming strength; and although I have been accused of advancing a paradox, while I maintained this proposition, I am convinced that the embarrassment stated as an evidence of decline was a proof of the reality and the magnitude of our resources. I do not state these circumstances to give any one an idea that I do not ardently wish for peace, but to show that we are not yet arrived at so deplorable a state of wretchedness and abasement as to be compelled to make any insecure and dishonourable compromise.

What, on the other hand, was the situation of the enemy? They at first, indeed, were enabled to employ gigantic means of support, which from their extravagant nature were temporary, not permanent. They find also the additional expedient of disseminating new, unheard of, destructive principles; these they poured forth from the interior of France into all the quarters of Europe, where no rampart could be raised to oppose the dangerous, the fatal inundation. Although madness and fanaticism carried them thus far for a time, yet no rational man will deny that those persons formed a fair and reasonable conclusion, who thought that such resources could not be attended with either duration or stability. I need hardly recur to the subject of French finance, though it has a very considerable effect indeed upon the question. I have on this subject been accused of bringing forward groundless surmises, of using fanciful reasoning, of stating elaborate theories without authority. I have even been complimented on my dexterity at this sort of argument, for the kind purpose of afterwards converting it into ridicule. But I shall not now stop to confirm what in this respect I have formerly asserted: I may surely, however, suppose that the admissions of the executive Directory are true, particularly when officially conveyed in the form of a message to one of their councils. Are we not told by themselves, that the only pay of their troops are the horrors of nakedness and famine; that their State contractors, their judges, and all other public functionaries, receive no part of their salaries; that the roads are impassable, that the public hospitals and general interests of charity are totally neglected, that nothing, in short, remains in a state of organization but murder and assassination? Is this a true picture drawn by themselves, and can this be the time for Europe to prostrate itself at the foot of France, suppliantly to bow the knee, and ignominiously to receive its law?

If these considerations would not have justified this country in refusing to treat unless upon the principle of restoring to the Emperor the territories of which he has been stripped, at least it is sufficient reason to entitle us to refuse to the French Republic in the moment of debilitated power and exhausted resource, what we should have disdained to grant to France in the proudest days of her prosperous and flourishing monarchy. It was reason enough why we should not desert our allies, nor abandon our engagements, and why we should not agree to yield up to France for the pretence of preventing future wars, what for two centuries our ancestors thought it wise to contend to prevent the French from obtaining possession of;[1] and why, after the recorded weakness of the Republic, we ought not to resign without a struggle what the power and the riches of France in other times could never extort. What then were we to attain by the conquests we had achieved? For ourselves, we had nothing to ask; we demanded the return of no ancient possessions; we sued not for liberty to maintain our independence, to reject the fraternal embrace, and prevent the organization of treason. These do not rest upon the permission of the enemy; they depend upon the valour, the intrepidity, and the patriotism of the people of this country. We desired, Sir, only to preserve our good faith inviolate, and were ready to sacrifice all our own advantages to obtain what we could not honourably give away without the consent of the Emperor. Could we possibly ask less at the outset of a negotiation? I touch, no doubt, upon a delicate subject, but I ask, could we even have demanded the consent of the Emperor to ask less? Whatever might have been the disposition of the Emperor to peace, would he have been content to agree to inferior terms, when the campaign was not yet closed, when the enemy were yet struck with the

[1] The Netherlands.

effects of the brilliant and glorious success with which the Imperial arms have lately been attended on the side of the Rhine, when the exertions in Italy might have been expected to communicate to the affairs of Austria in that quarter the same tide of victory by which the frontiers of Germany were distinguished? Could we have asked less, consistently with the good faith we owe to that ally to whose exertions and to whose victories we have been so much indebted; that ally to whom we are so closely bound by congenial feelings, with whom we participate in the glory of adversity retrieved and of prosperity restored? In doing this, I am confident the House will agree in thinking that we do not do too much.

By the terms proposed, all the territory between the Rhine and the Moselle was to be ceded by France, subject to future modification. When the French conquests in Italy were stated as objects of restitution, it was not from that to be inferred that Savoy and Nice were included, for in no geographical view could they be considered as component parts of that country. All the propositions underwent discussion between the plenipotentiary of His Majesty and the French minister; only the British minister informed the minister of France, that as to the Netherlands His Majesty could, on no account, retract any part of his propositions, but that everything else should be subject to modification. These offers, Sir, I maintain to have been extremely liberal in their principle, and more so, when we consider the application of it. We carried the principle of compensation to the fullest extent, when we offered to give up all that we had taken, reserving one subject only for consideration, which depended on a treaty, and which I shall presently mention; and we asked no more than what, by the strictest ties of justice and honour, we were bound to demand. Let me appeal to every one present if this conduct was not fair, just, and reasonable; if it did not bespeak sincere intentions and an anxious wish on the part of His Majesty to procure peace, consistently with good faith and security to himself and his allies, and if it was not entitled to a candid reception from the enemy.

As to the value of the French possessions which we offered to give up, it must be confessed that the same evils with which France has been afflicted have been extended to the colonial possessions; they have undoubtedly been much depreciated, much impoverished; but after all, they are of infinite importance to the commerce and marine of France. The valuable post of St. Domingo; the military and commercial advantages of Martinique; the peculiarly favourable military situation of St. Lucia; the importance of Tobago to this country; when we combine these, and place them in a united point of view, we have some reason to doubt whether there was not some degree of boldness on the part of His Majesty's ministers to make such overtures; we have some reason to suspect the wisdom of the measure, rather than to cavil at the insufficiency of the offer.

Pitt then explained that he had offered to restore not only the captured French colonies to France, but also the captured Dutch colonies [1] to Holland, practically the

[1] The Cape had been captured in 1795; Ceylon, Malacca, Amboyna, and Banda early in 1796.

subject of France, with the exception of strategic positions, such as the Cape of Good Hope and Ceylon, the control of which by France would threaten the British hold on India.

We ought to consider that those possessions, with regard to which no relation was to be admitted, were to be retained, in order that they might not become acquisitions to the French Government. In refusing to yield them up, we only refuse to put into the hands of the enemy the means of carrying into effect the deep-laid schemes of ambition they have long cherished, and the plan they have conceived of undermining our Indian Empire and destroying our Indian commerce, by ceding out of our own hands what may be deemed the bulwark of the wealth of this country and the security of the Indian Empire. These, indeed, were refused to be given up to our enemies; but everything else which the valour and the arms of this country had acquired, which was valuable, was proposed to be made matter of negotiation. This, Sir, was the nature of the propositions made at the very first moment when the negotiation was commenced: and I again submit to the final decision of the House, whether a proposition, including the restoration of everything valuable which we had acquired, except that which we could not forgo without manifest detriment to the most important interests of the country, was not founded in liberality and sincerity.

Sir, I must beg leave to observe, that on this part of the subject I have been the more anxious to be explicit because it is that part on which I lay the more particular stress, as tending to prove to the House, that everything was done at the commencement, everything distinctly stated, on which this country was willing to enter upon a negotiation. I am the more desirous of impressing the House with this part of my argument, because I feel it material in order to enable them to form a determinate precise idea of the character and prominent features of the negotiation itself. In return to the statements of compensation proposed by this country, the French Government presented no *projet* of their own, they afforded no room for discussion, because they were actuated by motives very distant from conciliation.

This much I have thought it necessary to state, in vindication of the character of myself and colleagues, that the House may be enabled to see that we never lost sight of the idea of a peace advantageous for our allies, safe for Europe, and honourable to this country. With regard to any specific terms of peace, which it might be proper to adopt or refuse, I do not think it would be wise for the House to pronounce. This may still be considered as a dormant negotiation, capable of being renewed; and it would be impolitic to give a pledge to any specific terms to which it might be impossible to adhere, and which can never be incurred without rashness. No man can be pledged to any particular terms, because in these he must be guided by a view of collateral circumstances and a comparative statement of resources. All that I wish Parliament to pronounce is, that they will add their testimony to the sincerity with which His Majesty has endeavoured to restore peace to Europe, and their approbation of the steps which were employed for its attainment.

But even after their rejection of every proposition that was advanced, after all the difficulties they started, after all the cavils they employed, after all the discouragements which they presented, when, at last, the French Government had been compelled to open the discussion, the first thing that happens, after requiring a note containing specific proposals, is a captious demand to have it signed by Lord Malmesbury. This demand was complied with to deprive them of every pretence for breaking off the negotiation, and immediately they call for an *ultimatum* in twenty-four hours. The impossibility of complying with such a demand is obvious. Was it possible to reconcile discordances, to smooth opposition, or pronounce good understanding in this manner? Does it come within the scope of the negotiation? Is an *ultimatum*, which means that demand which is to come the nearest to the views of all parties and to state the lowest terms which could be offered, thus to be made out at random, without knowing what the enemy would concede on their part or what they would accept on ours? A proposal, drawn up in such a manner, without explanation, without information, could have no good effect. It is a demand contrary to all reason and to all principle. With such a demand, therefore, it was impossible to comply; and in consequence of this, Lord Malmesbury received orders to quit Paris in forty-eight hours and the territories of the Republic as soon as possible.

Perhaps, however, I shall be told that the negotiation is not broken off, and that the French Government have pointed out a new basis upon which they are still willing to proceed. There are two things upon this subject not unworthy of consideration—the time at which they propose this new basis, and what sort of basis it is that they propose. After having approved and acted upon the basis proposed by His Majesty's Government; after having acknowledged, and, to all appearance, cordially acquiesced in it, as the ground of negotiation; after having demanded an *ultimatum* at the very commencement of this negotiation, and before any discussion had taken place, to be delivered in to the Directory in the space of twenty-four hours; and after dismissing the ambassador of the King with every mark of ignominy and insult, they propose a new basis, by which the negotiation is to be carried on by means of couriers. And what is the reason they assign for this new basis? Because Lord Malmesbury acted in a manner purely passive, and because he could assent to nothing without dispatching couriers to obtain the sanction of his Court. Here one cannot help remarking the studied perverseness of the temper of the French Government. When a courier was dispatched to Paris, at the instance of the minister of a neutral Power, in order to get a passport from the French Government, it was denied. A courier could not even obtain a passport, though the application was made to the executive Directory through the medium of the Danish minister. The request of the Danish minister was not enough; nothing could satisfy them but a British minister. Well, a British minister was sent. At the commencement of the negotiation he had occasion frequently to send dispatches to his Court, because it is very well known that there are a great number of difficulties which attend the opening of every negotiation, and because Lord Malmesbury had been sent to Paris before the preliminaries, which are usually settled by means of couriers, were arranged. While these preliminaries were in a course of settling, Lord Malmesbury's presence was barely endured, and the frequent dispatches of his couriers were subjects of animadversion; but no sooner were these preliminaries settled, and the British minister delivered in a *projet*, when there was less necessity for dispatching couriers, when the period for discussion was arrived, when the personal presence of an ambassador was particularly necessary, and when the King's minister announced to the French Government that he was prepared to enter into discussion upon the official memorials containing his *projet*, than he was ordered to quit Paris and leave the negotiation to be carried on by means of couriers. Such is the precise form, and it was impossible to devise a better, in which a studied insult, refined and matured by the French Directory, was offered to His Britannic Majesty.

I now come to state the broad plain ground on which the question rests, as far as the terms, upon which we are invited to treat on this new basis, are concerned. After having started a variety of captious objections at the opening of the negotiation, after the preliminaries were with much difficulty adjusted, after an *ultimatum* was demanded almost before discussion had commenced, after the King's minister was ordered, in the most insulting manner, to leave the territories of France, after a retraction by the executive Directory of the original basis of negotiation and the substitution of a new one in its place, they demand, not as an *ultimatum*, but as a preliminary, to be permitted to retain all those territories of which the chance of war has given them a temporary possession, and respecting which they have thought proper, contrary to every principle of equity and the received laws of nations, to pass a constitutional law, declaring, as they interpret it, that they shall not be alienated from the Republic.

Now whether this be the principle of their constitution or not, upon which I shall afterwards have occasion to make some observations, it was at least naturally to be supposed that the principle had been virtually set aside when the former basis of negotiation was recognized by the French Directory; for it must have been a strange admission of the principle of reciprocal compensations indeed, if they were obliged by the rules of their constitution to retain all those conquests which we were most bound in duty and in honour to insist upon their giving up (not by any mystery of a new constitution, which is little known and even among those who know it of doubtful interpretation, but by public and known engagements), and if they were under the same constitutional necessity, which they certainly are, of demanding the restitution of those colonies formerly in their possession, but which they have lost in the course of the war. Notwithstanding, however, their disavowal of this principle in the admission of the former basis of the negotiation, it is now alleged as a ground for the pretension, that they are entitled, as a matter of right, to demand from this country, not as an *ultimatum*, but as a preliminary to the discussion of any articles of treaty, that we shall make no proposals inconsistent with the laws and constitution of France.

I know of no law of nations which can in the remotest degree countenance such a perverse and monstrous claim. The annexation of territory to any State by the Government of that State during the continuance of the war in which it has been acquired, can never confer a claim which supersedes the treaties of their powers, and the known and public obligations of the different nations of Europe. It is impossible, in the nature of things, that the separate act of a separate Government can operate to the dissolution of the ties subsisting between other Governments, and to the abrogation of treaties previously concluded : and yet this is the pretension to which the French Government lay claim, and the acknowledgement of which they hold out not as an *ultimatum*, but as a preliminary of negotiation to the King of Great Britain and his allies. In my opinion, there is no principle of the law of nations clearer than this, that, when in the course of war any nation acquires new possessions, such nation has only temporary right to them, and they do not become property till the end of the war. This principle is incontrovertible, and founded upon the nature of things. For, supposing possessions thus acquired to be immediately annexed to the territory of the State by which the conquest was made, and that the conqueror was to insist upon retaining them, because he had passed a law that they should not be alienated, might not the neighbouring Powers, or even the hostile Power, ask— Who gave you a right to pass this law ? What have we to do with the regulations of your municipal law ? Or, what authority have you, as a separate State, by any annexation of territory to your dominions, to cancel existing treaties, and to destroy the equilibrium established among nations? Were this pretension to be tolerated, it would be a source of eternal hostility, and a perpetual bar to negotiation between the contending parties; because the pretensions of the one would be totally irreconcileable with those of the other.

This pretension in the instance of France has been as inconsistent in its operations as it was unfounded in its origin. The possessions which they have lost in the West Indies in the course of the war, they made independent Republics; and what is still more singular, Tobago, which they have lost in the war and which is retained by British arms, is a part of indivisible France. I should not be surprised to hear that Ireland, in consequence of the rumour which has been circulated of their intention to attempt an invasion upon that country, is constitutionally annexed to the territories of the Republic, or even that the city of Westminster is a part of indivisible France.

Pitt then referred to the text of the French constitution, and argued from it that the demand of the Directory, in any case unacceptable, was in reality a subterfuge, since the constitution 'leaves the Government entirely at liberty to dispose of the possessions, which they have acquired in war, in any way they may think proper'. He went on:

But this is not all the sacrifice they demand. This is not all the degradation to which they would have us submit. You must also engage, and as a preliminary too, to make no propositions which are contrary to the laws of the constitution and the *treaties* which bind the Republic. Here they introduce a new and extraordinary clause, imposing a restriction still more absurd and unreasonable than the other. The Republic of France may have made secret treaties which we know nothing about, and yet that Government expects that we are not to permit our propositions to interfere with these treaties. In the former instance we had a text upon which to comment, but here we are in the state of those diviners who were left to guess at the dreams which they were called upon to interpret. How is it possible for this country to know what secret articles there may be in the treaty between France and Holland? How can we know what the Dutch may have ceded to France, or whether France may not have an oath in heaven never to give up the territories ceded to her by Holland? Who can know but her treaty with Spain contains some secret article guaranteeing to the latter the restitution of Gibraltar, or some important possession now belonging to His Majesty? And how can I know whether the performance of all these engagements may not be included under the pretension which the French Government now holds out? How is it possible for me to sound where no line can fathom? And even after you have acceded to these preliminaries, in what situation do you stand? After accepting of terms of which you are entirely ignorant, and giving up all that it is of importance for you to keep, you at last arrive at a discussion of the government which France may choose to give to Italy, and of the fate which she may be pleased to assign to Germany.

In fact, the question is not, how much you will give for peace, but how much disgrace you will suffer at the outset, how much degradation you will submit to as a preliminary. In these circumstances, then, are we to persevere in the war with a spirit and energy worthy of the British name and of the British character; or are we, by sending couriers to Paris, to prostrate ourselves at the feet of a stubborn and supercilious Government, to do what they require, and to submit to whatever they may impose? I hope there is not a hand in His Majesty's councils that would sign the proposals, that there is not a heart in this House that would sanction the measure, and that there is not an individual in the British dominions who would act as the courier.

Pitt then moved an address to the King confirming the policy of the Government, and assuring His Majesty that he would be effectively supported in the rigorous prosecution of the war. An amendment was moved by the Opposition censuring the conduct of ministers in the negotiations. It was lost by 212 to 37, and the address was then agreed to.

11

The Mutiny in the Fleet

June 2, 1797 [1]

NEVER since the days of the Spanish Armada had England been in such peril as in the period which followed the breakdown of Malmesbury's negotiations at Paris. She was soon bereft of her last ally on the Continent. In the early months of 1797, Buonaparte finally crushed the Austrian power in North Italy and then marched

[1] *Speeches*, vol. iii, p. 141.

south to overwhelm the Pope. Returning northwards, he drove the Austrians over the Alps, followed close upon their heels, and dictated a preliminary peace at Leoben, within a hundred miles of Vienna. It was confirmed, on October 17, by the Treaty of Campo Formio. The Emperor was granted most of Venetia, which Buonaparte had conquered in the spring, and of the possessions of Venice in the Adriatic, but Buonaparte retained the Ionian Islands as useful stepping-stones towards Egypt and the East. On the other hand, Austria ceded her Belgic provinces to France, and in secret articles undertook to recognize a French occupation of the left bank of the Rhine. The First Coalition was thus finally extinct, and France could concentrate all her strength on carrying out the plans already formed for breaking British sea-power and invading England.

Meantime the safety of the country was almost as gravely threatened from within as from without. Four years of war, taxes steadily increasing, high cost of living, uncertain employment, a dearth of food, combined with the effects of the repressive legislation of the Government for the suppression of sedition to rouse the people of England to a dangerous discontent. The feeling in Scotland was still more disturbed. And Ireland was on the brink of rebellion. To crown all, the working of the whole machine of government was threatened by a sudden financial crisis, mainly due to the heavy export of gold to subsidize the Austrian efforts against France. The crisis had been postponed in the autumn of 1796 by the patriotic subscription of a State loan of £18,000,000 on easy terms, but it recurred in February 1797, and the Bank of England was directed by the Government to suspend cash payments. The only ray of light in that gloomy month was given by the victory of Jervis over the Spaniards [1] off Cape St. Vincent, a victory

[1] Spain had declared war on Britain in October 1796.

which prevented the combination of the French, Dutch, and Spanish fleets in a joint armada against England.

Scarcely had a general financial crash been averted, when the country was suddenly paralysed by the loss of its only protection against invasion. Most of them, to start with, victims of the press-gang, and disgusted, not without reason, at the low pay, miserable rations, and brutal discipline in the navy of that day, the men of the Channel Fleet at Spithead mutinied. After weeks of terrible suspense, the quarrel was settled in May by a generous policy of pardon and concession; but, a few days before the settlement, a similar mutiny broke out in the Nore Fleet at Sheerness. The danger here was still more acute, since in the Texel, just across the North Sea, the Dutch fleet was preparing to set sail, and the mouth of the Thames lay open to the enemy. Strong action was required, and when the mutineers declined the terms offered at Spithead, order was restored by drastic measures. For a moment the trouble threatened to spread to the army, but for a moment only. In June the crisis was over.

Pitt's health never recovered from these months of strain, but he did not falter, and to those who marked his calm, determined bearing he seemed to carry with him, embodied in his person, the courage of the nation. Such was the spirit in which he appealed on June 2 to the House of Commons, and through the House to the people, to rally to the assistance of the Government for the prevention and punishment of sedition. When the King's message had been read, he spoke as follows :

Important as the present occasion is, I feel that it will not be necessary for me to detain the House with a long detail upon the subject of the gracious communication from the Throne which has now been read to us. By that communication we learn that all the benefit of His Majesty's gracious favour, which restored satisfaction to part of His Majesty's forces, was attended with every mark of duty and gratitude by that part, and was extended to the whole of His Majesty's fleet; but that, nevertheless, there are now at the Nore deluded persons who have persisted in disobedience, and proceeded to open acts of mutiny and disorder, although all the same benefits have been allowed to them; the same liberal allowance, which was agreed upon by Parliament, and His Majesty's most gracious pardon have been offered to them in the same generous manner as it was to those who have returned to their duty. We have the mortification now to learn that mutiny is carried on to the most dangerous and criminal excess, to such a length that the persons concerned in it have gone into open and undisguised hostility against His Majesty's forces acting under orders and commands from regular authority. Much as we must deplore such events, much as we must feel them as an aggravation of the public difficulties with which we have to contend, yet I am sure we all feel it to be the duty of the House of Commons to show to its constituents, and to the world at large, that there is no difficulty which they will not meet with firmness and resolute decision; that we will take measures to extricate the country from its difficulties in a manner that is worthy of the representatives of a great, a brave, a powerful, and a free people.

I am persuaded that, under our present circumstances, we can have no hesitation in laying at the foot of the Throne an address of assurance, that we will afford

His Majesty every effectual support in our power; that we will counteract, as far as we can, so fatal an example as has, by the most consummate wickedness, been set to His Majesty's naval force; that we will show that we feel a just indignation against a conduct so unworthy of, so inconsistent with, the manly and generous character of British seamen; that we feel resentment at so ungrateful a return to the generosity of a liberal Parliament, and the mildness and benignity of an illustrious throne. I trust that we shall recollect what our duty is in such a conjuncture. I trust too, that as these late proceedings are utterly repugnant to the real spirit of the British sailor, contrary to the conduct which has established the glory of the British navy, and the renown of the British nation, it will appear that it was not in the hearts of British seamen that such mutinous principles originated. I trust that we shall show also, that if there are among us those who are enemies to the fundamental interests of this country, to its glory, to its safety, and to its existence as a nation, whose malignity is directed to the honour and even existence of our navy, who carry on their diabolical artifice by misrepresentation of facts, to pervert the dispositions and change the principles of the seamen by instilling into their minds false alarms and apprehensions, and prevail upon them to do acts contrary to their instinct, and that too when they are called upon to contend with an enemy—I trust, I say, that if there be among us such foes, they may be detected and dealt with as they deserve. Our indignation should be more active against the seducers than the seduced and misguided.

Whether, according to the existing law against the open attempts that we have seen made upon another branch of His Majesty's service to shake its loyalty, but which, to the honour of that body, remains unmoved, and I trust is immovable, we possess power enough to punish, as they deserve, such wicked offenders, may be a matter perhaps of doubt. I shall, however, instantly proceed to that part of the recommendation in His Majesty's message, and to state my ideas upon the law against persons who shall excite His Majesty's forces to mutiny or disobedience. It is not necessary for me to enter now into particulars upon that subject; but I feel it my duty to declare, that if the address which I shall propose shall meet, as I hope and confidently trust it will, the unanimous sense of the House, I shall immediately move for leave to bring in a Bill for the better prevention of the crime I have already stated. There is, I am persuaded, in this House, but one sense of the great guilt of this offence, of the notoriety of its practice, and of the danger of its consequences; in short, there exists every ground upon which penal law can be applied to any offence, viz. the mischief of the act itself, and the frequency of its commission. The remedy which I mean to propose for the consideration of Parliament will, I trust, be sufficiently efficacious to attain its object, without o'erstepping the moral guilt and real malignity of the crime.

While, however, we all feel it to be our duty to enter on the consideration of such legislative provision, while Parliament is not wanting in its duty at such a crisis of public affairs, I trust also that we shall not be disappointed in our expectation of the spirit of the public collectively or individually; that they will not be wanting in their exertions in such a crisis; that they will be animated, collectively and individually, with a spirit that will give energy and effect to their exertions; that every man who boasts and is worthy of the name of an Englishman, will stand forth in the metropolis and in every part of the kingdom, to maintain the authority of the laws and enforce obedience to them, to oppose and counteract the machinations of the disaffected, and to preserve a due principle of submission to legal authority. I trust that all the inhabitants of the kingdom will unite in one common defence against internal enemies, to maintain the general security of the kingdom, by providing for the local security of each particular district; that we shall all remember, that by so doing we shall give the fullest scope to His Majesty's forces against foreign enemies, and also the fullest scope to the known valour and unshaken fidelity of the military force of the kingdom against those who shall endeavour to disturb its internal tranquillity. Such are the principles which I feel, and upon which I shall act for myself, and such are the principles and will be the conduct, I hope, of every man in this House and out of it; such are the sentiments that are implanted in us all; such the feelings that are inherent in the breast of every Englishman. I should insult the House by showing that I distrusted its character, and the character of the country, if I said more, and I should have neglected my duty if I had said less. I now move, Sir,

'That an humble address be presented to His Majesty

to return His Majesty the thanks of this House for his most gracious message.

'To express to His Majesty the concern and indignation which we must feel in common with His Majesty, at the heinous and criminal conduct of the crews of some of His Majesty's ships, notwithstanding the offer so repeatedly made to them of His Majesty's most gracious pardon, and the proofs of the paternal regard of His Majesty, and of the liberality of Parliament, which they have received in common with the rest of His Majesty's fleet.

'To assure His Majesty, that we are ready and determined to afford to His Majesty our utmost assistance in repressing such dangerous and criminal proceedings, and to adopt every measure which can tend, at this conjuncture, to provide for the public security: with this view we shall proceed, without delay, in pursuance of the recommendation of His Majesty, to consider of such further provision as it may be necessary to make, for the more effectual prevention and punishment of all traitorous attempts to excite mutiny in any part of His Majesty's forces, or to withdraw them from their duty and allegiance, and from that obedience and discipline which are so important to the prosperity and the safety of the British Empire.

'That we have the fullest reliance, that all His Majesty's faithful subjects, from sentiments of loyalty and attachment to His Majesty, and a just anxiety for their dearest interests, will be eager to manifest, at so important a crisis, a full determination to contribute, on every occasion, their utmost exertions for the support of legal authority, the maintenance of peace and order, and the general protection and defence of His Majesty's kingdoms.'

The course of the debate having revealed no opposition to his policy, Pitt appealed in his reply for complete unanimity.

In expressing my anxiety for unanimity in voting the proposed address, I am influenced indeed by the most important considerations. I wish for such a unanimity as will lay a just foundation for future prosperity, for one on which I place the most favourable augury, the unanimity of the nation at large—a unanimity not in support of the administration, but in support of the constitution itself, and of all those laws by which it is guarded. The country is called upon to be unanimous in a contest which embraces everything that is most valuable to its dearest interests. Whatever difference of opinion may prevail in the minds of gentlemen on former points, there cannot exist a shadow of doubt with respect to the present question. It is now indispensably necessary for us to unite in one common cause ; it is incumbent on us to consolidate our efforts, to reconcile our different views, to concentrate our individual exertions, and to give energy and vigour to the laws, without which it is impossible there can be any solid happiness. It is not merely by declarations that we are bound to proceed, but by a spirit and promptitude of action, and a firm resolution and readiness to support the execution of the laws by military subordination and legal obedience. It becomes our duty to give a resistless efficacy to this conduct through every corner of the metropolis and through every part of the kingdom. By such measures we can alone disappoint the dark and malignant efforts of the enemy; and I am proud to say that to so glorious a unanimity there is nothing that I would not cheerfully sacrifice.

The address was agreed to *nemine contradicente.*

The worst storm was past, but the sky was still black. Stimulated by the naval mutiny, the first rising had just occurred in Ireland. Its suppression only postponed a general rebellion, and had the mutiny persisted, had the French been able to land in Ireland in the summer of 1797, they would have found its occupation an easy task, and the end of the British Empire would have been at hand. It is little wonder that Pitt was willing to make one more effort for peace, and in the autumn negotiations were resumed. Their initiation brings to a close the first phase of the long struggle; their failure marks the opening of a new phase. The war with the revolutionary Governments of the French Republic is ended. The war with Napoleon begins.

THE WAR: SECOND PHASE
1797-1802

The Renewal of the War: an Appeal for National Unity

November 10, 1797 [1]

MALMESBURY crossed once more to France and met the representatives of the Directory at Lille in July. He was authorized to surrender more than he had offered in the previous year. Preliminaries of peace between France and Austria had been signed at Leoben in April, and the impending surrender of Belgium by its old rulers made it impossible for Great Britain, almost in extremities herself, to hold out any longer for its restoration. No objection, therefore, was raised to the retention by France of all her conquests on the Continent. Pitt was now ready, moreover, to give up everything British arms had won except the Cape and Trinidad.

Never again had France an opportunity of concluding peace on such triumphant terms. And Pitt was right in believing that the mass of Frenchmen would have joyfully accepted an offer which practically amounted on our side to a confession of defeat. The conclusion of peace was, in fact, the first aim of the 'Constitutional' party, which possessed a majority both in the Legislative Chambers and in the country. But four

[1] *Speeches*, vol. iii, p. 153.

out of the five Directors, and most of the Ministers dependent on them, belonged to the 'Revolutionary' party, which stood for war. As long as the party conflict was undecided, peace hung in the balance. On September 17, thirteen days after Buonaparte's intervention[1] had decided it, the French delegates at Lille informed Malmesbury that, unless he possessed authority, and used it, to surrender everything, he must leave France within twenty-four hours.

It was to be war then, and war to the knife. When Buonaparte returned to Paris to grasp the despotic power which was waiting for his hand, he was greeted by the revolutionaries as the appointed conqueror of England.[2]

But before his return the crushing defeat of the Dutch fleet off Camperdown (October 11) had already made the conquest of England more difficult. The fleets at the disposal of France in the neighbourhood of the Channel were now not strong enough to cover an invasion until they could be joined by those at Cadiz and Toulon. The Battle of Camperdown, therefore, could be set in the balance against the Treaty of Campo Formio (October 17) when, on November 10, Pitt explained to the House of Commons the failure of the Lille negotiations, and made his historic appeal for national unity in face of the gravest danger the country had yet known.

Dundas moved that the House do concur with the address of the House of Lords. After Sir John Sinclair, who moved an amendment, and Lord Temple, Pitt's cousin, had spoken, Pitt rose.

Sir—Having come to this House with the firm persuasion that there never existed an occasion when the unanimous concurrence of the House might be more

---

[1] Introduction, p. xxxiv.   [2] Introduction, p. xliii.

justly expected, than on a proposal to agree in the sentiments contained in the address which has been read, I must confess myself considerably disappointed, in some degree, even by the speech of my noble relation (much as I rejoice in the testimony which he has given of his talents and abilities), and still more by the speech of the honourable baronet, and by the amendment which he has moved. I cannot agree with the noble lord in the extent to which he has stated his sentiments, that we ought to rejoice that peace was not made ; much less, Sir, can I feel desirous to accept, on the part of myself or my colleagues, either from my noble kinsman, or any other person, the approbation which he was pleased to express of the manner in which we have concluded the negotiation. *We* have not concluded the negotiation— the negotiation has been concluded by others ; we have not been suffered to continue it ; our claim to merit, if we have any, our claim to the approbation of our country is, that we persisted in every attempt to conduct that negotiation to a pacific termination, as long as our enemies left us not the prospect but the chance or possibility of doing so, consistent with our honour, our dignity, and our safety. We lament and deplore the disappointment of the sincere wishes which we felt, and of the earnest endeavours which we employed. Yet we are far from suffering those sentiments to induce us to adopt the unmanly line of conduct that has been recommended by the honourable baronet. This is not the moment to dwell only on our disappointment, to suppress our indignation, or to let our courage, our constancy, and our determination be buried in the expression of unmanly fear or unavailing regret. Between these two extremes it is that I trust our conduct is directed; and in calling upon the House to join in sentiments between those extremes, I do trust, that if we cannot have the unanimous opinion, we shall have the general and ready concurrence both of the House and of the country.

Sir, before I trouble the House, which I am not desirous of doing at length, with a few points which I wish to recapitulate, let me first call to your minds the general nature of the amendment which the honourable baronet has, under these circumstances, thought fit to propose, and the general nature of the observations by which he introduced it. He began with deploring the calamities of war, on the general topic that all war is calamitous. Do I object to this sentiment? No: but is it our business at a moment when we feel that the continuance of that war is owing to the animosity, the implacable animosity of our enemy, to the inveterate and insatiable ambition of the present frantic Government of France, not of the people of France, as the honourable baronet unjustly stated it—is it our business at that moment to content ourselves with merely lamenting in commonplace terms the calamities of war, and forgetting that it is part of the duty which, as representatives of the people, we owe to our Government and our country, to state that the continuance of those evils upon ourselves, and upon France too, is the fruit only of the conduct of the enemy; that it is to be imputed to them, and not to us?

Sir, the papers which were ordered to be laid on the

table have been in every gentleman's hand, and on the materials which they furnish we must be prepared to decide. Can there be a doubt that all the evils of war, whatever may be their consequences, are to be imputed solely to His Majesty's enemies? Is there any man here prepared to deny that the delay in every stage of the negotiation, and its final rupture, are proved to be owing to the evasive conduct, the unwarrantable pretensions, the inordinate ambition, and the implacable animosity of the enemy? I will shortly state what are the points, though it is hardly necessary that I should state them, for they speak loudly for themselves, on which I would rest that proposition; but if there is any man who doubts it, is it the honourable baronet? Is it he who makes this amendment, leaving out everything that is honourable to the character of his own country, and seeming to court some new complaisance on the part of the French Directory?—the honourable baronet, who, as soon as he has stated the nature of his amendment, makes the first part of his speech a charge against His Majesty's Ministers, for even having commenced the negotiation in the manner and under the circumstances in which they did commence it—who makes his next charge, their having persevered in it, when violations of form and practice were insisted upon in the earliest stage of it? Does he discover that the French Government, whom we have accused with insincerity, have been sincere from the beginning to the end of the negotiation? Or, after having accused His Majesty's Ministers for commencing and persevering in it, is the honourable baronet so afraid of being misconstrued into an idea of animosity against the people of France, that he must disguise the truth, must do injustice to the character and cause of his own country, and leave unexplained the cause of the continuance of this great contest? Let us be prepared to probe that question to the bottom, to form our opinion upon it, and to render our conduct conformable to that opinion. This, I conceive, to be a manly conduct, and, especially at such a moment, to be the indispensable duty of the House. But let not the honourable baronet imagine there is any ground for his apprehension, that by adopting the language of the address, which ascribes the continuance of the war to the ambition of the enemy, we shall declare a system of endless animosity between the nations of Great Britain and France. I say directly the contrary. He who scruples to declare that in the present moment the Government of France are acting as much in contradiction to the known wishes of the French nation, as to the just pretensions and anxious wishes of the people of Great Britain—he who scruples to declare them the authors of this calamity, deprives us of the consolatory hope which we are inclined to cherish, of some future change of circumstances more favourable to our wishes.

It is a melancholy spectacle, indeed, to see in any country, and on the ruin of any pretence of liberty however nominal, shallow, or delusive, a system of tyranny erected, the most galling, the most horrible, the most undisguised in all its parts and attributes that has stained the page of history, or disgraced the annals of the world; but it would be much more unfortunate, if when we see that the same cause carries desolation through France, which extends disquiet and fermentation through Europe, it would be worse, indeed, if we attributed to the nation of France that which is to be attributed only to the unwarranted and usurped authority which involves them in misery, and would, if unresisted, involve Europe with them in one common ruin and destruction. Do we state this to be animosity on the part of the people of France? Do we state this in order to raise up an implacable spirit of animosity against that country? Where is one word to that effect in the declaration to which the honourable gentleman has alluded? He complains much of this declaration, because it tends to perpetuate animosity between two nations which one day or other must be at peace—God grant that day may be soon! But what does that declaration express upon the subject? Does it express that, because the present existing Government of France has acted as it has acted, we forgo the wish or renounce the hope that some new situation may lead to happier consequences? On the contrary, His Majesty's language is distinctly this: 'While this determination continues to prevail on the part of his enemies, His Majesty's earnest wishes and endeavours to restore peace to his subjects must be fruitless; but his sentiments remain unaltered; he looks with anxious expectation to the moment when the Government of France may show a temper and spirit in any degree corresponding with his own.' I wish to know whether words can be found in the English language which more expressly state the contrary sentiment to that which the honourable baronet imputes; they **not** only disclaim animosity against the people of France in consequence of the conduct of its rulers, but do not go the length of declaring, that after all this provocation, even with the present rulers, all treaty is impracticable. Whether it is probable that, acting on the principles upon which they have acquired their power, and while that power continues, they will listen to any system of moderation or justice at home or abroad, it is not now necessary to discuss; but for one, I desire to express my cordial concurrence in the sentiment, so pointedly expressed in that passage of the declaration, in which His Majesty, notwithstanding all the provocation he has received, and even after the recent successes which, by the blessing of Providence, have attended his arms, declares his readiness to adhere to the same moderate terms and principles which he proposed at the time of our greatest difficulties, and to conclude peace on that ground, if it can now be obtained, even with this very Government.

I am sensible that, while I am endeavouring to vindicate His Majesty's servants against the charges of the honourable baronet, which are sufficiently, however, refuted by the early part of his own speech, I am incurring, in some degree, the censure of the noble lord to whom I before alluded. According to his principles and opinions, and those of some few others in this country, it is matter of charge against us that we even harbour in our minds at this moment a wish to conclude peace upon the terms which we think admissible with the present rulers of France. I am not one of those who can or will join in that sentiment. I have no difficulty in repeating what I stated before, that in their present spirit, after what they have said, and still more after what they have done, I can entertain little hope of so desirable an event. I have no hesitation in avowing, for it would be idleness and hypocrisy to conceal it, that for the sake of mankind in general, and to gratify those sentiments which can never be eradicated from the human heart, I should see with pleasure and satisfaction the termination of a Government whose conduct and whose origin is such as we have seen that of the Government of France. But that is not the object, that ought not to be the principle, of the war, whatever wish I may entertain in my own heart; and whatever opinion I may think it fair or manly to avow, I have no difficulty in stating that, violent and odious as is the character of that Government, I verily believe, in the present state of Europe, that if we are not wanting to ourselves, if, by the blessing of Providence, our perseverance and our resources should enable us to make peace with France upon terms in which we taint not our character, in which we do not abandon the sources of our wealth, the means of our strength, the defence of what we already possess; if we maintain our equal pretensions, and assert that rank which we are entitled to hold among nations—the moment peace can be obtained on such terms, be the form of government in France what it may, peace is desirable, peace is then anxiously to be sought. But unless it is attained on such terms, there is no extremity of war, there is no extremity of honourable contest, that is not preferable to the name and pretence of peace, which must be in reality a disgraceful capitulation, a base, an abject surrender of everything that constitutes the pride, the safety, and happiness of England.

These, Sir, are the sentiments of my mind on this leading point, and with these sentiments I shape my conduct between the contending opinions of the noble lord and of the honourable baronet. But there is one observation of the honourable baronet on which I must now more particularly remark. He has discovered that we state the Directory of France to have been all along insincere, and yet take merit for having commenced a negotiation, which we ought never to have commenced without being persuaded of their sincerity. This supposed contradiction requires but a few words to explain it. I believe that those who constitute the *present* Government of France never were sincere for a moment in the negotiation. From all the information I have obtained, and from every conjecture I could form, I for one never was so duped as to believe them sincere. But I did believe, and I thought I knew, that there was a general prevailing wish for peace, and a predominant sense of its necessity growing and confirming itself in France, and founded on the most obvious and most pressing motives. I did see a spirit of reviving moderation gradually gaining ground, and opening a way to the happiest alterations in the general system of that country. I did believe that the violence of that portion of the Executive Government, which, by the late strange revolution of France, unhappily for France itself and for the world, has gained the ascendancy, would have been restrained within some bounds; that ambition must give way to reason; that even frenzy itself must be controlled and governed by necessity. These were the hopes and expectations I entertained. I did, notwithstanding, feel that even from the outset, and in every step of that negotiation, those who happily had not yet the full power to cut it short in the beginning, who dared not trust the public eye with the whole of their designs, who could not avow all their principles, unfortunately, nevertheless, did retain from the beginning power enough to control those who had a better disposition; to mix in every part of the negotiation, which they could not then abruptly break off, whatever could impede, embarrass, and perplex, in order to throw upon us, if possible, the odium of its failure.

Sir, the system of France is explained by the very objections that are made against our conduct. The violent party could not, as I have stated, at once break off the treaty on their part, but they wished to drive England to the rupture. They had not strength enough to reject all negotiation, but they had strength enough to mix in every step those degradations and insults, those inconsistent and unwarranted pretensions in points even of subordinate importance, which reduced ministers to that opinion which I have described; but which they decided in a way that has exposed them to the censure of the honourable baronet. They chose rather to incur the blame of sacrificing punctilios (at some times essential) rather than afford the enemy an opportunity of evading this plain question—Is there any ground, and, if any, what, upon which you are ready to conclude peace? To that point it was our duty to drive them. We have driven them to that point. They would tell us no terms, however exorbitant and unwarrantable, upon which they would be ready to make peace.

What would have been the honourable baronet's expedient to avoid this embarrassment? It would have been, as he has this day informed us, an address which he had thought of moving in the last session, and which, indeed, I should have been less surprised had he moved, than if the House had concurred in it; he would have moved that no *projet* should be given in till the enemy were prepared to present a *contre projet*. If it was a great misfortune that that address was not moved, I am afraid some of the guilt belongs to me, because the honourable baronet did suggest such an idea, and I did with great sincerity and frankness tell him that, if he was really a friend to peace, there was no motion he could make so little calculated to promote that object; and I did prevail upon the honourable baronet to give up the intention. If I am right in the supposition I have stated; if I am right in thinking that our great object was to press France to this point, and to put the question—if you have any terms to offer, what are they? —was there any one way by which we could make it so difficult for them to retain any pretence of a desire of peace, as to speak out ourselves, and call upon them either for agreement, or for modification, or for some other plan in their turn? By not adopting the honourable baronet's plan, we have put the question beyond dispute, whether peace was attainable at last, and whether our advances would or would not be met on the part of France; and I shall, to the latest hour of my life, rejoice that we were fortunate enough to place this question in the light which defies the powers of misrepresentation, in which no man can attempt to perplex it, and in which it presents itself this day for the decision of the House and of the nation, and calls upon every individual who has at stake the public happiness and his own, to determine for himself, whether this is or is not a crisis which requires his best exertions in the defence of his country.

To show which, I shall now proceed, notwithstanding the reproach which has been thrown on our line of conduct, to show the system even of obstinate forbearance, with which we endeavoured to overcome preliminary difficulties, the determined resolution on our part to overlook all minor obstacles, and to come to the real essence of discussion upon the terms of peace. To show this, it is not necessary to do more than to call to the recollection of the House the leading parts of the declaration of His Majesty. I mean to leave that part of the subject also without the possibility of doubt or difference of opinion. It is certainly true that, even previous to any of the circumstances that related to the preliminary forms of the negotiation, the prior conduct of France had offered to any Government that was not sincerely and most anxiously bent upon peace, sufficient ground for the continuance of hostilities. It is true that, in the former negotiation at Paris, Lord Malmesbury was finally sent away, not upon a question of terms of peace, not upon a question of the cession of European or colonial possessions, but upon the haughty demand of a previous preliminary, which should give up everything on the part of the allies, and which should leave them afterwards everything to ask, or rather to require. It is true it closed in nearly the same insulting manner as the second mission. It is true, too, that, subsequent to that period, in the preliminaries concluded between the Emperor and France, it was agreed to invite the allies of each party to a congress, which, however, was never carried into execution. It was under these circumstances that His Majesty, in the earnest desire of availing himself of that spirit of moderation which had begun to show itself in France, determined to renew those proposals which had been before slighted and rejected. But when this step was taken, what was the conduct of those who have gained the ascendancy in France? On the first application to know on what ground they were disposed to negotiate, wantonly, as will be shown by the sequel, and for no purpose but to prevent even the opening of the conferences, they insisted upon a mode of negotiation very contrary to general usage and convenience, contrary to the mode in which they had terminated war with any of the belligerent Powers, and directly contrary to any mode which they themselves afterwards persisted in following in this very negotiation with us. They began by saying, they would receive no proposals for preliminaries, but that conferences should be held for the purpose of concluding at once a definitive treaty.

His Majesty's answer was, that it was his desire to adopt that mode only which was most likely to accelerate the object in view, and the powers of his plenipotentiary would apply to either object, either preliminary or definitive. They appeared content with his answer:

but what was the next step? In the simple form of granting a passport for the minister—at the moment they were saying they preferred a definitive peace, because it was the most expeditious—in that very passport, which in all former times has only described the character of the minister, without entering into anything relating to the terms or mode of negotiating, they insert a condition relative to his powers, and that inconsistent with what His Majesty had explained to be the nature of the powers he had intended to give, and with which they had apparently been satisfied; they made it a passport not for a minister coming to conclude peace generally, but applicable only to a definitive and separate peace.

This proceeding was in itself liable to the most obvious objection; but it is more important as an instance to show how, in the simplest part of the transaction, the untractable spirit of France discovered itself; it throws light upon the subsequent part of the transaction, and shows the inconsistencies and contradictions of their successive pretensions. As to the condition then made in the passport for the first time, that the negotiation should be for a separate peace, His Majesty declared that he had no choice between a definitive and a preliminary treaty, but as to a separate peace, his honour and good faith, with regard to his ally the Queen of Portugal,[1] would not permit it: he therefore stated his unalterable determination to agree to no treaty in which Portugal should not be included, expressing at the same time his

[1] In August, during the course of the negotiations, Portugal made a separate peace with France.

readiness that France should treat on the part of Holland and Spain.

On this occasion, the good faith of this country prevailed; the system of violence and despotism was not then ripe, and therefore His Majesty's demand to treat for Portugal was acquiesced in by the Directory. They, at the same time, undertook to treat on their part for their allies, Holland and Spain, as well as for themselves, though in the subsequent course of the negotiation they pretended to be without sufficient power to treat for either.

I must here entreat the attention of the House to the next circumstance which occurred. When the firmness of His Majesty, his anxious and sincere desire to terminate the horrors of war, and his uniform moderation, overcame the violence and defeated the designs of the members of the Executive Government of France, they had recourse to another expedient—the most absurd, as well as the most unjustifiable. They adverted to the rupture of the former negotiation, as if that rupture was to be imputed to His Majesty; and this insinuation was accompanied with a personal reflection upon the minister who was sent by His Majesty to treat on the part of this country. His Majesty, looking anxiously as he did to the conclusion of peace, disdained to reply otherwise than by observing, that this was not a fit topic to be agitated at the moment of renewing a negotiation, and that the circumstances of the transaction were well enough known to Europe and to the world. And the result of this negotiation has confirmed what the former had sufficiently proved, that His Majesty could not have selected, in the ample field of talents which his dominions furnish, any person better qualified to do justice to his sincere and benevolent desire to promote the restoration of peace, and his firm and unalterable determination to maintain the dignity and honour of his kingdoms.

In spite of these obstacles, and others more minute, the British plenipotentiary at length arrived at Lille; the full powers were transmitted to the respective Governments, and were found unexceptionable, though the supposed defect of these full powers is, three months after, alleged as a cause for the rupture of the negotiation; and what is more remarkable, it did so happen, that the French full powers were, on the face of them, much more limited than ours, for they only enabled the commissioners of the Directory to act according to the instructions they were to receive from time to time. On this point it is not necessary now to dwell, but I desire the House to treasure it in their memory, when we come to the question of pretence for the rupture of the negotiation.

Then, Sir, I come to the point in which we have incurred the censure of the honourable baronet, for delivering in on our part a *projet*. To his opinion I do not subscribe, for the reasons that I stated before. But can there be a stronger proof of His Majesty's sincerity, than his waiving so many points important in themselves rather than suffer the negotiation to be broken off? What was our situation? We were to treat with a Government that had in the outset expressed that they would treat only definitively; and from every part of their conduct which preceded the meeting of our plenipotentiary and their commissioners, we might have expected that they would have been prepared to answer our *projet* almost in twenty-four hours after it was delivered. We stood with respect to France in this predicament—we had nothing to ask of them; the question only was, how much we were to give of that which the valour of His Majesty's arms had acquired from them and from their allies. In this situation, surely, we might have expected that, before we offered the price of peace, they would at least have condescended to say what were the sacrifices which they expected us to make. But, Sir, in this situation, what species of *projet* was it that was presented by His Majesty's minister? A *projet* the most distinct, the most particular, the most conciliatory and moderate, that ever constituted the first words spoken by any negotiator; and yet of this *projet* what have we heard in the language of the French Government? What have we seen dispersed through all Europe by that press in France which knows no sentiments but what French policy dictates? What have we seen dispersed by that English press which knows no other use of English liberty, but servilely to retail and transcribe French opinions? We have been told, that it was a *projet* that refused to embrace the terms of negotiation. Gentlemen have read the papers—how does that fact stand? In the original *projet* we agreed to give up the conquests we had made from France and her allies, with certain exceptions. For those exceptions a blank was left, in order to ascertain whether France was desirous that the exceptions should be divided between her and her allies, or whether she continued to insist upon a complete compensation, and left England to look for compensation only to her allies. France, zealous as she pretends to be for her allies, had no difficulty in authorizing her ministers to declare that she must retain everything for herself. This blank was then filled up, and it was then distinctly stated, how little, out of what we had, we demanded to keep. In one sense, it remains a blank still; we did not attempt to preclude France from any other mode of filling it up: but while we stated the utmost extent of our own views, we left open to full explanation whatever points the Government of France could desire. We called upon them, and repeatedly solicited them, to state something as to the nature of the terms which they proposed, if they objected to ours. It was thus left open to modification, alteration, or concession.

But this is not the place, this is not the time, in which I am to discuss, whether those terms, in all given circumstances, or in the circumstances of that moment, were or were not the ultimate terms upon which peace ought to be accepted or rejected. If it were once brought to the point when an ultimatum could be judged of, I will not argue whether some great concession might not have been made with the certainty of peace, or whether the terms proposed constituted an offer of peace upon more favourable grounds for the enemy than His Majesty's ministers could justify. I argue not the one question or the other; it would be inconsistent with the public interest and our duty, that we should here state or discuss it. All that I have to discuss is, whether the terms, upon the face of them, appear honourable, open, frank, distinct, sincere, and a pledge of moderation; and I leave it to the good sense of the House, whether there can exist a difference of opinion upon this point.

Sir, what was it we offered to renounce to France? In one word, all that we had taken from them. What did this consist of? The valuable, and almost, under all circumstances, the impregnable island of Martinique, various other West India possessions, St. Lucia, Tobago, the French part of St. Domingo, the settlements of Pondicherry and Chandernagore, all the French factories and means of trade in the East Indies, and the islands of St. Pierre and Miquelon; and for what were these renunciations to be made? For peace, and for peace only. And to whom? To a nation which had obtained from His Majesty's dominions in Europe nothing in the course of the war, which had never met our fleets but to add to the catalogue of our victories, and to swell the melancholy lists of their own captures and defeats. To a Power which had never separately met the arms of this country by land, but to carry the glory and prowess of the British name to a higher pitch: and to a country whose commerce is unheard of, whose navy is annihilated, whose distress, confessed by themselves (however it may be attempted to be dissembled by their panegyrists in this or any other country), is acknowledged by the sighs and groans of the people of France, and proved by the expostulations and remonstrances occasioned by the violent measures of its Executive Government.

Such was the situation in which we stood, such the

situation of the enemy, when we offered to make these important concessions as the price of peace. What was the situation of the allies of France? From Spain, who, from the moment she had deserted our cause and enlisted on the part of the enemy, only added to the number of our conquests and to her own indelible disgrace, we made claim of one island, the island of Trinidad, a claim not resting on the mere naked title of possession to counterbalance the general European aggrandizement of France, but as the price of something that we had to give by making good the title to the Spanish part of St. Domingo, which Spain had ceded without right, and which cession could not be made without our guarantee.[1] To Holland, having in our hands the whole means of their commerce, the whole source of their wealth, we offered to return almost all that was valuable and lucrative to them in the mere consideration of commerce. We desired in return to keep what to them, in a pecuniary view, would be only a burthen, in a political view worse than useless, because they had not the means to keep it; what, had we granted it, would have been a sacrifice, not to them, but to France; what would in future have enabled her to carry on her plan of subjugation against the Eastern possessions of Holland itself, as well as against those of Great Britain. All that we asked was, not indemnification for what we had suffered, but the means of preserving our own possessions and the strength of our

[1] By the Treaty of Utrecht (1713) Spain was bound not to alienate any of her possessions in the West Indies or America without the consent of Great Britain.

naval empire. We did this at a time when our enemy was feeling the pressure of war—and who looks at the question of peace without some regard to the relative situation of the country with which you are contending? Look then at their trade; look at their means; look at the posture of their affairs; look at what we hold, and at the means we have of defending ourselves, and our enemy of resisting us, and tell me, whether this offer was or was not a proof of sincerity and a pledge of moderation. Sir, I should be ashamed of arguing it, I confess; I am apprehensive we may have gone too far on the first proposals we made, rather than show any backwardness in the negotiation; but it is unnecessary to argue this point.

Our proposal was received and allowed by the French plenipotentiaries, and transmitted for the consideration of the Directory; months had elapsed in sending couriers weekly and daily from Paris to Lille, and from Lille to Paris; they taught us to expect, from time to time, a consideration of this subject, and an explicit answer to our *projet*. But the first attempt of the Directory to negotiate, after having received our *projet*, is worthy of remark. They required that we, whom they had summoned to a definitive treaty, should stop and discuss preliminary points, which were to be settled without knowing whether, when we had agreed to them all, we had advanced one inch; we were to discuss, whether His Majesty would renounce the title of King of France, a harmless feather, at most, in the crown of England; we were to discuss, whether we would restore those ships taken at Toulon, the acquisition of valour, and which we were entitled upon every ground to hold ; we were to discuss, whether we would renounce the mortgage which we might possess on the Netherlands, and which engaged much of the honourable baronet's attention : but it does so happen, that what the honourable baronet considered as so important, was of no importance at all. For a mortgage on the Netherlands, we have none, and consequently we have none to renounce ; therefore, upon that condition, which they had no right to ask, and we had no means of granting, we told them the true state of the case, and that it was not worth talking about.

The next point which occurred is of a nature which it is difficult to dwell upon without indignation. We were waiting the fulfilment of a promise which had been made repeatedly, of delivering to our ambassador a *contre projet,* when they, who had desired us to come for the purpose of concluding a definitive treaty, propose that we should subscribe as a *sine qua non* preliminary, that we were ready, in the first instance, to consent to give up all that we had taken, and then to hear what they had further to ask. Is it possible to suppose that such a thing could be listened to by any country that was not prepared to prostrate itself at the feet of France, and in that abject posture to adore its conqueror, to solicit new insults, to submit to demands still more degrading and ignominious, and to cancel at once the honour of the British name ? His Majesty had no hesitation in refusing to comply with such insolent and unwarrantable demands. Here again the House will see that the spirit of the violent part of the French Government, which had the insolence to advance this proposition, had not acquired power and strength in that state of the negotiation to adhere to it. His Majesty's explanations and remonstrances for a time prevailed, and an interval ensued, in which we had a hope that we were advancing to a pacification.

His Majesty's refusal of this demand was received by the French plenipotentiaries with assurances of a pacific disposition, was transmitted to their Government, and was seconded by a continued and repeated repetition of promises that a *contre projet* should be presented, pretending that they were under the necessity of sending to their allies an account of what passed, and that they were endeavouring to prevail on them to accede to proposals for putting an end to the calamities of war —to terminate the calamities of that war into which those allies were forced, in which they were retained by France alone, and in which they purchased nothing but sacrifices to France and misery to themselves. We were told, indeed, in a conference that followed, that they had obtained an answer, but that, not being sufficiently satisfactory, it was sent back to be considered. This continued, during the whole period, until that dreadful catastrophe of September 4. Even after that event, the same pretence was held out; they peremptorily promised the *contre projet* in four days; the same pacific professions were renewed, and our minister was assured that the change of circumstances in France should not be a bar to the pacification.

Such was the uniform language of the plenipotentiaries in the name of the Government. How it is proved by their actions I have already stated to the House. After this series of professions, what was the first step taken to go on with the negotiation in this spirit of conciliation? Sir, the first step was to renew, as His Majesty's declaration has well stated, in a shape still more offensive, the former inadmissible and rejected demand; the rejection of which had been acquiesced in by themselves two months before, and during all which time we had been impatiently waiting for the performance of their promises. That demand was the same that I have already stated in substance, that Lord Malmesbury should explain to them, not only his powers, but also his instructions; and they asked not for the formal extent of his power, which would give solidity to what he might conclude in the King's name, but they asked an irrevocable pledge, that he would consent to give up all that we had taken from them and from their allies, without knowing how much more they had afterwards to ask. It is true they endeavoured to convince Lord Malmesbury that, although an avowal of his instructions was demanded, it would never be required that he should act upon it, for there was a great difference between knowing the extent of the powers of a minister and insisting upon their exercise.

And here I would ask the honourable baronet, whether he thinks, if, in the first instance, we had given up all to the French plenipotentiaries, they would have given it all back again to us? Suppose I was ambassador from the French Directory, and the honourable baronet was ambassador from Great Britain, and I were to say to him, 'Will you give up all you have gained? It would only be a handsome thing in you, as an Englishman, and no ungenerous use shall be made of it.' Would the honourable baronet expect me, as a French ambassador, to say, ' I am instructed, from the good nature of the Directory, to say, you have acted handsomely, and I now return you what you have so generously given'? Should we not be called children and drivellers, if we could act in this manner? And indeed the French Government could be nothing but children and drivellers, if they could suppose that we should have acceded to such a proposal.

But they are bound, it seems, by sacred treaties; they are bound by immutable laws; they are sworn, when they make peace, to return everything to their allies; and who shall require of France, for the safety of Europe, to depart from its own pretensions to honour and independence?

If any person can really suppose that this country could have agreed to such a proposition, or that such a negotiation was likely to lead to a good end, all I can say is, that with such a man I will not argue. I leave others to imagine what was likely to have been the end of a negotiation, in which it was to have been settled as a preliminary, that you were to give up all that you have gained; and when, on the side of your enemy, not a word was said of what he had to propose afterwards. They demand of your ambassador to show to them not only his powers, but also his instructions, before they explain a word of theirs; and they tell you too, that you are never to expect to hear what their powers are, until you shall be ready to concede everything which the Directory may think fit to require. This is certainly the substance of what they propose; and they tell you also, that they are to carry on the negotiation from the instructions which their plenipotentiaries are to receive from time to time from them. You are to have no power to instruct your ambassador; you are to show to the enemy at once all you have in view, and they will only tell you from time to time, as to them shall seem meet, what demands they shall make.

It was thus it was attempted, on the part of the French, to commence the negotiation. In July this demand was made to Lord Malmesbury. He stated that his powers were ample. In answer to this, they went no farther than to say that, if he had no such power as what they required, he should send to England to obtain it. To which he replied, that he had not, nor should he have it if he sent. In this they acquiesce, and attempt to amuse us for two months. At the end of that time, the plenipotentiaries say to Lord Malmesbury, not what they said before, 'Send to England for power to accede to proposals which you have already rejected,' but 'Go to England yourself for such powers, in order to obtain peace.'

Such was the winding up of the negotiation; such was the way in which the prospect of peace has been disappointed by the conduct of France; and I must look upon the dismissal of Lord Malmesbury as the last stage of the negotiation, because the undisguised insult, by which it was pretended to be kept up for ten days after Lord Malmesbury was sent away, was really below comment. You, France, send him to ask for those powers which you were told he had not, and in the refusal of which you acquiesced. You have asked, as a preliminary, that which is monstrous and exorbitant. That preliminary, you were told, would not be complied with, and yet the performance of that preliminary you made the *sine qua non* condition of his return! Such was the last step by which the French Government has shown that it had feeling enough left to think it necessary to search for some pretext to colour its proceedings: but they are such proceedings that no pretext or artifice can cover them, as will appear more particularly from the papers officially communicated to the House.

But here the subject does not rest. If we look to the whole complexion of this transaction, the duplicity, the arrogance and the violence which has appeared in the course of the negotiation, if we take from thence our opinion of its general result, we shall be justified in our conclusion, not that the people of France, not that the whole Government of France, but that that part of the Government which had too much influence and has now the whole ascendancy, never was sincere; was determined to accept of no terms of peace but such as would make it neither durable nor safe, such as could only be accepted by this country by a surrender of all its interests, and by a sacrifice of every pretension to the character of a great, a powerful, or an independent nation.

This, Sir, is inference no longer, you have their own open avowal. You have it stated in the subsequent declaration of France itself, that it is not against your commerce, it is not against your wealth, it is not against your possessions in the East or colonies in the West, it is not against even the source of your maritime greatness, it is not against any of the appendages of your Empire, but against the very essence of your liberty, against the foundation of your independence, against the citadel of your happiness, against your constitution itself, that their hostilities are directed. They have themselves announced and proclaimed the proposition, that what they mean to bring with their invading army is the genius of *their* liberty—I desire no other word to express the subversion of the British constitution, and the substitution of the most malignant and fatal contrast—and the annihilation of British liberty, and the obliteration of everything that has rendered you a great, a flourishing, and a happy people.

This is what is at issue; for this are we to declare ourselves in a manner that deprecates the rage which our enemy will not dissemble and which will be little moved by our entreaty. Under such circumstances, are we ashamed or afraid to declare, in a firm and manly tone, our resolution to defend ourselves, or to speak the language of truth with the energy that belongs to Englishmen united in such a cause? Sir, I do not scruple for one to say, if I knew nothing by which I could state to myself a probability of the contest terminating in our favour, I would maintain, that the contest with its worst chances is preferable to an acquiescence in such demands.

If I could look at this as a dry question of prudence, if I could calculate it upon the mere grounds of interest,

I would say, if we love that degree of national power which is necessary for the independence of the country and its safety; if we regard domestic tranquillity, if we look at individual enjoyment, from the highest to the meanest among us, there is not a man, whose stake is so great in the country, that he ought to hesitate a moment in sacrificing any portion of it to oppose the violence of the enemy; nor is there, I trust, a man in this happy and free nation, whose stake is so small, that would not be ready to sacrifice his life in the same cause. If we look at it with a view to safety, this would be our conduct; but if we look at it upon the principle of true honour, of the character which we have to support, of the example which we have to set to the other nations of Europe, if we view rightly the lot in which Providence has placed us, and the contrast between ourselves and all the other countries in Europe, gratitude to that Providence should inspire us to make every effort in such a cause. There may be danger; but on the one side there is danger accompanied with honour, on the other side there is danger with indelible shame and disgrace. Upon such an alternative Englishmen will not hesitate.

I wish to disguise no part of my sentiments upon the grounds on which I put the issue of the contest. I ask whether, up to the principles I have stated, we are prepared to act. Having done so, my opinion is not altered; my hopes, however, are animated from the reflection that the means of our safety are in our own hands. For there never was a period when we had more to encourage us; in spite of heavy burdens, the radical strength of the nation never showed itself more conspicuous; its revenue never exhibited greater proofs of the wealth of the country. The same objects, which constitute the blessings we have to fight for, furnish us with the means of continuing them. But it is not upon that point I rest it. There is one great resource, which I trust will never abandon us. It has shone forth in the English character, by which we have preserved our existence and fame as a nation, which I trust we shall be determined never to abandon under any extremity, but shall join hand and heart in the solemn pledge that is proposed to us, and declare to His Majesty, that we know great exertions are wanting, that we are prepared to make them, and at all events determined to stand or fall by the laws, liberties, and religion of our country.

The amendment was withdrawn, and the address was passed unanimously. Thus, at last, the gravity of the situation and the Prime Minister's great appeal had broken down in one field, at any rate, the divisions of party and united the House of Commons in support of a national war-policy.

2

Strength the only basis of Security
December 5, 1797 [1]

In the course of the prolonged debate on the Budget, Pitt spoke of terminating 'the present contest in a way that might afford us a chance of having a secure interval of peace—real, genuine, not a nominal or delusive, peace'. An honourable member, Mr. Hussey, declared that the one thing needful was peace, and expressed his alarm at the words 'nominal or delusive'. He also

[1] *Speeches*, vol. iii, p. 217.

reminded Pitt of his mistaken belief in the continuance of peace five years previously.[1] Pitt replied as follows:

I remember the declaration to which the honourable gentleman refers. It was made by me in the year 1792. It was at a time when I proposed, what was extremely agreeable to me, a diminution in the existing burdens of the public, and a continuation of the sum allotted to the discharge of the public debt. I did not pretend to assure the House that peace was at all events to be uninterrupted for any given number of years—that would have been an extravagant and ill-founded assurance—but I thought, under the then apparent obvious political circumstances of all Europe, there never appeared a fairer prospect of the continuance of peace for a long interval. That in that conjecture I was disappointed, is most undoubtedly true; for which, however, I ought not to take shame to myself upon the suggestion of the honourable gentleman, since he himself acknowledges he was deceived also.

Why were we both deceived? Because many of us beheld, with a degree of favourable feeling, the rising establishment of what was then a popular Government in France, and saw principles of a pleasing nature in their appearance, but the extent of which, and the views of their professors, were not then developed—principles which professed economy at home and peace abroad. We did not then see the seeds of that widespread harvest which has since been reaped; of that unbounded ambition abroad, and profligate profusion and plunder at home. What then is the inference? Because I thought

[1] See *supra*, p. 16.

that there was a prospect of peace in 1792, when appearances were in its favour, was I to conclude that I should be disappointed by a subsequent appearance of ambition, turbulence, and frenzy? Are we to say now, that we ought to have scruples in opposing that violence; that we are not to judge of present as well as past appearances?

I am as impatient for the hour of peace as that honourable gentleman, or as any man in this House, or in this country. I have as much reason as any man in this country can have, for wishing to see peace return, when it is accompanied by security. But when I say, I do not wish to see a ' nominal and delusive peace ', it is because I value peace. I do not wish to have peace proclaimed for a moment, in order to unnerve your strength, to slacken your efforts, to disband your force, to expose you to sudden and violent hostility, without your present means of defence or any effectual resistance. Should peace be proclaimed without security, you may indeed have a peace that is nominal and delusive.

I wish, for the benefit of Europe—I wish, for the benefit of the world at large, and for the honour of mankind, as well as for the happiness of the people of France, although now your enemies, but who are objects of compassion—I wish, I say, that the present spirit of their rulers, and the principles they cherish, may be extinguished, and that other principles may prevail there. But whether they do so or not is more immediately their concern than ours. It is not to any alteration in that country, but to the means of security in this, that I look with anxiety and care. I wish for peace, whether their principles be good or bad; but not to trust to their forbearance. Our defence should be in our own hands. In that we shall find the bulwark of our safety against France, whatever may be the pride, ambition, or animosity of that Power against us, and which it has manifested in almost all the periods of its history; and I agree with what has been lately said, that its tone was never higher than it is at present.

Certainly much depends upon the posture in which you converse of peace. What is the real foundation of the strength of a nation? Spirit, security, and conscious pride, that cannot stoop to dishonour. It comprehends a character that will neither offer nor receive an insult. Give me peace consistently with that principle, and I will not call it a peace 'nominal or delusive'; and there is no man who will go farther than I will to obtain it. To anything dishonourable I will never submit; nor will this country ever submit to it, I trust. There can be no man who has an English heart within his bosom who can wish it; or can wish that you may, by an untimely diminution of your strength, expose yourselves to the renewal, with aggravated insults, of those evils which we have already had too much reason to deplore.

3

The Spirit of 'Mercantile' Britain: an Example to Europe

December 3, 1798 [1]

THE aggressive character of the party now controlling the destinies of France was not slow to assert itself. In February, 1798, French troops occupied Rome: the

---

[1] *Speeches*, vol. iii, p. 300.

Pope was removed as a prisoner, and a Roman Republic was declared. At the same time a French army invaded Switzerland in support of a 'unionist' rebellion; the country was reconstructed as the Helvetic Republic; Geneva and Mulhouse were annexed, and the treasuries of the chief towns were plundered, as Rome had been, to help Buonaparte to pay for his ships and men.

Meanwhile the situation in Ireland grew rapidly worse, and various parts of the country soon broke out in open insurrection. The dispersion of the rebels by themselves was an easy matter, but the French made three attempts to help them. Only one, however, achieved a landing, and the invaders were soon forced to surrender. Their plans lacked the controlling force of a master-mind, and Buonaparte, after reviewing the preparations at the northern ports, had decided to postpone a direct attack on the British Isles till he had fulfilled his dream of winning an empire in the East, and thus indirectly crippling Britain by cutting off at its source her main supply of commerce. In May he sailed from Toulon and captured Malta, and in June, evading the pursuit of Nelson's squadron, which, despite the menace of invasion, Pitt had boldly dispatched to the Mediterranean, he landed in Egypt. But on the night of August 1, Nelson at last caught and destroyed his fleet at the battle of the Nile.

The victory seemed for the moment to have turned the whole tide of war. The command of the Mediterranean had passed at a blow from French to British ships. Buonaparte was cooped up in Egypt. And the hands of Pitt were strengthened in his efforts to bring Austria and Russia into a new coalition against France.

The financial crisis, too, was over, and Pitt had already in 1797 brought forward his famous proposals for meeting the cost of war as far as possible by the efforts of the existing generation, in other words by taxation, instead of raising loans. 'We ought to consider', he said on November 24, 1797,[1] 'how far the efforts we shall exert to preserve the blessings we enjoy will enable us to transmit the inheritance to posterity unencumbered with those burdens which would cripple their vigour and prevent them from asserting that rank in the scale of nations which their ancestors so long and so gloriously maintained.' His chief suggestion for giving effect to these principles was a graduated income tax.[2]

The measure raised a storm of opposition, but, after bitter debates, it was ultimately passed in January 1798. More gratifying was the reception given to a proposal, put forward by Addington, the Speaker, that the Bank of England should be empowered to receive voluntary gifts to meet the needs of the State. The nation rose to the occasion. The King subscribed £20,000 a year. Robert Peel, a calico printer and father of the future Prime Minister, gave £10,000; Pitt himself, though he was always in financial difficulties, £2,000; the City of London, £10,000; the Bank of England, £200,000; and the less wealthy classes contributed in proportion to their capacity.

The blackest days were over, and in Pitt's mind suspense gave place to elation at the patriotic spirit of the country, at the unanimity of classes and of parties, and, above all, at the effect on Europe of Nelson's victory. It was in this temper that he expounded his new Budget to the Commons on December 3, 1798. The greater part of his speech was devoted to financial detail. He estimated the total supply required for the coming year at nearly £30,000,000. To meet this, he

---

[1] *Speeches*, vol. iii, p. 180.

[2] Incomes under £60 were to be exempt. Incomes between £60 and £65 were to pay 2*d.* in the pound: and the tax rose proportionately to 2*s.* in the pound for incomes of £200 or over.

calculated the yield of existing taxes and of the growing produce of the consolidated fund at about £6,000,000. He proposed to obtain the remainder partly by renewing the income tax levied in the previous year. Its yield had so far been disappointing, and, owing to the practice of evasion and fraud, the estimated amount (£7,500,000) had only been attained by adding in the voluntary contributions to which he alluded as follows:

Not only in this country but in every part of the British dependencies the patriotic spirit has displayed itself, and wherever they were placed, the subjects of England have shown themselves worthy of the relations by which they are connected with their country. Instead of £1,500,000 the voluntary contributions already exceed two millions; and the sum of seven millions and a half, for which credit was taken, has been effective to the public service.

To improve its yield he proposed to bring forward a revised scheme for the income tax and to appoint special Commissioners to superintend its assessment and collection. He estimated the taxable income of the country at £102,000,000,[1] and he expected the tax to

[1] Pitt gave the following interesting details of his estimate:

	£
The land rental, after deducting one-fifth	20,000,000
The tenant's rental of land, deducting two-thirds of the rack rent	6,000,000
The amount of tithes, deducting one-fifth	4,000,000
The produce of mines, canal-navigation, &c., deducting one-fifth	3,000,000
The rental of houses, deducting one-fifth	5,000,000
The profits of professions	2,000,000

yield £10,000,000, or about 10 per cent. The sum required being £24,000,000, this would leave £14,000,000 to be raised by loan; but, as the operation of the Sinking Fund would account for £4,500,000, only £9,500,000 would be added to the national debt.

Having finished his financial statement, Pitt concluded his speech as follows:

I trust that it will not be necessary for me to go into any detail of argument to convince the committee of the advantages of the beneficial mode adopted last session of raising a considerable part of the supplies within the year. The propriety of the measure has been recognized and felt in a way the most gratifying to the feelings and to the pride of every Englishman. The principle has been proved to be the most wise and beneficial, though in the manner of carrying it into practice it has been so shamefully and grossly evaded. The experience which we have had points out the propriety of correcting the errors of that plan, and of enforcing and extending the principle. If we have been able, from the benefits of that measure, so evaded and crippled, to do so much,

	£
The rental of Scotland, taking it at one-eighth of that of England	5,000,000
The income of persons resident in Great Britain, drawn from possessions beyond seas	5,000,000
The amount of annuities from the public funds, after deducting one-fifth for exemptions and modifications	12,000,000
The profits on the capital employed in our foreign commerce	12,000,000
The profits on the capital employed in domestic trade, and the profits of skill and industry	28,000,000
In all	£102,000,000

it is obviously our duty to seek for the means of perfecting the plan upon which we are set out ; and if we can find regulations and checks against the abuses that have been committed, it is surely wise and proper that they should be made to apply to a more general and extensive scheme than that which we have already tried. It no longer rests upon theory or upon reasoning ; it is recommended to us by the surest test of experience : and if, by the efficacy of this plan, we have been able to disappoint the enemy; to rise above all the attempts which they made to disturb our domestic tranquillity ; to remove the apprehensions of the despondent, and to show them that all their fears of our being unable to continue the contest were vain ; to assert the high and proud distinction which we took in the maintenance of genuine government and social order ;—if we have been able thereby to animate the public spirit of Europe, to revive its dismayed energy, and to give a turn to the political aspect of the world favourable to the cause of humanity, shall we not persevere in a course which has been so fruitful of good ? If we have proved that, at the end of the sixth year of war, unsubdued by all the exertions and sacrifices we have made, our commerce is flourishing beyond the example of any year even of peace ; if our revenues are undiminished ; if new means of vigour are daily presenting themselves to our grasp ; if our efforts have been crowned with the most perfect success ; if the public sentiment be firm and united in the justice and necessity of the cause in which we are embarked ; if every motive to exertion continues the same, and every effort we have made in the cause is a source only of exultation and pride to the heart; if, by the efficacy of those efforts, we have now the expectation of accomplishing the great object of all our sacrifices and all our labours; if despondency be dissipated at home, and confidence created abroad, shall we not persevere in a course so fairly calculated to bring us to a happy issue?

Let us do justice to ourselves. It is not merely owing to the dazzling events of the campaign that we are indebted for the proud station in which we now stand. Great and glorious as those achievements have been, which cannot fail to be a source of exultation to every British bosom, I shall not detract from the high renown of all those persons to whose skill, vigour, and determination we are indebted for the achievements that have astonished and aroused Europe, when I say, that it is not altogether owing to them that we now feel ourselves in a situation so proud and consoling. The grand and important changes which have been effected in Europe are not merely to be ascribed to the promptitude, vigilance, skill, and vigour of our naval department, whose merits no man can feel, or can estimate, more highly than I do; nor to the heroism, zeal, patriotism, and devotion of our transcendent commanders—and I speak particularly of that great commander [1] whose services fill every bosom with rapturous emotion, and who will never cease to derive from the gratitude of his countrymen the tribute of his worth—nor is it to the unparalleled perseverance, valour, and wonders performed by our gallant fleets, which have raised the British name to a distinction unknown even to her former annals, that

[1] Nelson.

we are to ascribe all the advantages of our present posture. No, we must also do justice to the wisdom, energy, and determination of the Parliament who have furnished the means and the power, by which all the rest was sustained and accomplished. Through them all the departments of His Majesty's Government had the means of employing the force whose achievements have been so brilliant; through the wisdom of Parliament the resources of the country have been called forth, and its spirit embodied in a manner unexampled in its history. By their firmness, magnanimity, and devotion to the cause, not merely of our own individual safety, but of the safety of mankind in general, we have been enabled to stand forth the saviours of the earth. No difficulties have stood in our way; no sacrifices have been thought too great for us to make; a common feeling of danger has produced a common spirit of exertion, and we have cheerfully come forward with a surrender of a part of our property as a salvage, not merely for recovering ourselves, but for the general recovery of mankind. We have presented a phenomenon in the character of nations.

It has often been thought, and has been the theme of historians, that as nations became mercantile, they lost in martial spirit what they gained in commercial avidity; that it is of the essence of trade to be sordid, and that high notions of honour are incompatible with the prosecution of traffic. This hypothesis has been proved to be false; for in the memorable era of the past year Great Britain has exhibited the glorious example of a nation showing the most universal spirit of military heroism at a time when she had acquired the most flourishing degree of national commerce. In no time of the proudest antiquity could the people of Great Britain exhibit a more dignified character of martial spirit than they have during the last year, when they have also risen to the greatest point of commercial advantage. And, Mr. Chairman, they are not insensible of the benefits, as well as of the glory, they have acquired. They know and feel that the most manly course has also been the most prudent, and they are sensible that, by bravely resisting the torrent with which they were threatened, instead of striking balances on their fate, and looking to the averages of profit and loss, on standing out or on yielding to the tempest, they have given to themselves not merely security, but lustre and fame. If they had, on the contrary, submitted to purchase a suspension of danger and a mere pause of war, they feel that they could only have purchased the means of future and more deplorable mischief, marked with the stamp of impoverishment and degradation. They feel therefore that, in pursuing the path which duty and honour prescribed, they have also trod in the path of prudence and economy. They have secured to themselves permanent peace and future repose, and have given an animating example to the world of the advantages of vigour, constancy, and union. If the world shall not be disposed to take the benefit of this example, Great Britain has at least the consolation to know that she has given them the power.

And if I were disposed, Sir, to pay regard to drier and colder maxims of policy, I should say that every regard even to prudent economy would point out the course which we have taken, as the most advantageous for a people to pursue. It will be manifest to every gentleman on the slightest consideration of the subject, that, in the end, the measure of raising the supplies within the year is the cheapest and the most salutary course that a wise people can pursue ; and when it is considered that there is a saving of at least one-twelfth upon all that is raised, gentlemen will not suffer a superstitious fear and jealousy of the danger of exposing the secrecy of income to combat with a measure that is so pregnant with benefits to the nation. If gentlemen will take into their consideration the probable duration of peace and war, calculated from the experience of past times, they will be convinced of the immeasurable importance of striving to raise the supplies within the year, rather than accumulating a permanent debt. The experience of the last hundred, fifty, or forty years, will show how little confidence we can have in the duration of peace, and it ought to convince us how important it is to establish a system, that will prepare us for every emergency, give stability to strength, and perpetual renovations to resource. I think, I could make it apparent to gentlemen, that in any war of the duration of six years the plan of funding all the expenses to be incurred in carrying it on would leave at the end of it a greater burden permanently upon the nation than they would have to incur for the six years only of its continuance and one year beyond it, provided that they made the sacrifice of a tenth of their income. In the old, unwise, and destructive way of raising the supplies by a permanent fund, without any provision for its redemption, a war so carried on entails the burden upon the age and upon their posterity for ever. This has, to be sure, in a great measure, been done away and corrected by the salutary and valuable system which has been adopted of the redemption fund.[1] But that fund cannot accomplish the end in a shorter period than forty years, and during all that time the expenses of a war so funded must weigh down and press upon the people. If, on the contrary, it had at an early period of our history been resolved to adopt the present mode of raising the supplies within the year; if, for instance, after the Peace of Aix-la-Chapelle,[2] the scheme of redemption even had been adopted and persevered in to this time, we should not now, for the seventh year of the war, have had more to raise from the pockets of the people than what we have now to pay of permanent taxes, together with about a fourth of what it would be necessary to lay on in addition for this year. Fortunately we have at last established the redemption fund: the benefits of it are already felt; they will every year be more and more acknowledged; and in addition to this it is only necessary that, instead of consulting a present advantage and throwing the burden, as heretofore, upon posterity, we shall fairly meet it ourselves, and lay the foundation of a system that shall make us independent of all the future events of the world.

I am sure that, in deliberating upon the advantages of this system, gentlemen whose liberal and exalted

[1] i. e. the Sinking Fund.
[2] The Peace of Aix-la-Chapelle in 1748 between England and France and their respective allies brought to a close the War of the Austrian Succession.

views go beyond the mere present convenience of the moment and are not limited to the period of the interest which they may themselves take in public affairs, or even to the period of their own existence, but look with a provident affection to the independence and happiness of a generation unborn, will feel and recognize the wisdom of a system that has for its principle the permanency of British grandeur. You will feel that it is not only to the splendour of your arms, to the achievements of your fleets, that you are indebted for the high distinction which you at present enjoy; but also to the wisdom of the councils you have adopted in taking advantage of the influence which your happy constitution confers beyond the example of any other people, and by which you have given a grand and edifying lesson to dismayed Europe, that safety, honour, and repose must ever depend upon the energy with which danger is met and resisted. You have shown a power of self-defence which is permanent and unassailable. Standing upon the principles you have assumed, the wild and extravagant hopes of the enemy will be thwarted; Europe will be aroused and animated to adopt a course so honourable; and surely with the means of persevering thus obvious, you will not think it prudent or necessary to shrink from the principles you have adopted, or take shelter in a peace which might be obtained by a more temporizing conduct, but which would be neither safe nor durable.

But, Sir, I cannot encourage any sentiment so degrading. I feel in common with every gentleman who hears me the proud situation in which we have been placed, and the importance it has given us in the scale of nations.

The rank that we now hold, I trust, we shall continue to cherish, and, pursuing the same glorious course, we shall all of us feel it to be a source of pride and consolation that we are the subjects of the King of Great Britain.

Pitt then moved his financial resolutions, which were agreed to.

4

At War with Armed Opinions

June 7, 1799 [1]

IN the course of a debate on our alliance with Russia,[2] Pitt was criticized for attempting not merely to overcome the power of France but to force her to change her political opinions. To this charge Pitt replied as follows:

We are not in arms against the opinions of the closet nor the speculations of the school. We are at war with armed opinions. We are at war with those opinions which the sword.of audacious, unprincipled, and impious innovation seeks to propagate amidst the ruins of empires, the demolition of the altars of all religion, the destruction of every venerable and good and liberal institution, under whatever form of polity it has been raised:— and this, in spite of the dissenting reason of men, in

---

[1] *Speeches*, vol. iii, p. 421.   [2] See *infra*, p. 246.

contempt of that lawful authority which, in the settled order, superior talents and superior virtues attain, crying out to them not to enter on holy ground, nor to pollute the stream of eternal justice, admonishing them of their danger, whilst like the genius of evil they mimic their voice, and, having succeeded in drawing upon them the ridicule of the vulgar, close their day of wickedness and savage triumph with the massacre and waste of whatever is amiable, learned, and pious in the districts they have over-run.

Whilst the principles avowed by France, and acted upon so wildly, held their legitimate place confined to the circles of a few ingenious and learned men; whilst these men continued to occupy those heights which vulgar minds could not mount; whilst they contented themselves with abstract inquiries concerning the laws of matter or the progress of mind, it was pleasing to regard them with respect; for, while the simplicity of the man of genius is preserved untouched, if we will not pay homage to his eccentricity, there is, at least, much in it to be admired. Whilst these principles were confined in that way and had not yet bounded over the common sense and reason of mankind, we saw nothing in them to alarm, nothing to terrify. But their appearance in arms changed their character. We will not leave the monster to prowl the world unopposed. He must cease to annoy the abode of peaceful men. If he retire into the cell, whether of solitude or repentance, thither we will not pursue him; but we cannot leave him on the throne of power.

5

Buonaparte

February 3, 1800 [1]

For the greater part of 1799 Buonaparte was still caged in Egypt. His attempt to break north and attack Turkey by way of Syria was baffled by Sir Sidney Smith's defence of Acre (March to May), and he returned to Cairo. But in the autumn he learned that France was hard pressed by the allies and the Directory once more menaced by a royalist reaction. He straightway decided to abandon his Eastern enterprise, and leaving his army to its fate, he secretly took ship and reached Paris in October.

Paris needed him. The campaigns undertaken by the Directory during his absence had at first gone well. The last desperate resistance of the Swiss among their mountains had been overcome and a new centralized government imposed on them. Practically the whole of Italy had been subjected and reorganized in a group of subservient republics. But the tide of success had stopped there. Alarmed by this aggressive advance towards two sides of his dominions, the Hapsburg Emperor declared war in March. And already, in the previous December, Pitt had persuaded the Czar Paul of Russia, irritated by Buonaparte's seizure of Malta, which he considered to be under his special protection as Grand Master of the Knights of St. John, to form an alliance with Great Britain, the basis of which was a determination to force France back within her ancient frontiers. The three

---

[1] *Speeches*, vol. iv, p. 1.

Powers, supported by Portugal, Naples, and Turkey, constituted the Second Coalition. Prussia still remained obstinately isolated, hampering the co-operation of the allies and in the end ensuring its own doom.

The Second Coalition, like the First, prospered at the outset. The Austro-Russian armies overwhelmed the French in Italy. Everywhere the Italians threw off the yoke. At the end of June the French, all Italy lost, stood at bay on the Ligurian coast.

And then the Second Coalition, like the First, began to break down through the jealousy and selfishness of the allies. In September the failure of co-operation between Austrians and Russians enabled Masséna to inflict a crushing defeat on the latter at Zürich. Disease proved more disastrous than jealousy in the Anglo-Russian campaign in Holland, and in October the allied forces, stricken with fever and having achieved nothing but the destruction of the Dutch fleet, were withdrawn under the Convention of Alkmaar.

Meanwhile, Buonaparte was back in Paris. By the *coup d'état* of Brumaire (November 10) he overthrew the Directory. In December he became First Consul under a new constitution. Names and forms aside, he had made himself the absolute monarch of France.[1]

On Christmas Day he wrote to Francis II and George III, as it were to his brother monarchs, proposing peace. Pitt agreed with Thugut, the Austrian Chancellor, that the proposals were merely a device for separating Austria and Britain, but he has been criticized by some authorities for not welcoming what they consider to have been a truly statesmanlike offer. He was hotly assailed at the time in the press, in pamphlets, and in the House. To all these attacks he made an exhaustive reply in his speech of February 3, 1800. On that day Dundas moved an address to the King approving the

[1] Introduction, pp. xxxiv–xxxv.

Government's rejection of the overtures from Paris. Whitbread and Erskine opposed it. Canning supported it. Then Pitt spoke.

He began by declaring that any one who thought that the French overtures should have been accepted, must belong to one of three classes:

He must either believe that the French Revolution neither does now exhibit, nor has at any time exhibited, such circumstances of danger, arising out of the very nature of the system and the internal state and condition of France, as to leave to foreign Powers no adequate ground of security in negotiation; or, secondly, he must be of opinion that the change which has recently taken place, has given that security, which, in the former stages of the Revolution, was wanting; or, thirdly, he must be one who, believing that the danger existed, not undervaluing its extent, nor mistaking its nature, nevertheless thinks, from his view of the present pressure on the country, from his view of its situation and its prospects, compared with the situation and prospects of its enemies, that we are, with our eyes open, bound to accept of inadequate security for everything that is valuable and sacred, rather than endure the pressure, or incur the risk, which would result from a farther prolongation of the contest.

To controvert the opinions of those who might belong to the first of these classes, Pitt entered on a detailed review of the diplomatic history of the war from its beginning. He pointed out once again that the war was made by France and not by England; that its immediate cause was 'a demand made by France upon Holland, to open the navigation of the Scheldt, on the ground of a general and national right, in violation of a positive treaty'.

On the same arbitrary notion (he said) they soon afterwards discovered that sacred law of nature, which made the Rhine and the Alps the legitimate boundaries of France, and assumed the power, which they have affected to exercise through the whole of the Revolution, of superseding by a new code of their own all the recognized principles of the law of nations. . . . As to Holland, they contented themselves with telling us that the Scheldt was too insignificant for us to trouble ourselves about, and therefore it was to be decided as they chose, in breach of a positive treaty, which they had themselves guaranteed, and which we, by our alliance, were bound to support. If, however, after the war was over, Belgium should have consolidated its liberty—a term of which we now know the meaning from the fate of every nation into which the arms of France have penetrated—then Belgium and Holland might, if they pleased, settle the question of the Scheldt by separate negotiation between themselves. With respect to aggrandizement, they assured us that they would retain possession of Belgium by arms no longer than they should find it necessary for the purpose already stated of consolidating its liberty.

Pitt then pointed out that the real ambitions of the revolutionary Government had been manifested to the world by the decrees of November 19 and December 15, 1792, the latter of which declared that in all countries, into which the armies of France should come, the existing régime should be replaced by a system on the French model. This really amounted ' to a universal declaration of war against all thrones and against all civilized Governments '.

If any doubt is entertained, whither the armies of France were intended to come, if it is contended that they referred only to those nations with whom they were then at war, or with whom in the course of this contest they might be driven into war; let it be remembered that, at this very moment, they had actually given orders to their generals to pursue the Austrian army from the Netherlands into Holland, with whom they were at that time at peace. Or, even if the construction contended for is admitted, let us see what would have been its application; let us look at the list of their aggressions, which was read by my right honourable friend [1] near me. With whom have they been at war since the period of this declaration? With all the nations of Europe save two,[2] and if not with those two, it is only because, with every provocation that could justify defensive war, those countries have hitherto acquiesced in repeated violations of their rights, rather than recur to war for their vindication. Wherever their arms have been carried, it will be a matter of short subsequent inquiry to trace whether they have faithfully applied these principles. If in terms this decree is a denunciation of war against all Governments; if in practice it has been applied against every one with which France has come into contact; what is it but the deliberate code of the French Revolution, from the birth of the Republic, which has never once been

---

[1] Dundas.   [2] Sweden and Denmark.

departed from, which has been enforced with unremitted rigour against all the nations that have come into their power? .

Such, Sir, was the nature of the system. Let us examine a little farther, whether it was from the beginning intended to be acted upon, in the extent which I have stated. At the very moment when their threats appeared to many little else than the ravings of madmen, they were digesting and methodizing the means of execution, as accurately as if they had actually foreseen the extent to which they have since been able to realize their criminal projects. They sat down coolly to devise the most regular and effectual mode of making the application of this system the current business of the day, and incorporating it with the general orders of their army; for (will the House believe it) this confirmation of the decree of the nineteenth of November was accompanied by an exposition and commentary addressed to the general of every army of France, containing a schedule as coolly conceived and as methodically reduced, as any by which the most quiet business of a justice of peace or the most regular routine of any department of state in this country could be conducted. Each commander was furnished with one general blank formula of a letter for all the nations of the world! 'The people of France to the people of . . . . . greeting. We are come to expel your tyrants.' Even this was not all. One of the articles of the decree of December 15 was expressly, 'that those who should show themselves so brutish and so enamoured of their chains as to refuse the restoration of their rights, to renounce liberty and equality, or to preserve, recall, or treat with their prince or privileged orders, were not entitled to the distinction which France, in other cases, had justly established between Government and people; and that such a people ought to be treated according to the rigour of war and of conquest.' Here is their love of peace; here is their aversion to conquest; here is their respect for the independence of other nations!

It was then, after receiving such explanations as these, after receiving the ultimatum of France, and after M. Chauvelin's credentials had ceased, that he was required to depart. Even after that period, I am almost ashamed to record it, we did not on our part shut the door against other attempts to negotiate. But this transaction was immediately followed by the declaration of war, proceeding not from England in vindication of its rights, but from France as the completion of the injuries and insults they had offered. And on a war thus originating, can it be doubted, by an English House of Commons, whether the aggression was on the part of this country or of France? Or whether the manifest aggression on the part of France was the result of anything but the principles which characterize the French Revolution?

Pitt next reminded the House that, up to this point, England had observed the strictest neutrality—a fact which the French Government itself admitted in a decree published on the eve of the declaration of war.

To Prussia, with whom we were in connexion, and still more decisively to Holland, with whom we were in close and intimate correspondence, we uniformly stated our unalterable resolution to maintain neutrality and avoid interference in the internal affairs of France, as long as France should refrain from hostile measures against us and our allies.

More than that. Pitt had actually proposed to Russia that the two Powers should attempt a joint mediation between France and the allies—Prussia and Austria— then at war with her.

At that period, Russia had at length conceived, as well as ourselves, a natural and just alarm for the balance of Europe, and applied to us to learn our sentiments on the subject. In our answer to this application, we imparted to Russia the principles upon which we then acted, and we communicated this answer to Prussia, with whom we were connected in defensive alliance. I will state shortly the leading part of those principles. A dispatch was sent from Lord Grenville to His Majesty's Minister in Russia, dated December 29, 1792, stating a desire to have an explanation set on foot on the subject of the war with France. I will read the material parts of it.

'The two leading points, on which such explanation will naturally turn, are the line of conduct to be followed previous to the commencement of hostilities, and with a view, if possible, to avert them; and the nature and amount of the forces which the Powers engaged in this concert might be enabled to use, supposing such extremities unavoidable.

'With respect to the first, it appears on the whole,

subject, however, to future consideration and discussion with the other Powers, that the most advisable step to be taken would be that sufficient explanation should be had with the Powers at war with France, in order to enable those not hitherto engaged in the war to propose to that country terms of peace. That these terms should be the withdrawing their arms within the limits of the French territory; the abandoning their conquests; the rescinding any acts injurious to the sovereignty or rights of any other nations, and the giving in some public and unequivocal manner a pledge of their intention no longer to foment troubles or to excite disturbances against other Governments. In return for these stipulations, the different Powers of Europe, who should be parties to this measure, might engage to abandon all measures or views of hostility against France, or interference in their internal affairs, and to maintain a correspondence and intercourse of amity with the existing powers in that country, with whom such a treaty may be concluded.'

Having thus determined whose was the responsibility for bringing England into the conflict, Pitt enumerated the several States against which France had proceeded to make war, or by threat of war to bring under her domination: up to 1793, the Papal States (at Avignon), Austria, Prussia, the German Empire; from 1793 onwards, Great Britain, Holland, Spain, Portugal, and practically all the Italian States.

Let these facts and these dates be compared with what we have heard. The honourable gentleman [1] has

[1] Erskine.

told us, and the author[1] of the note from France has told us also, that all the French conquests were produced by the operations of the allies. It was when they were pressed on all sides, when their own territory was in danger, when their own independence was in question, when the confederacy appeared too strong; it was then they used the means with which their power and their courage furnished them; and, 'attacked upon all sides, they carried everywhere their defensive arms.' I do not wish to misrepresent the learned gentleman,[2] but I understood him to speak of this sentiment with approbation. The sentiment itself is this, that if a nation is unjustly attacked in any one quarter by others, she cannot stop to consider by whom, but must find means of strength in other quarters, no matter where; and is justified in attacking, in her turn, those with whom she is at peace, and from whom she has received no species of provocation.

Pitt then described the efforts he had made in 1796 and 1797 to obtain peace on secure and reasonable conditions. To what Erskine had said with regard to the failure of the first negotiations, he replied as follows:

He maintains that the single point on which the negotiation was broken off, was the question of the possession of the Austrian Netherlands; and that it is, therefore, on that ground only, that the war has, since that time, been continued. When this subject was before under discussion, I stated, and I shall state again

---

[1] Talleyrand.   [2] Erskine.

(notwithstanding the learned gentleman's accusation of my having endeavoured to shift the question from its true point), that the question then at issue was not whether the Netherlands should, in fact, be restored; though even on that question I am not, like the learned gentleman, unprepared to give any opinion; I am ready to say, that to leave that territory in the possession of France would be obviously dangerous to the interests of this country, and is inconsistent with the policy which it has uniformly pursued, at every period in which it has concerned itself in the general system of the Continent. But it was not on the decision of this question of expediency and policy that the issue of the negotiation then turned. What was required of us by France was not merely that we should acquiesce in her retaining the Netherlands, but that, as a preliminary to all treaty, and before entering upon the discussion of terms, we should recognize the principle that whatever France, in time of war, had annexed to the Republic, must remain inseparable for ever, and could not become the subject of negotiation. I say that, in refusing such a preliminary, we were only resisting the claim of France to arrogate to itself the power of controlling, by its own separate and municipal acts, the rights and interests of other countries, and moulding, at its discretion, a new and general code of the law of nations.

In 1797, he continued, we had gone to the extreme limit of concession. We had offered to surrender everything except Trinidad and the Cape of Good Hope, which was 'necessary for the security of our Indian possessions'. But France had repulsed us.

Let us look at the conduct of France immediately subsequent to this period. She had spurned at the offers of Great Britain; she had reduced her continental enemies to the necessity of accepting a precarious peace; she had (in spite of those pledges repeatedly made and uniformly violated) surrounded herself by new conquests on every part of her frontier but one. That one was Switzerland. The first effect of being relieved from the war with Austria, of being secured against all fears of continental invasion on the ancient territory of France, was their unprovoked attack against this unoffending and devoted country. This was one of the scenes which satisfied even those who were the most incredulous, that France had thrown off the mask, 'if indeed she had ever worn it.' It collected, in one view, many of the characteristic features of that revolutionary system which I have endeavoured to trace. The perfidy which alone rendered their arms successful, the pretext of which they availed themselves to produce division and prepare the entrance of Jacobinism in that country, the proposal of an armistice, one of the known and regular engines of the Revolution, which was, as usual, the immediate prelude to military execution, attended with cruelty and barbarity, of which there are few examples,—all these are known to the world. The country they attacked was one which had long been the faithful ally of France, which, instead of giving cause of jealousy to any other Power, had been for ages proverbial for the simplicity and innocence of its manners, and which had acquired and preserved the esteem of all the nations of Europe; which had almost, by the common consent of mankind, been exempted from the sound of war, and marked out as a land of Goshen, safe and untouched in the midst of surrounding calamities.

Look then at the fate of Switzerland, at the circumstances which led to its destruction; add this instance to the catalogue of aggression against all Europe; and then tell me whether the system I have described has not been prosecuted with an unrelenting spirit, which cannot be subdued in adversity, which cannot be appeased in prosperity, which neither solemn professions, nor the general law of nations, nor the obligation of treaties (whether previous to the Revolution or subsequent to it), could restrain from the subversion of every State into which, either by force or fraud, their arms could penetrate. Then tell me whether the disasters of Europe are to be charged upon the provocation of this country and its allies, or on the inherent principle of the French Revolution, of which the natural result produced so much misery and carnage in France, and carried desolation and terror over so large a portion of the world. . . .

After this, it remains only shortly to remind gentlemen of the aggression against Egypt, not omitting, however, to notice the capture of Malta, in the way to Egypt.

Inconsiderable as that island may be thought, compared with the scenes we have witnessed, let it be remembered that it is an island, of which the Government had long been recognized by every State of Europe, against which France pretended no cause of war, and whose independence was as dear to itself and as sacred as that of any country in Europe. It was in fact not unimportant from its local situation to the other Powers of Europe, but in proportion as any man may diminish its importance, the instance will only serve the more to illustrate and confirm the proposition which I have maintained. The all-searching eye of the French Revolution looks to every part of Europe and every quarter of the world, in which can be found an object either of acquisition or plunder. Nothing is too great for the temerity of its ambition, nothing too small or insignificant for the grasp of its rapacity.

From hence Buonaparte and his army proceeded to Egypt. The attack was made, pretences were held out to the natives of that country in the name of the French King, whom they had murdered; they pretended to have the approbation of the Grand Seignior whose territories they were violating; their project was carried on under the profession of a zeal for Mohammedanism; it was carried on by proclaiming that France had been reconciled to the Mussulman faith, had abjured that of Christianity, or, as he in his impious language termed it, of '*the sect of the Messiah*'.

The only plea which they have since held out to colour this atrocious invasion of a neutral and friendly territory, is that it was the road to attack the English Power in India. It is most unquestionably true that this was one and a principal cause of this unparalleled outrage; but another, and an equally substantial cause (as appears by their own statements), was the division and partition of the territories of what they thought a falling Power.

It is impossible to dismiss this subject without observing that this attack against Egypt was accompanied by an attack upon the British possessions in India, made on true revolutionary principles. In Europe, the propagation of the principles of France had uniformly prepared the way for the progress of its arms. To India, the lovers of peace had sent the messengers of Jacobinism, for the purpose of inculcating war in those distant regions on Jacobin principles, and of forming Jacobin clubs, which they actually succeeded in establishing, and which in most respects resembled the European model, but which were distinguished by this peculiarity, that they were required to swear in one breath, *hatred to tyranny, the love of liberty, and the destruction of all kings and sovereigns—except the good and faithful ally of the French Republic,* CITIZEN TIPPOO.[1]

What then was the nature of this system? Was it anything but what I have stated it to be—an insatiable love of aggrandizement, an implacable spirit of destruction directed against all the civil and religious institutions of every country? This is the first moving and acting spirit of the French Revolution; this is the spirit which animated it at its birth, and this is the spirit which will not desert it till the moment of its dissolution, ' which grew with its growth, which strengthened with its strength,' but which has not abated under its misfortunes, nor declined in its decay. It has been invariably the same in every period, operating more or less, according as accident or circumstances might assist it; but it has been inherent in the Revolution in all its stages, it has equally belonged to Brissot, to Robespierre, to Tallien, to Reubel, to Barras, and to every one of the leaders of

[1] Introduction, p. xliv.

the Directory, but to none more than to Buonaparte, in whom now all their powers are united. What are its characters? Can it be accident that produced them? No, it is only from the alliance of the most horrid principles with the most horrid means, that such miseries could have been brought upon Europe. It is this paradox, which we must always keep in mind when we are discussing any question relative to the effects of the French Revolution. Groaning under every degree of misery, the victim of its own crimes, and, as I once before expressed it in this House, asking pardon of God and of man for the miseries which it has brought upon itself and others, France still retains (while it has neither left means of comfort nor almost of subsistence to its own inhabitants) new and unexampled means of annoyance and destruction against all the other Powers of Europe.

Its first fundamental principle was to bribe the poor against the rich, by proposing to transfer into new hands, on the delusive notion of equality and in breach of every principle of justice, the whole property of the country. The practical application of this principle was to devote the whole of that property to indiscriminate plunder and to make it the foundation of a revolutionary system of finance, productive in proportion to the misery and desolation which it created.

It has been accompanied by an unwearied spirit of proselytism, diffusing itself over all the nations of the earth; a spirit which can apply itself to all circumstances and all situations, which can furnish a list of grievances, and hold out a promise of redress equally to all nations, which inspired the teachers of French liberty with the hope of alike recommending themselves to those who live under the feudal code of the German Empire; to the various States of Italy, under all their different institutions; to the old republicans of Holland, and to the new republicans of America; to the Catholic of Ireland, whom it was to deliver from Protestant usurpation; to the Protestant of Switzerland, whom it was to deliver from popish superstition; to the Mussulman of Egypt, whom it was to deliver from Christian persecution; to the remote Indian, blindly bigoted to his ancient institutions; and to the natives of Great Britain, enjoying the perfection of practical freedom and justly attached to their constitution, from the joint result of habit, of reason, and of experience.

The last and distinguishing feature is a perfidy, which nothing can bind, which no tie of treaty, no sense of the principles generally received among nations, no obligation, human or divine, can restrain.

Thus qualified, thus armed for destruction, the genius of the French Revolution marched forth, the terror and dismay of the world. Every nation has in its turn been the witness, many have been the victims of its principles, and it is left for us to decide, whether we will compromise with such a danger, while we have yet resources to supply the sinews of war, while the heart and spirit of the country is yet unbroken, and while we have the means of calling forth and supporting a powerful co-operation in Europe.

Pitt now passed to the second stage of his argument, and met the second class of his critics—those who believed that the accession of Buonaparte to absolute power had given to the French Government a security it had hitherto lacked. He had reviewed the state of France as it *was*, under its successive Governments. 'Let us now examine', he said, 'what it *is*.'

In the first place, we see, as has been truly stated, a change in the description and form of the sovereign authority; a supreme power is placed at the head of this nominal Republic, with a more open avowal of military despotism than at any former period; with a more open and undisguised abandonment of the names and pretences under which that despotism long attempted to conceal itself. The different institutions, republican in their form and appearance, which were before the instruments of that despotism, are now annihilated; they have given way to the absolute power of one man, concentrating in himself all the authority of the State, and differing from other monarchs only in this, that, as my honourable friend [1] truly stated it, he wields a sword instead of a sceptre. What then is the confidence we are to derive either from the frame of the Government, or from the character and past conduct of the person who is now the absolute ruler of France?

Had we seen a man, of whom we had no previous knowledge, suddenly invested with the sovereign authority of the country, invested with the power of taxation, with the power of the sword, the power of war and peace, the unlimited power of commanding the resources, of disposing of the lives and fortunes of every man in France; if we had seen, at the same moment, all the inferior machinery of the Revolution, which, under the variety of successive shocks, had kept the system in motion, still

[1] Canning.

remaining entire, all that, by requisition and plunder, had given activity to the revolutionary system of finance and had furnished the means of creating an army, by converting every man, who was of age to bear arms, into a soldier, not for the defence of his own country, but for the sake of carrying unprovoked war into surrounding countries; if we had seen all the subordinate instruments of Jacobin power subsisting in their full force, and retaining (to use the French phrase) all their original organization; and had then observed this single change in the conduct of their affairs, that there was now one man, with no rival to thwart his measures, no colleague to divide his powers, no council to control his operations, no liberty of speaking or writing, no expression of public opinion to check or influence his conduct;—under such circumstances, should we be wrong to pause, or wait for the evidence of facts and experience, before we consented to trust our safety to the forbearance of a single man, in such a situation, and to relinquish those means of defence which have hitherto carried us safe through all the storms of the Revolution?—if we were to ask what are the principles and character of this stranger, to whom Fortune has suddenly committed the concerns of a great and powerful nation?

But is this the actual state of the present question? Are we talking of a stranger of whom we have heard nothing? No, Sir; we have heard of him; we and Europe and the world have heard both of him and of the satellites by whom he is surrounded; and it is impossible to discuss fairly the propriety of any answer which could be returned to his overtures of negotiation, without taking into consideration the inferences to be drawn from his personal character and conduct.

Pitt now developed his attack on 'the character and conduct' of Buonaparte. He dealt first with his pretensions as a peace-maker. The French note had claimed that his present overtures were his second attempt at a general pacification. What was his first attempt? The conclusion of a *separate* treaty with Austria. What is his second attempt? A proposal for a *separate* treaty with Great Britain. These facts alone throw suspicion on his sincerity, and the suspicion is intensified in the mind of any one who recalls the message he sent by two trusted friends to inform the Directory of the conclusion of the Treaty of Campo Formio. They announced that the war with Austria was at an end and that France was now free to attack Great Britain.

They used, on this occasion (Pitt continued), the memorable words, '*the Kingdom of Great Britain and the French Republic cannot exist together.*' This, I say, was the solemn declaration of the deputies and ambassadors of Buonaparte himself, offering to the Directory the first fruits of this first attempt at general pacification.

So much for his disposition towards general pacification. Let us look next at the part he has taken in the different stages of the French Revolution, and let us then judge whether we are to look to him as the security against revolutionary principles; let us determine what reliance we can place on his engagements with other countries, when we see how he has observed his engagements to his own. When the constitution of the third year was established under Barras, that constitution was imposed by the arms of Buonaparte, then commanding the army of the Triumvirate in Paris.[1] To that constitution he then swore fidelity. How often he has repeated the same oath I know not; but twice, at least, we know that he has not only repeated it himself, but tendered it to others, under circumstances too striking not to be stated.

Sir, the House cannot have forgotten the Revolution of the fourth of September,[2] which produced the dismissal of Lord Malmesbury from Lille. How was that Revolution procured? It was procured chiefly by the promise of Buonaparte (in the name of his army), decidedly to support the Directory in those measures which led to the infringement and violation of everything that the authors of the constitution of 1795, or its adherents, could consider as fundamental, and which established a system of despotism inferior only to that now realized in his own person. Immediately before this event, in the midst of the desolation and bloodshed of Italy, he had received the sacred present of new banners from the Directory. He delivered them to his army with this exhortation: 'Let us swear, fellow soldiers, by the *manes* of the patriots who have died by our side, eternal hatred to the enemies of the constitution of the third year:'— that very constitution which he soon after enabled the Directory to violate, and which, at the head of his grenadiers, he has now finally destroyed. Sir, that oath was again renewed in the midst of that very scene to which I have last referred; the oath of fidelity to the constitution of the third year was administered to all the members of the assembly then sitting (under the terror

[1] Introduction, pp. xxxiv-xxxv. [2] Introduction, p. xxxiv.

of the bayonet), as the solemn preparation for the business of the day; and the morning was ushered in with swearing attachment to the constitution that the evening might close with its destruction.

If we carry our views out of France, and look at the dreadful catalogue of all the breaches of treaty, all the acts of perfidy at which I have only glanced, and which are precisely commensurate with the number of treaties which the Republic have made (for I have sought in vain for any one which it has made and which it has not broken); if we trace the history of them all from the beginning of the Revolution to the present time, or if we select those which have been accompanied by the most atrocious cruelty and marked the most strongly with the characteristic features of the Revolution, the name of Buonaparte will be found allied to more of them than that of any other that can be handed down in the history of the crimes and miseries of the last ten years. His name will be recorded with the horrors committed in Italy, in the memorable campaign of 1796 and 1797, in the Milanese, in Genoa, in Modena, in Tuscany, in Rome, and in Venice.

His entrance into Lombardy was announced by a solemn proclamation, issued on April 27, 1796, which terminated with these words: 'Nations of Italy! the French army is come to break your chains; the French are the friends of the people in every country; your religion, your property, your customs, shall be respected.' This was followed by a second proclamation, dated from Milan, May 20, and signed 'Buonaparte', in these terms: ' Respect for property and personal security, respect for the religion of countries : these are the sentiments of the Government of the French Republic, and of the army of Italy. The French, victorious, consider the nations of Lombardy as their brothers.' In testimony of this fraternity, and to fulfil the solemn pledge of respecting property, this very proclamation imposed on the Milanese a provisional contribution to the amount of twenty millions of livres, or near one million sterling ; and successive exactions were afterwards levied on that single State to the amount, in the whole, of near six millions sterling. The regard to religion and to the customs of the country was manifested with the same scrupulous fidelity. The churches were given up to indiscriminate plunder. Every religious and charitable fund, every public treasure was confiscated. The country was made the scene of every species of disorder and rapine. The priests, the established form of worship, all the objects of religious reverence, were openly insulted by the French troops. At Pavia, particularly, the tomb of St. Augustine, which the inhabitants were accustomed to view with peculiar veneration, was mutilated and defaced. This last provocation having roused the resentment of the people, they flew to arms, surrounded the French garrison, and took them prisoners, but carefully abstained from offering any violence to a single soldier. In revenge for this conduct, Buonaparte, then on his march to the Mincio, suddenly returned, collected his troops, and carried the extremity of military execution over the country: he burnt the town of Benasco and massacred eight hundred of its inhabitants ; he marched to Pavia, took it by storm, and delivered it over to general plunder, and published, at the same moment, a proclamation of May 26, ordering his troops to shoot all those who had not laid down their arms and taken an oath of obedience, and to burn every village where the *tocsin* should be sounded, and to put its inhabitants to death.

Having described the similar treatment inflicted on Modena, Tuscany, Genoa, and Rome, Pitt passed on to Venice.

But of all the disgusting and tragical scenes which took place in Italy, in the course of the period I am describing, those which passed at Venice are perhaps the most striking and the most characteristic. In May 1796 the French army under Buonaparte, in the full tide of its success against the Austrians, first approached the territories of this Republic, which from the commencement of the war had observed a rigid neutrality. Their entrance on these territories was as usual accompanied by a solemn proclamation in the name of their general. 'Buonaparte to the Republic of Venice. It is to deliver the finest country in Europe from the iron yoke of the proud House of Austria that the French army has braved obstacles the most difficult to surmount. Victory in union with justice has crowned its efforts. The wreck of the enemy's army has retired behind the Mincio. The French army, in order to follow them, passes over the territory of the Republic of Venice; but it will never forget that ancient friendship unites the two Republics. Religion, government, customs, and property shall be respected. That the people may be without apprehension, the most severe discipline shall be maintained. All that may be provided for the army shall be faithfully paid for in money. The general-in-chief engages the officers of the Republic of Venice, the magistrates, and the priests, to make known these sentiments to the people, in order that confidence may cement that friendship which has so long united the two nations, faithful in the path of honour as in that of victory. The French soldier is terrible only to the enemies of his liberty and his Government. Buonaparte.'

This proclamation was followed by exactions similar to those which were practised against Genoa, by the renewal of similar professions of friendship, and the use of similar means to excite insurrection. At length, in the spring of 1797, occasion was taken from disturbances thus excited, to forge, in the name of the Venetian Government, a proclamation hostile to France; and this proceeding was made the ground for military execution against the country, and for effecting by force the subversion of its ancient Government and the establishment of the democratic forms of the French Revolution. This revolution was sealed by a treaty, signed in May 1797, between Buonaparte and commissioners appointed on the part of the new and revolutionary Government of Venice. By the second and third secret articles of this treaty, Venice agreed to give as a ransom, to secure itself against all farther exactions or demands, the sum of three millions of livres in money, the value of three millions more in articles of naval supply, and three ships of the line; and it received in return the assurances of the friendship and support of the French Republic.

Immediately after the signature of this treaty, the arsenal, the library, and the palace of St. Mark were ransacked and plundered, and heavy additional contributions were imposed upon its inhabitants: and, in not more than four months afterwards, this very Republic of Venice, united by alliance to France, the creature of Buonaparte himself, from whom it had received the present of French liberty, was by the same Buonaparte transferred under the Treaty of Campo Formio, to 'that iron yoke of the proud House of Austria', to deliver it from which he had represented in his first proclamation to be the great object of all his operations.

Sir, all this is followed by the memorable expedition into Egypt, which I mention, not merely because it forms a principal article in the catalogue of those acts of violence and perfidy in which Buonaparte has been engaged; not merely because it was an enterprise peculiarly his own, of which he was himself the planner, the executor, and the betrayer; but chiefly because, when from thence he retires to a different scene to take possession of a new throne, from which he is to speak upon an equality with the kings and governors of Europe, he leaves behind him, at the moment of his departure, a specimen, which cannot be mistaken, of his principles of negotiation. The intercepted correspondence, which has been alluded to in this debate, seems to afford the strongest ground to believe that his offers to the Turkish Government to evacuate Egypt were made solely with a view '*to gain time*'; that the ratification of any treaty on this subject was to be delayed with the view of finally eluding its performance, if any change of circumstances favourable to the French should occur in the interval. But whatever gentlemen may think of the intention with which these offers were made, there will at least be no question with respect to the credit due to those professions by which he endeavoured to prove in Egypt his pacific dispositions. He expressly enjoins his successor strongly and steadily to insist in all his intercourse with the Turks that he came to Egypt with no hostile design, and that he never meant to keep possession of the country; while, on the opposite page of the same instructions, he states in the most unequivocal manner his regret at the discomfiture of his favourite project of colonizing Egypt and of maintaining it as a territorial acquisition. Now, Sir, if in any Note addressed to the Grand Vizier or the Sultan Buonaparte had claimed credit for the sincerity of his professions, that he forcibly invaded Egypt with no view hostile to Turkey and solely for the purpose of molesting the British interests, is there any one argument now used to induce us to believe his present professions to us, which might not have been equally urged on that occasion to the Turkish Government? Would not those professions have been equally supported by solemn asseverations, by the same reference which is now made to personal character, with this single difference, that they would then have been accompanied with one instance less of that perfidy, which we have had occasion to trace in this very transaction?

It is unnecessary to say more with respect to the credit due to his professions, or the reliance to be placed on his general character: but it will, perhaps, be argued, that, whatever may be his character or whatever has been his past conduct, he has now an interest in making and observing peace. That he has an interest in making peace is at best but a doubtful proposition, and that he has an interest in preserving it is still more uncertain. That it is his interest to negotiate, I do not indeed deny. It is his interest above all to engage this country in separate negotiation, in order to loosen and dissolve the whole system of the confederacy on the Continent, to palsy at once the arms of Russia or of Austria, or of any other country that might look to you for support; and then either to break off his separate treaty, or if he should have concluded it, to apply the lesson which is taught in his school of policy in Egypt; and to revive, at his pleasure, those claims of indemnification which ' *may have been reserved to some happier period*'.

This is precisely the interest which he has in negotiation; but on what grounds are we to be convinced that he has an interest in concluding and observing a solid and permanent pacification? Under all the circumstances of his personal character and his newly acquired power, what other security has he for retaining that power but the sword? His hold upon France is the sword, and he has no other. Is he connected with the soil, or with the habits, the affections, or the prejudices of the country? He is a stranger, a foreigner, and a usurper; he unites in his own person everything that a pure Republican must detest; everything that an enraged Jacobin has abjured; everything that a sincere and faithful Royalist must feel as an insult. If he is opposed at any time in his career, what is his appeal?

He appeals to his fortune; in other words, to his army and his sword. Placing, then, his whole reliance upon military support, can he afford to let his military renown pass away, to let his laurels wither, to let the memory of his achievements sink in obscurity? Is it certain that, with his army confined within France and restrained from inroads upon her neighbours, he can maintain at his devotion a force sufficiently numerous to support his power? Having no object but the possession of absolute dominion, no passion but military glory, is it certain that he can feel such an interest in permanent peace as would justify us in laying down our arms, reducing our expense, and relinquishing our means of security, on the faith of his engagements? Do we believe that after the conclusion of peace he would not still sigh over the lost trophies of Egypt, wrested from him by the celebrated victory of Aboukir [1] and the brilliant exertions of that heroic band of British seamen whose influence and example rendered the Turkish troops invincible at Acre? Can he forget that the effect of these exploits enabled Austria and Russia, in one campaign, to recover from France all which she had acquired by his victories, to dissolve the charm which, for a time, fascinated Europe, and to show that their generals, contending in a just cause, could efface by their success and their military glory even the most dazzling triumphs of his victories and desolating ambition?

Can we believe, with these impressions on his mind, that if, after a year, eighteen months, or two years, of

[1] i.e. the Battle of the Nile.

peace had elapsed, he should be tempted by the appearance of a fresh insurrection in Ireland, encouraged by renewed and unrestrained communication with France, and fomented by the fresh infusion of Jacobin principles; if we were at such a moment without a fleet to watch the ports of France, or to guard the coasts of Ireland, without a disposable army, or an embodied militia, capable of supplying a speedy and adequate reinforcement, and that he had suddenly the means of transporting thither a body of twenty or thirty thousand French troops:—can we believe that at such a moment his ambition and vindictive spirit would be restrained by the recollection of engagements or the obligation of treaty? Or, if in some new crisis of difficulty and danger to the Ottoman Empire, with no British navy in the Mediterranean, no confederacy formed, no force collected to support it, an opportunity should present itself for resuming the abandoned expedition to Egypt, for renewing the avowed and favourite project of conquering and colonizing that rich and fertile country, and of opening the way to wound some of the vital interests of England and to plunder the treasures of the East, in order to fill the bankrupt coffers of France, would it be the interest of Buonaparte under such circumstances, or his principles, his moderation, his love of peace, his aversion to conquest, and his regard for the independence of other nations—would it be all, or any of these that would secure us against an attempt, which would leave us only the option of submitting without a struggle to certain loss and disgrace, or of renewing the contest which we had prematurely terminated, and renewing it without allies, without preparation, with diminished means, and with increased difficulty and hazard?

Hitherto I have spoken only of the reliance which we can place on the professions, the character, and the conduct of the present First Consul; but it remains to consider the stability of his power. The Revolution has been marked throughout by a rapid succession of new depositaries of public authority, each supplanting his predecessor; what grounds have we as yet to believe that this new usurpation, more odious and more undisguised than all that preceded it, will be more durable? Is it that we rely on the particular provisions contained in the code of the pretended constitution, which was proclaimed as accepted by the French people, as soon as the garrison of Paris declared their determination to exterminate all its enemies, and before any of its articles could even be known to half the country, whose consent was required for its establishment?

I will not pretend to inquire deeply into the nature and effects of a constitution, which can hardly be regarded but as a farce and a mockery. If, however, it could be supposed that its provisions were to have any effect, it seems equally adapted to two purposes; that of giving to its founder for a time an absolute and uncontrolled authority, and that of laying the certain foundation of future disunion and discord, which, if they once prevail, must render the exercise of all the authority under the constitution impossible, and leave no appeal but to the sword.

Is then military despotism that which we are accustomed to consider as a stable form of government? In all ages of the world, it has been attended with the least stability to the persons who exercised it, and with the most rapid succession of changes and revolutions. The advocates of the French Revolution boasted in its outset that by their new system they had furnished a security for ever, not to France only but to all countries in the world, against military despotism; that the force of standing armies was vain and delusive; that no artificial power could resist public opinion; and that it was upon the foundation of public opinion alone that any government could stand. I believe that in this instance, as in every other, the progress of the French Revolution has belied its professions; but so far from its being a proof of the prevalence of public opinion against military force, it is instead of the proof the strongest exception from that doctrine which appears in the history of the world. Through all the stages of the Revolution military force has governed; public opinion has scarcely been heard. But still I consider this as only an exception from a general truth; I still believe, that in every civilized country (not enslaved by a Jacobin faction) public opinion is the only sure support of any government. I believe this with the more satisfaction from a conviction that, if this contest is happily terminated, the established Governments of Europe will stand upon that rock firmer than ever; and whatever may be the defects of any particular constitution, those who live under it will prefer its continuance to the experiment of changes which may plunge them in the unfathomable abyss of revolution, or extricate them from it, only to expose them to the terrors of military despotism. And to apply this to France, I see no reason to believe that the present usurpation will be more permanent than any other military despotism which has been established by the same means and with the same defiance of public opinion.

What, then, is the inference I draw from all that I have now stated? Is it that we will in no case treat with Buonaparte? I say no such thing. But I say, as has been said in the answer returned to the French note, that we ought to wait for *experience and the evidence of facts*, before we are convinced that such a treaty is admissible. The circumstances I have stated would well justify us if we should be slow in being convinced; but on a question of peace and war, everything depends upon degree and upon comparison. If, on the one hand, there should be an appearance that the policy of France is at length guided by different maxims from those which have hitherto prevailed; if we should hereafter see signs of stability in the Government, which are not now to be traced; if the progress of the allied army should not call forth such a spirit in France, as to make it probable that the act of the country itself will destroy the system now prevailing; if the danger, the difficulty, the risk of continuing the contest should increase, while the hope of complete ultimate success should be diminished; all these, in their due place, are considerations, which, with myself and (I can answer for it) with every one of my colleagues, will have their just weight. But at present these considerations all operate one way; at present there is nothing from which we can presage a favourable disposition to change in the French councils.

If, he went on to argue, such a change did take place, if the authority of Buonaparte, ' this last adventurer in the lottery of revolutions ', should be overthrown, if the Bourbon monarchy should be restored, then indeed a secure peace might be obtained. But failing such a change and failing actual evidence of a transformation in Buonaparte's character, the war must be continued.

It is true, indeed, that even the gigantic and unnatural means by which the Revolution has been supported are so far impaired; the influence of its principles and the terror of its arms so far weakened; and its power of action so much contracted and circumscribed, that against the embodied force of Europe, prosecuting a vigorous war, we may justly hope that the remnant and wreck of this system cannot long oppose an effectual resistance. But supposing the confederacy of Europe prematurely dissolved, supposing our armies disbanded, our fleets laid up in our harbours, our exertions relaxed, and our means of precaution and defence relinquished, do we believe that the revolutionary power, with this rest and breathing-time given it to recover from the pressure under which it is now sinking, possessing still the means of calling suddenly and violently into action whatever is the remaining physical force of France, under the guidance of military despotism—do we believe that this power, the terror of which is now beginning to vanish, will not again prove formidable to Europe? Can we forget that, in the ten years in which that power has subsisted, it has brought more misery on surrounding nations and produced more acts of aggression, cruelty, perfidy, and enormous ambition, than can be traced in the history of France for the centuries which have elapsed since the foundation of its monarchy, including all the wars which, in the course of that period, have been waged by any of those sovereigns, whose projects of aggrandizement and violations of treaty afford a constant theme of general reproach against the ancient government of France? And with these considerations before us, can we hesitate whether we have the best prospect of permanent peace, the best security for the independence and safety of Europe, from the restoration of the lawful government, or from the continuance of revolutionary power in the hands of Buonaparte?

In compromise and treaty with such a power, placed in such hands as now exercise it and retaining the same means of annoyance which it now possesses, I see little hope of permanent security. I see no possibility at this moment of concluding such a peace as would justify that liberal intercourse which is the essence of real amity; no chance of terminating the expenses or the anxieties of war, or of restoring to us any of the advantages of established tranquillity. And as a sincere lover of peace, I cannot be content with its nominal attainment. I must be desirous of pursuing that system which promises to attain, in the end, the permanent enjoyment of its solid and substantial blessings for this country and for Europe. As a sincere lover of peace, I will not sacrifice it by grasping at the shadow, when the reality is not substantially within my reach——

Cur igitur pacem nolo? Quia infida est, quia periculosa, quia esse non potest.[1]

[1] Cicero, *Philippics*, vii. 3. 'Why, then, do I refuse peace? Because it is deceptive, because it is dangerous, because it cannot be.'

The war, then, Pitt concluded, must be continued: and we shall continue it with every prospect of success.

When we consider the resources and the spirit of the country, can any man doubt that, if adequate security is not now to be obtained by treaty, we have the means of prosecuting the contest without material difficulty or danger, and with a reasonable prospect of completely attaining our object ? I will not dwell on the improved state of public credit, on the continually increasing amount (in spite of extraordinary temporary burthens) of our permanent revenue, on the yearly accession of wealth to a degree unprecedented even in the most flourishing times of peace, which we are deriving, in the midst of war, from our extended and flourishing commerce ; on the progressive improvement and growth of our manufactures ; on the proofs which we see on all sides of the uninterrupted accumulation of productive capital; and on the active exertion of every branch of national industry, which can tend to support and augment the population, the riches, and the power of the country.

As little need I recall the attention of the House to the additional means of action which we have derived from the great augmentation of our disposable military force, the continued triumphs of our powerful and victorious navy, and the events which, in the course of the last two years, have raised the military ardour and military glory of the country to a height unexampled in any period of our history.

In addition to these grounds of reliance on our own strength and exertions, we have seen the consummate skill and valour of the arms of our allies proved by that series of unexampled successes which distinguished the last campaign, and we have every reason to expect a co-operation on the Continent, even to a greater extent, in the course of the present year.

If we compare this view of our own situation with everything we can observe of the state and condition of our enemy; if we can trace him labouring under equal difficulty in finding men to recruit his army or money to pay it; if we know that in the course of the last year the most rigorous efforts of military conscription were scarcely sufficient to replace to the French armies, at the end of the campaign, the numbers which they had lost in the course of it; if we have seen that the force of the enemy, then in possession of advantages which it has since lost, was unable to contend with the efforts of the combined armies; if we know that, even while supported by the plunder of all the countries which they had overrun, the French armies were reduced, by the confession of their commanders, to the extremity of distress, and destitute not only of the principal articles of military supply, but almost of the necessaries of life; if we see them now driven back within their own frontiers, and confined within a country whose own resources have long since been proclaimed by their successive governments to be unequal either to paying or maintaining them; if we observe that, since the last revolution, no one substantial or effectual measure has been adopted to remedy the intolerable disorder of their finances, and to supply the deficiency of their credit and resources; if we see, through large and populous districts of France, either open war levied against the present usurpation, or evident marks of disunion and distraction, which the first occasion may call forth into a flame; if, I say, Sir, this comparison be just, I feel myself authorized to conclude from it, not that we are entitled to consider ourselves certain of ultimate success, not that we are to suppose ourselves exempted from the unforeseen vicissitudes of war, but that, considering the value of the object for which we are contending, the means for supporting the contest, and the probable course of human events, we should be inexcusable if at this moment we were to relinquish the struggle on any grounds short of entire and complete security against the greatest danger which has ever yet threatened the world; that from perseverance in our efforts under such circumstances, we have the fairest reason to expect the full attainment of that object; but that at all events, even if we are disappointed in our more sanguine hopes, we are more likely to gain than to lose by the continuation of the contest; that every month to which it is continued, even if it should not in its effects lead to the final destruction of the Jacobin system, must tend so far to weaken and exhaust it, as to give us at least a greater comparative security in any other termination of the war; that, on all these grounds, this is not the moment at which it is consistent with our interest or our duty to listen to any proposals of negotiation with the present ruler of France; but that we are not therefore pledged to any unalterable determination as to our future conduct; that in this we must be regulated by the course of events; and that it will be the duty of His Majesty's Ministers from time to time to adapt their measures to any variation of circumstances, to consider how far the effects of the military operations of the allies, or of the internal disposition of France, correspond with our present expectations; and, on a view of the whole, to compare the difficulties or risks which may arise in the prosecution of the contest, with the prospect of ultimate success or of the degree of advantage which may be derived from its farther continuance, and to be governed by the result of all these considerations in the opinion and advice which they may offer to their sovereign.

The address was carried by 265 to 64.

6
The Watchword: 'Security'
February 17, 1800 [1]

IN the course of a debate, a fortnight later, on a subsidy to Austria, Tierney challenged Pitt to define the real object of the war. 'It is not', he concluded, 'the destruction of Jacobin principles; it may be the restoration of the House of Bourbon; but I would wish the right honourable gentleman in one sentence to state, if he can, without his *ifs* and *buts* and special pleading ambiguity, what this object is. I am persuaded he cannot, and that he calls us to prosecute a war, and to lavish our treasure and blood in its support, when no one plain satisfactory reason can be given for its continuance.' Pitt at once replied.

The observation with which the honourable gentle-

[1] *Speeches*, vol. iv, p. 61.

man concluded his speech, appears to me one of the strangest I ever heard advanced, and first challenges my attention. He defies me to state, in one sentence, what is the object of the war. I know not whether I can do it in one sentence; but in one word I can tell him that it is *security*: security against a danger, the greatest that ever threatened the world. It is security against a danger which never existed in any past period of society. It is security against a danger which in degree and extent was never equalled; against a danger which threatened all the nations of the earth; against a danger which has been resisted by all the nations of Europe, and resisted by none with so much success as by this nation, because by none has it been resisted so uniformly and with so much energy.

A little later in his speech, he reverted to Tierney's challenge.

The honourable gentleman took another ground of argument, to which I shall now follow him. He said that the war could not be just, because it was carried on for the restoration of the House of Bourbon; and, secondly, that it could not be necessary, because we had refused to negotiate for peace when an opportunity for negotiation was offered us. As to the first proposition, that it cannot be just, because it is carried on for the restoration of the House of Bourbon, he has assumed the foundation of the argument, and has left no ground for controverting it, or for explanation, because he says that any attempt at explanation upon this subject is the mere ambiguous unintelligible language of *ifs* and *buts*, and of special pleading. Now, Sir, I never had much liking to special pleading; and if ever I had any,[1] it is by this time almost entirely gone. He has besides so abridged me in the use of particles, that though I am not particularly attached to the sound of an *if* or a *but*, I would be much obliged to the honourable gentleman if he would give me some others to supply their places. Is this, however, a light matter, that it should be treated in so light a manner? The restoration of the French monarchy, I will still tell the honourable gentleman, I consider as a most desirable object, because I think that it would afford the strongest and best security to this country and to Europe. *But* this object may not be attainable; and *if* it be not attainable, we must be satisfied with the best security which we can find independent of it. Peace is most desirable to this country; *but* negotiation may be attended with greater evils than could be counterbalanced by any benefits which would result from it. And *if* this be found to be the case; *if* it afford no prospect of security; *if* it threaten all the evils which we have been struggling to avert; *if* the prosecution of the war afford the prospect of attaining complete security; and *if* it may be prosecuted with increasing commerce, with increasing means, and with increasing prosperity, except what may result from the visitations of the seasons; then I say that it is prudent in us not to negotiate at the present moment. These are my *buts* and my *ifs*. This is my plea, and on no other do I wish to be tried by God and my country.

---

[1] Pitt was called to the Bar in 1780, but the demands of his political career soon put an end to his practice.

At the conclusion of his speech Pitt rebuked those who were raising an agitation for peace in the country by declaring that the present scarcity was due entirely to the war and would cease with its cessation.

If any man thinks he sees the means of bringing the contest to an earlier termination than by vigorous effort and military operations, he is justified in opposing the measures which are necessary to carry it on with energy. Those who consider the war to be expedient cannot, with consistency, refuse their assent to measures calculated to bring it to a successful issue. Even those who may disapprove of the contest, which they cannot prevent by their votes, cannot honestly pursue that conduct which could tend only to render its termination favourable to the enemy. God forbid I should question the freedom of thought or the liberty of speech! But I cannot see how gentlemen can justify a language and a conduct which can have no tendency but to disarm our exertions and to defeat our hopes in the prosecution of the contest. They ought to limit themselves to those arguments which could influence the House against the war altogether, not dwell upon topics which can tend only to weaken our efforts and betray our cause. Above all, nothing can be more unfair in reasoning, than to ally the present scarcity with the war, or to insinuate that its prosecution will interfere with those supplies which we may require. I am the more induced to testify thus publicly the disapprobation which such language exacts in my mind, when I observe the insidious use that is made of it in promoting certain measures out of doors; a language, indeed, contrary to all honest principle, and repugnant to every sentiment of public duty.

7

Sea-Law and the Neutral Powers

February 2, 1801 [1]

THE progress of the war in 1800 was marked by the recovery of the French position on the Continent and by the appearance of a new danger to British sea-power.

The spring opened with a great effort by Austria to complete the expulsion of the French from Italy. The attempt was thwarted by the strategy of Buonaparte, who unexpectedly crossed the Alps by the St. Bernard, took the Austrian forces in the rear, and crushed them at Marengo (June 14). Five days later, Moreau drove the Austrians from Ulm, and on December 3 he won a decisive victory at Hohenlinden. Austria was compelled to sue for peace, and in the following February the Treaty of Lunéville was signed.

It marked the end of the Second Coalition, for Russia had already fallen out of line. Jealousy of Austria, annoyance at the failure of the Anglo-Russian campaign in Holland, and long-felt irritation at the claims enforced by England over neutral shipping, had caused Paul I to yield to the timely flattery of the victorious Buonaparte, to abandon his allies, and to renew, with the other Northern Powers, Sweden and Denmark, the old Armed Neutrality League of 1780 in defence of the rights of neutrals.

The powers claimed by belligerents to interfere with neutral shipping were more drastic in the eighteenth century than they are now. In accordance with the previous practice of herself and other States in previous wars, Great Britain insisted on the right to search neutral ships, whether convoyed by a neutral man-of-

[1] *Speeches*, vol. iv, p. 134.

war or not: to seize enemy goods found on them, destined for an enemy port, although the blockade of that port might be only nominal: and to seize contraband-of-war under any circumstances whatever.

The British capture of Malta in September still further inflamed the temper of the Czar, for Buonaparte, perceiving its fall to be imminent, cunningly offered to restore it to the Grand Master of the Order of St. John. Paul now induced Prussia to join the league, laid an embargo on all British ships in Russian harbours, and imprisoned many British seamen. Under these circumstances the British Government naturally prepared for war, and on February 2, 1801, Pitt explained to the House of Commons the nature of the issues at stake and the legal basis of the British claim. In reply to an amendment to the Address, moved by Grey, he spoke as follows:

The honourable gentleman has, in the course of his speech, introduced several topics which, he says, have been frequently discussed before, and which he expresses his hope will again be investigated. Upon both these grounds, I am not disposed to trouble the House at length, upon any of these subjects, at present. There is, indeed, but one new question before the House, I mean that which has been announced to us in His Majesty's most gracious Speech from the Throne, respecting our differences with the Northern Powers. Sir, I must confess that the manner in which the honourable gentleman has treated every part of this subject has really filled me with astonishment, both when I consider the general plan of his speech, and the particular statements into which he went in support of his argument. The honourable gentleman thought it right, in the first place, to express his doubts of the justice of our claim with respect to neutral vessels; and in the next place (which appeared to me fully as singular) to question the importance of the point now at issue. But though the honourable gentleman seemed disposed to entertain doubts on points upon which I believe there is hardly another man to be found in this country who would hesitate for a moment, yet there were other points upon which his mind appeared to be free from doubt and his opinion completely made up. If, after a full discussion of this question, it should appear that the claim which this country has made is founded on the clearest and most indisputable justice—if it should be proved that our greatness, nay, our very existence as a nation, and everything that has raised us to the exalted situation which we hold, depends upon our possessing and exercising this right—if, I say, all this should be proved in the most satisfactory manner, still the honourable gentleman is prepared seriously to declare in this House that such are the circumstances in which we stand, that we ought publicly and explicitly to state to the world that we are unequal to the contest, and that we must quietly give up for ever an unquestionable right, and one upon which not only our character, but our very existence as a maritime Power depends. This is the conduct which the honourable gentleman advises us to pursue at once, without determining, without investigating, whether it is compatible with our safety. I really find much difficulty, Sir, in reconciling this language to that sort of spirit which the honourable gentleman talks of in another part of his speech, in which he says he is far from wishing to make the country despond.—[*Mr. Grey here said across the table, that he had been misunderstood.*]—Sir, I am stating what the honourable gentleman said, and I shall be happy to find that he did not mean what he said.

I shall now, Sir, endeavour to follow the honourable gentleman through his argument, as far as I can recollect it, upon the important question of the Northern confederacy. In following the order which he took, I must begin with his doubts and end with his certainties; and I cannot avoid observing that the honourable gentleman was singularly unfortunate upon this subject; for he entertained doubts where there was not the slightest ground for hesitation, and he contrives to make up his mind to absolute certainty, upon points in which both argument and fact are decidedly against him.

That part of the question upon which the honourable gentleman appears to be involved in doubt, is with respect to the justice of our claim in regard to neutral vessels. In commenting upon this part of the subject, the honourable gentleman gave us a lesson in politics, which is more remarkable for its soundness than its novelty, namely, that a nation ought not to enforce a claim that is not founded in justice, and that nothing would be found to be consistent with true policy that was not conformable to strict justice. I thought, however, I heard the honourable gentleman in another part of his speech, where he was arguing the question of the expediency and propriety of our negotiating a separate peace with France, contend that no consideration of good faith to Austria ought to prevent us from entering into such a negotiation.—[*Mr. Grey said, he had not laid that down as a principle, but merely with respect to the circumstances under which we stood with regard to Austria.*]— I am glad to hear the honourable gentleman contradict me, but I certainly understood him to say so. I am also glad to find that, when the issue of fact is found against him, he has no demurrer in reserve upon the principle. Upon the justice, however, of our claim, the honourable gentleman states himself to be wholly in doubt.

There is, Sir, in general, a degree of modesty in doubting that conciliates very much, and a man is seldom inclined to bear hard upon an antagonist whose attack does not exceed the limits of a doubt. But, Sir, when a gentleman doubts that which has been indisputably established for more than a century—when he doubts that which has been an acknowledged principle of law in all the tribunals of the kingdom which are alone competent to decide upon the subject, and which Parliament has constantly known them to act upon—when he doubts principles which the ablest and wisest statesmen have uniformly adopted—I say, Sir, the doubt that calls in question principles so established, without offering the slightest ground for so doing, shows a great deal of that pert presumption which, as often as modesty, leads to scepticism. I wish to ask every gentleman in the House whether it has not been always known that such was the principle upon which our courts were acting from the commencement of the present war up to the moment that I am speaking? I ask whether that principle has not been maintained in every war? Let me at the same time ask, whether, in the course of the speeches of the gentlemen on the other side of the House, any one topic of alarm has been omitted, which either fact could furnish or ingenuity supply? I believe I shall not be answered in the negative, and yet I believe I may safely assert that it never occurred to any one member to increase the difficulties of the country by stating a doubt upon the question of right; and it will be a most singular circumstance that the honourable gentleman and his friends should only have begun to doubt when our enemies are ready to begin to combat. But though I have heard doubts expressed upon a subject on which it appeared to me that a doubt could hardly have entered the mind of an Englishman, I have not heard one word to show on what ground there can exist a doubt upon the justice of our claim—a claim which, until this House decides the contrary, I shall consider as part of the law of the land; for I consider the maritime law and the law of nations, as acted upon in our courts, to be part of the law of the land. I speak in the presence of some learned gentlemen who are conversant in the practice of the courts to which I allude, and who, I am sure, will contradict me if I state that which is incorrect. I ask any of these learned gentlemen whether they would suffer the principle, upon which our claim rests, to be called in question in any of their courts? But when we come to consider this question as applying to the contest in which we may be engaged, there are so many considerations that are decisive upon the subject, that I am really convinced by the manner in which the honourable gentleman treated it, that his doubts have all arisen from his not having looked into the question.

There are two ways in which this subject is to be considered. The first is, what has been the general law of nations upon this subject, independent of any particular treaties which may have been made? The next is, how far any precise treaties affect it, with regard to the particular Powers who are the objects of the present dispute? With respect to the law of nations, I know that the principle upon which we are now acting, and for which I am now contending, has been universally admitted and acted upon, except in cases where it has been restrained or modified by particular treaties between different States. And here I must observe that the honourable gentleman has fallen into the same error which constitutes the great fallacy in the reasoning of the advocates for the Northern Powers, namely, that every exception from the general law by a particular treaty proves the law to be as it is stated in that treaty; whereas the very circumstance of making an exception by treaty proves what the general law of nations would be, if no such treaty were made to modify or alter it. The honourable gentleman alludes to the treaty made between this country and France in the year 1787, known by the name of the Commercial Treaty. In that treaty it certainly was stipulated that in the event of Great Britain being engaged in a war, and France being neutral, she should have the advantage now claimed, and vice versa; but the honourable gentleman confesses that he recollects that the very same objection was made at that time, and was fully answered, and that it was clearly proved that no part of our stipulation in that treaty tended to a dereliction of the principle for which we are now contending. Besides, when it is considered how far the interests of this country can be implicated in a naval war in which France is neutral, it will not afford any proof either that we considered the principle as unimportant or that we gave it up. I could, without in the slightest degree weakening the cause which I am endeavouring to support, give to the honourable gentleman all the benefit he can possibly derive from the Commercial Treaty with France and from particular treaties with other States, and I should be glad to know what advantage he could derive from such an admission. If he could show treaties with any given number of States, still, if there were any State in Europe with whom no such treaty was in existence, with that State the law of nations, such as I am now contending for, must be in full force. Still more, it will be allowed to me that, if there is any nation that has forborne to be a party of these treaties, that maintained this principle and has enforced its rights, in such a case no inference that can be drawn from treaties with other Powers can have any weight.

The utmost the honourable gentleman could argue, and even in that I do not think he would be founded in justice, would be this—that, if there was no general consent with respect to the principles, particular treaties ought to serve as a guide in other cases. But what will the honourable gentleman say, if, instead of my stating an imaginary case, I give to him this short answer, that with every one of the three Northern Powers with whom we are at present in dispute, independent of the law of nations, of our uniform practice, and of the opinions of our courts, we have the strict letter of engagements by which they are bound to us? What will he say, if I show that their present conduct to us is as much a violation of positive treaties with us, as it is of the law of nations? With respect to Denmark and Sweden, nobody here, I am sure, has to learn that the treaties of 1661 and 1670 are now in full force, and nobody can read those treaties without seeing that the right of carrying enemies' property is completely given up. With regard to Russia, the right of this country never was given by us. It undoubtedly was very much discussed during the time that the Treaty of Commerce with Russia was negotiating; but I will not rest my argument upon negative evidence. In the Convention signed between Great Britain and Russia at the commencement of the present war, the latter bound herself not merely to observe this principle by a convention (not done away, unless we have unjustly commenced hostilities against her), but she engaged to use her efforts to prevent neutral Powers from protecting the commerce of France on the seas or in the ports of France. Laying aside, then, every other ground upon which I contend that the principle I am now maintaining is supported, still I say that the treaties with these three Powers, Russia, Sweden, and Denmark, are now in full force, and I ask whether it is possible to suggest any one ground upon which it can be contended that these Powers are released from their engagements to us? So much for the justice of the claim.

I will not, Sir, take up much more of the time of the House, because there will be papers laid before the House which will place the subject in a clearer point of view than can be done in the course of a debate : but I must say, that with regard to these Powers the case does not stop here. What will the honourable gentleman say I if show him, that in the course of the present war, both Denmark and Sweden have distinctly expressed their readiness to agree in that very principle, against which they are disposed to contend, and that they made acknowledgements to us for not carrying the claim so far as Russia was disposed to carry it? What will the honourable gentleman say, if I show him that Sweden, who in the year 1780 agreed to the Armed Neutrality, has since been at war herself, and then acted upon a principle directly contrary to that which she agreed to in the year 1780, and to that upon which she is now disposed to act? In the war between Sweden and Russia, the former distinctly acted upon that very principle for which we are now contending. What will the honourable gentleman say, if I show him that in the last autumn Denmark, with her fleets and arsenals at our mercy, entered into a solemn pledge not again to send vessels with convoy, until the principle was settled ; and that, notwithstanding this solemn pledge, this State has entered into a new convention, similar to that which was agreed to in 1780 ? One of the engagements of that treaty is, that its stipulations are to be maintained by force of arms. Here then is a nation, bound to us by treaty and who has recently engaged not even to send a convoy until the point should be determined, that tells us she has entered into an engagement by which she is bound to support that principle by force of arms.

Is this, or is it not, war? Is it not that which, if we

had not heard the honourable gentleman this night, would lead a man to think he insulted an Englishman by questioning his feelings upon the subject? But, Sir, when all these circumstances are accompanied by armaments, prepared at a period of the year when they think they have time for preparation without being exposed to our navy, His Majesty informs you that these Courts have avowed the principles of the Treaty of 1780, known by the name of the Armed Neutrality. But then the honourable gentleman says, 'We do not know the precise terms of the present treaty, and therefore we ought to take no steps until we are completely apprised of its contents.' It is true, we do not know the exact terms of the treaty; but I should think if we demand to know whether they have made engagements which we consider as hostile to our interests, and they tell us they have, but do not tell us what exceptions are made in our favour, we are not, I should think, bound to guess them, or to give them credit for them until they are shown to us. How far would the honourable gentleman push his argument? Will he say that we ought to wait quietly for the treaty, that we ought to take no step, until we have read it paragraph by paragraph, and that then we should acknowledge to those Powers that we are now dispirited and not prepared to dispute the point? Does he mean that we should give them time to assemble all their forces and enable them to produce something like a substitute for the fallen navy of France? Is this the conduct which the honourable gentleman would recommend to the adoption of this country? Are we to wait till we see the article itself, until we see the seal to the contract of our destruction, before we take any means to ensure our defence?

Sir, I will not trouble the House any longer upon the question of right; I come now to the question of expedience, and upon this part of the subject the honourable gentleman is not so much in doubt. The question is, whether we are to permit the navy of our enemy to be supplied and recruited—whether we are to suffer blockaded forts to be furnished with warlike stores and provisions—whether we are to suffer neutral nations, by hoisting a flag upon a sloop or a fishing boat, to convey the treasures of South America to the harbours of Spain, or the naval stores of the Baltic to Brest or Toulon? Are these the propositions which gentlemen mean to contend for? I really have heard no argument upon the subject yet. [*Mr. Sheridan and Dr. Laurence entered the House together, and sat down upon the opposite bench.*] I suppose I shall be answered by and by, as I see there is an accession of new members to the confederacy, who will, I have no doubt, add to the severity and to the length of the contest. I would ask, Sir, has there been any period since we have been a naval country, in which we have not acted upon this principle? The honourable gentleman talks of the destruction of the naval power of France, but does he really believe that her marine would have been decreased to the degree that it now is, if, during the whole of the war, this very principle had not been acted upon? And if the commerce of France had not been destroyed, does he believe that, if the fraudulent system of neutrals had not been prevented, her navy would not have been in a very different situation from that in which it now is? Does he not know that the naval preponderance, which we have by these means acquired, has given security to this country, and has more than once afforded chances for the salvation of Europe? In the wreck of the Continent and the disappointment of our hopes there, what has been the security of this country but its naval preponderance? And if that were once gone, the spirit of the country would go with it. If we had no other guide, if we had nothing else to look to but the experience of the present war, that alone proves, not the utility, but the necessity of maintaining a principle so important to the power and even to the existence of this country.

There was something rather singular in the manner in which the honourable gentleman commented upon, and argued from, the destruction of the naval power of France. He says, her marine is now so much weakened that we may now relinquish the means by which we have so nearly destroyed it; and, at the very same moment, he holds out the terrors of an invasion of Ireland. The honourable gentleman says, 'We are not now, as we were in the year 1780,[1] shrinking from the fleets of France and Spain in the Channel:' but, if that was our only excuse for not asserting the principle in the year 1780, we have not now, happily for this country, the same reason for not persisting in our rights; and the question now is, whether, with increased proofs of the necessity of acting upon that principle and with increased means of supporting it, we are for ever to give it up?

I think (Pitt concluded) the question of right in

[1] Introduction, p. xii.

dispute between us and the confederated Powers so eminently important, that it claims at this hour the undivided attention of this House. As to what has been said on other topics, of the censures which ought to be cast on the counsel we have had any share in giving for the prosecution of the war, I have the consolation of knowing what they are likely to be from a recollection of what they have repeatedly been—that they will most probably be put in the same way, and will admit of being answered in the same way, as they have been already answered as often as they were brought forward, and, I cannot help flattering myself, with the same success. I hope also that the public will feel, as they have repeatedly felt, that the calamities which have overspread Europe and which have affected to a certain degree this country, though much less than any other, have not been owing to any defect on our part, but that we have pursued principles best calculated for the welfare of human society, the nature and effect of which have been frequently commented upon by those who have opposed and by those who have supported these principles, and with whom I have had the honour to act, and still have the honour of acting; on which, I say, the power, the security, the honour of this nation has depended, and which, I trust, the perseverance and firmness of Parliament and the nation will not cease to pursue, while His Majesty's servants discharge their duty.

The amendment was negatived by 245 to 63.

On the day after this speech (February 3) Pitt intimated to the King his decision to resign the office he had held without a break since 1783. In the previous year he had carried the Act of Union with Ireland, and in the preliminary negotiations he had pledged himself to bring in a measure of Catholic emancipation, the necessary complement, in his opinion, to the Act of Union. But the King stubbornly refused to assent to any such measure; and Pitt, unable to redeem his pledge, considered himself bound to resign.

He declined to serve in the Cabinet of his successor, Addington, the ex-Speaker, but he promised to support him in Parliament, and urged his political friends to co-operate with the new Government.

It started under favourable auspices. The war with the League of Northern Powers was soon finished. By his bold attempt to force the defences of Copenhagen, on April 2, Nelson secured an armistice of fourteen weeks from the Danes. Ten days earlier, the Czar Paul had been assassinated, and his successor, Alexander, now hastened to come to an understanding with Great Britain. Some of the British claims were surrendered, and the League was dissolved in June.

By the summer, Buonaparte's designs in the East were finally frustrated. Tippoo had already been killed, and the French power in India broken by the capture of Seringapatam. The occupation of Malta had secured our hold on the Mediterranean. And in August, the French army in Egypt was forced to lay down its arms and return to France.

Britain's supremacy at sea was now unquestioned: but Buonaparte's supremacy on land, since the breakdown of the Second Coalition, was equally unassailable. Under these circumstances the continuance of the war seemed a fruitless waste of effort, and on October 1 the preliminaries of peace were signed.

Pitt supported the action of the Government in his speech of November 3.[1] He did not pretend that

[1] *Speeches*, vol. iv, p. 197.

the proposed peace fulfilled his earlier hopes. But he admitted that the dissolution of 'the confederacy of the States of Europe' rendered it inevitable. And after all, he argued, England would emerge from the conflict in full command of the sea. Security from attack being assured her by her maritime power, she should now husband her resources for future needs and not waste them in continuing a contest which could not, in the present state of Europe, be finally decided. The permanence of the peace would depend on Buonaparte. 'It would be affectation and hypocrisy in me', he said, 'to say that I have changed, or can change my opinion of the character of the person presiding in France, until I see a train of conduct which would justify that change.' If his object was 'to exercise a military despotism' Pitt ventured to predict that he would not first attack England. And, if he did, England would be ready. 'This country always was, and I trust always will be, able to check the ambitious projects of France and to give that degree of assistance to the rest of Europe which we have done on this occasion.' 'I am inclined to hope', he concluded, 'everything that is good. But I am bound to act as if I feared otherwise.'

The wisdom of this last remark was soon demonstrated. The Treaty of Amiens was signed on March 27, 1802. On May 17, 1803, relations between France and England were once more broken off. The war had entered on its third phase.

THE WAR: THIRD PHASE
1803–1806

The Impossibility of Peace
May 23, 1803 [1]

THE terms of the Treaty of Amiens were favourable to France, for England restored all her acquisitions oversea except Ceylon and Trinidad. On the other hand, Buonaparte's ambitions in the East were checked by the evacuation of Naples and of Egypt, the acknowledgement of the independence of the Ionian Isles, and the restoration of Malta to the Knights of St. John, under the express condition that its independence and neutrality were guaranteed in perpetuity by all the Great Powers.

Favourable as it was, Buonaparte was by no means inclined to leave the settlement as it stood. In May he took advantage of the new prestige the peace had won him to consolidate his personal power by securing a *plébiscite* appointing him First Consul for life, and henceforth, like his fellow monarchs, he styled himself by his first name. He soon showed that Napoleon was no more content than Buonaparte to limit his ambitions to the internal development of France. The Treaty of Amiens was not six months old before he boldly changed the map of Europe by annexing Piedmont and Elba, and, on pretence of mediation in its domestic disputes, ordered an army to occupy Switzerland. In March 1803 he swept away the Helvetic Republic and imposed yet another constitution on the Swiss, in accordance with which they were bound to provide levies for their

[1] *Speeches*, vol. iv, p. 221.

'Mediator's' wars. Moreover, he retained troops in Holland and in the Italian Republics in violation of the Treaty of Lunéville.

Undeterred by British protests at these actions, he now resumed his dreams of world-dominion. In the autumn of 1802 he dispatched Colonel Sebastiani on a mission to Egypt. It was called a 'commercial mission', but its true character was revealed by the publication of Sebastiani's report. He declared that the Ionian Islands would welcome the restoration of French rule, and that an army of 6,000 Frenchmen could easily achieve the conquest of Egypt.

This final provocation was met by the British Government with more than a mere protest: it declared (February 1803) that British troops would continue in occupation of Malta—the only safeguard of the Indian route, now that the Cape had been abandoned—until Sebastiani's report was satisfactorily explained and the *status quo* at the conclusion of the Treaty of Amiens re-established.

Napoleon believed, however, that England was in no mood to renew the war, and that Addington, so different a man from Pitt, would yield to threats and bluster. He told the British Ambassador that his Government was disputing about trifles, and he railed in coarse language against the perfidy of England.[1] He had misjudged the temper of the British people. A fresh *ultimatum* was presented, and his rejection of it was followed by war.

On May 23, the House of Commons was informed by a royal message of the recall of the ambassadors and the imminence of war. Pitt's speech on this occasion was considered by many as his finest effort; but, unfortunately, the alteration of the hour for the admission of strangers to the House accidentally prevented the reporters from attending the debate, and only a meagre outline of the speech has been preserved.

---

[1] 'He talked', reported Lord Whitworth, 'more like a captain of dragoons than the head of one of the greatest States of Europe.'

One of its most striking passages was the comparison of 'the irresistible force and overwhelming progress of French ambition to those dreadful convulsions of nature by which provinces and kingdoms are consumed and buried in ruins'. 'Can we contemplate', he asked, 'those scenes of havoc and destruction, without reflecting how soon that torrent of liquid fire may direct its ravages against ourselves?'

In another paragraph he denounced the practice of employing for secret service men who were officially admitted to the country as agents of the French Embassy.

The French Government (he said) then proceeded clandestinely to send these agents in the train of their ambassadors, and not content with this breach of the law of nations, they afterwards addressed to them instructions under the official character in which they had received admittance, and the object of these instructions was to direct them to take measures, in time of peace, for ascertaining the soundings of ports and for obtaining military information of districts—acts for which they would have been hanged as spies in time of war.

He concluded by calling on the Government to adopt not only the necessary naval and military measures, but also a strong financial policy. His peroration was somewhat as follows :

He repeated that he was aware that these measures could not be effected without material and extensive personal sacrifices and without great additional burthens, which must to a degree affect the ease, convenience, and even comfort of many classes of society. He lamented these consequences as much as any man, and if he saw any prospect that, by present concession, we could obtain a real and desirable interval of peace, security, and repose, he should be as anxious as any man to avoid the necessity of such arduous and painful exertions; but, under the present circumstances, a weak and timid policy could perhaps scarcely even postpone the moment when they would become indispensable for our existence, and would infallibly expose us to the certainty, at no distant period, of a similar struggle, with those means given out of our hands which we now possessed, and with the chance diminished of finally conducting it to a successful issue. We had not an option at this moment between the blessings of peace and the dangers of war. From the fatality of the times and the general state of the world, we must consider our lot as cast, by the decrees of Providence, in a time of peril and trouble. He trusted the temper and courage of the nation would conform itself to the duties of that situation—that we should be prepared, collectively and individually, to meet it with that resignation and fortitude, and, at the same time, with that active zeal and exertion, which, in proportion to the magnitude of the crisis, might be expected from a brave and free people; and that we should reflect, even in the hour of trial, what abundant reason we have to be grateful to Providence, for the distinction we enjoy over most of the countries of Europe, and for all the advantages and blessings which national wisdom and virtue have hitherto protected, and which it now depends on perseverance in the same just and honourable sentiments still to guard and to preserve.

At the close of the debate, an amendment to the address was rejected by 398 to 67.

2

The Undesirability of a Change of Government during War

June 3, 1803 [1]

On the outbreak of hostilities the general voice of the nation demanded the return to power of 'the pilot that weathered the storm'.[2] Pitt's position was delicate. He considered the Government's policy, and especially its financial measures, weak and dangerous. But he had promised to support Addington, and, unless Addington himself released him from his pledge, he declined to come forward. And, in any case, he considered it impolitic to force a Government from office in time of war unless the safety of the nation positively required it. When, therefore, a direct vote of censure was moved on June 3, he expressed his opinion as follows:

I am aware of the inconveniences that would result from supporting any measure which has the tendency of the present motion, unless the clearest necessity exists for it. Though I do not dispute the right of this House to address the King for the removal of ministers, yet nothing is more mischievous than a parliamentary interference by declared censure, rendering the continuance of ministers in office impossible, unless that interference is justified by extraordinary exigency of affairs. Not disputing the right of the House, I contend that the right is to be governed by a sound discretion and by the public interest. We must look to considerations of

---

[1] *Speeches*, vol. iv, p. 235.   [2] Canning's lines on Pitt.

public expediency and of public safety. There are some questions in the discussion of which gentlemen must feel more than they can well express, and this, with regard to the interference of Parliament for removing ministers, is one of them. Admitting even that there were considerable grounds of dissatisfaction at the conduct of ministers, would it tend to promote those exertions, to encourage those sacrifices, which the difficulty and danger of our situation require? Would our means of sustaining the struggle in which we are engaged, and of calling forth those resources necessary for our defence, be improved by cutting short the date of administration and unsettling the whole system of government? To displace one administration and to introduce a new one is not the work of a day. With all the functions of executive power suspended, with the regular means of communication between Parliament and the Throne interrupted, weeks, nay months, wasted in doubt, uncertainty and inaction,—how could the public safely consent to a state of things so violent and unnatural, as would result from Parliament rendering one administration incapable of exercising any public functions, without any other efficient Government being obtained in its stead?

I will venture to hint, also, that after such a step any administration that should succeed, be it what it might, (and what it would be must still depend upon the Crown) would feel itself placed in a most delicate situation. To put the matter as conscientiously and delicately as possible, would any set of men feel their introduction to power in these circumstances to be such as to enable them to discharge, in a manner satisfactory to themselves, the duties which so eventful a period must impose? These are considerations for the Crown and the public, and they outweigh all those which present themselves on a partial view of the advantages which could be hoped from a prosecution of that censure and dissolution of administration, to which the propositions tend.

The vote of censure was negatived by 275 to 34.

3

The Arming of the Nation

July 18, 1803 [1]

IN its first stages the new struggle was between France and England alone; and it was evident that Napoleon would now attempt at all costs to carry out his project of invasion. Measures were therefore taken to increase the military forces available for the defence of the country. The Army of Reserve or Additional Force Act provided for the raising by ballot of a new army of 50,000 men, to serve for four years as a Reserve for the Regular Army. The militia was re-embodied; and the Defence Act provided for the enrolment of a Volunteer Force.

On July 18, 1803, a bill was introduced 'to amend and render more effectual' the Defence Act. It provided for the enrolment by the Lords-Lieutenant in four classes of all men between the ages of 17 and 55. The first three classes—consisting of unmarried men under 50 and married men under 30 with not more than two children less than ten years old—were, under penalty of a fine, to

---

[1] *Speeches*, vol. iv, p. 240.

attend drill one day a week and to undergo from fourteen to twenty days' continuous training before the end of the year. Pitt supported the bill in the following speech :

I feel sincerely happy that this measure has been at length brought before the House, as it affords a prospect of that vigour which is necessary in the present conjuncture. I approve of its principle and object. It indeed is founded on the principles of the plan which, unconnected as I am with His Majesty's Government, I have thought it my duty to intimate to ministers. I have been always decidedly of opinion that such a measure was essentially necessary, in addition to our regular force, in order to put the question as to our domestic security entirely beyond all doubt. I am not now disposed, because, indeed, I do not think it necessary, to enter into any investigation of the degree of danger which the country has to apprehend, though I am aware it is material that the danger should not be underrated.

But to return to the measure before the House. I rejoice in its introduction as the most congenial in its spirit to the constitution of this country, and in its execution not at all likely to meet any obstacle from the character or disposition of the people. In its structure there is nothing new to our history ; in its tendency there is nothing ungrateful to our habits ; it embraces the interests, it avails itself of the energies, and it promises to establish the security of the country. It imposes no burthens, nor does it propose any arrangement of which it can be in the power of any class of the community to complain. Its object is the safety of all, without containing anything in its provisions offensive to any. It is perfectly agreeable to the best institutions of civilized society, and has for its basis the rudiments of our constitutional history.

It is obvious that, unless we make efforts adequate to the crisis in which we are placed, the country is insecure, and if those efforts cannot be effectual without compulsion, I trust no man can entertain a doubt of the propriety of resorting to it: but I have a confident expectation that compulsion will be unnecessary; that the number of voluntary offers will be sufficient to obviate the necessity of that disagreeable alternative. It is, however, an alternative of which I hope no man will disapprove, should the necessity arise, and least of all my right honourable friend,[1] who has not, on a former occasion, hesitated to recommend that compulsion. By His Majesty's prerogative he has it in his power, at any time that the country is threatened with invasion, to call out all his subjects for its defence; and the object of the measure before the House is, that the people, when called out, should be prepared to second his views, should be trained to military evolutions, should be ready to act with promptitude in any quarter where their services might be required, should be capable of conforming to orders without confusion or delay, of collecting with celerity and acting with decision. Such a plan is highly desirable; for it would be unwise to leave the defence of the country placed on our naval force, however superior, or in our regular army, however gallant and well disciplined, or even in the people armed *en masse*, unless previously drilled in military manœuvres and subject

[1] Windham.

to the directions of Government, who, by the measure before the House, are to be invested with ample powers of rendering the application of this force effectual, and of directing it to the several branches of public service which circumstances may call for.

The training of the people, however, should be prompt. No delay should be suffered, for there is not room to allow it. The efforts of those to be entrusted with the execution of this important duty should be unremitted, and indeed of all public and private individuals, until the country shall be completely secure against any attacks of the enemy. This security is certain, if every man will be active in his station; and of that activity I have not the least doubt, if Government will give the proper stimulus.

With respect to the observations of my noble friend,[1] upon the sentiments of my right honourable friend[2] as to the dangers of invasion, the noble lord seems to have quite mistaken his meaning; for my right honourable friend did not at all describe the danger in such a way as to damp the spirit of the country, but rather to excite its caution and energy, by removing the idea that an invasion is impracticable; and as soon as that delusive notion shall cease to prevail, I am quite certain that the whole tenor of my right honourable friend's remarks will be to produce confidence of security in the public mind, at the time when that feeling of confidence ought to exist, either with reference to the safety of the State or of individuals. The amount of our danger, therefore, it would be impolitic to conceal from the people. It was

---

[1] Lord Hawkesbury. [2] Windham.

the first duty of ministers to make it known, and after doing so, it should have been their study to provide against it, and to point out the means to the country by which it might be averted. It is quite impossible that a people will make adequate efforts to resist a danger, of the nature and extent of which they are studiously kept in ignorance. Upon those grounds I disapprove of the outcry so often raised against my right honourable friend and others, who have endeavoured by their speeches to rouse the energies of the country in the most effectual way, namely, by pointing out the necessity which existed for employing those energies. After, however, the grounds of apprehension shall have been extinguished, I have little doubt that the exertions of my right honourable friend will be to point the attention of ministers to such means of annoying the enemy as his ingenuity can suggest; and that those grounds will be removed with proper attention and activity on the part of ministers, I can have no doubt; for who can fear for the event, when millions of Englishmen are to be opposed to the detachment of the instruments of French ambition? And whatever the number of our invaders may be, they cannot, comparatively with the force I trust we shall have to oppose them, be more than a mere detachment.

I have not understood from the words of my right honourable friend that he had any fear as to the event, but that he wished solely to urge the adoption of such measures as might tend to give an effective direction to our natural strength. My right honourable friend has appeared to me very little to indulge in those gloomy presages which are ascribed to him by those of whose sluggishness, supineness, and inactivity he has been long in the habit of complaining. But I feel the most sincere gladness that the charge of supineness can no longer apply. His Majesty's ministers seem now determined upon rousing the spirit of the country, and upon giving that spirit a just and powerful direction. I hail, for the sake of my country, the appearance of this resolution. This is an auspicious day, though I cannot help expressing my surprise that this measure has not been submitted to the consideration of the House long ago: but even now I hope it will answer its purpose, that it will meet the approbation of Parliament, and that the people will promptly come forward to second its object. After the precise views of this country shall be made known, and after its dangers shall be fully understood, I am sure that no man will shrink from the calls of his country in this hour of peril, unless from motives such as he dare not avow.

Whether ministers ought sooner to have proposed this measure is a question into which I shall not now enter at large, but I will merely observe that, if it becomes necessary from a knowledge of the enemy's views, I believe no knowledge of that kind has been recently obtained— none of which ministers and the public were not aware at the time that war was declared, and even before. Why then was this important measure delayed? The danger to be looked for has been apprehended for a considerable time back, and upon the contingency of it my noble friend admits that, even during peace, a very large and expensive establishment was kept up. I cannot conceive any excuse that can be alleged for such procrastination.

It did not proceed, I suppose, from the desire of ministers to consider the scale and measure of our dangers, or from an opinion on their part, that it was better they should be tardy and gradual in their measures against the gigantic efforts of the enemy. This cannot have been the reason, and really I see no difference in the state of Europe, nor in the relative situation of this country with respect to France, from what it was at the commencement of the war. I am, therefore, at a loss to divine the motives which have influenced the conduct of ministers, and why this measure was not brought forward long since. If there was no necessity to be active, if there was leisure for slow deliberation, then of course the period is not such, in their estimation, as to call for any extraordinary promptitude of exertion, or such as ought to excite alarm; but, in truth, if there was any particular measure which claimed precedency, it was that now under consideration, which could not interfere with any other military arrangements. The question simply is this—was it prudent to postpone the introduction of a measure which had for its object to prepare the people for a general armament, and which preparation must necessarily consume some time before it could be efficient? Yet, in the wisdom of ministers, this is the particular measure which is to be delayed to the last.

I will not, however, stop to inquire into the time which has been already lost; but I shall express my earnest hope that no time will be wasted hereafter—that every instant will be actively engaged until the country be completely safe. I think that some arrangements should be made to connect the different departments of the executive authority, so that, upon orders issued from Government to the Lords-Lieutenant of counties, the people might be immediately set in motion; so that, without interfering with agriculture, which should not by any means be disturbed, the several classes might be disciplined, to attend the drill at least two days in each week, to assemble in particular places throughout the country; the limitation of distance from the residence of each man to the place of assembly, to be about six miles, the time of attendance to be not less than half a day. The distance I propose is not more than the stout English peasantry are in the habit of going, when led to a cricket match or any rural amusement. These men, in my conception, might be disciplined by soldiers on furlough, who, on being called back to their regiment, when danger should actually reach our shores, might be enabled to bring with them one hundred sturdy recruits, prepared for military action through their means.

With regard to the motion before the House, I must say that it is not liable to the objections advanced by my right honourable friend, on the ground that it would have a compulsory operation, for in fact it does not propose to resort to compulsion, if the object can be attained by voluntary offers; and I am of opinion that the purposes may be so effected. These voluntary offers may be promoted considerably by the presence of the nobility and gentry in their respective districts, and on that account, I rejoice in the prospect that we are soon to separate, not only with reference to this, but to the other measures which have passed the House, and to the execution of which the presence I have alluded to must materially contribute. The great men of the country to animate by their example, to countenance by their authority, and to assist by their advice the operations of the people, have it in their power to achieve the most important good, to excite a zeal and devotion to the public cause, and to diffuse their own spirit through all ranks of the community.

With a view to those desirable advantages, I wish that the session may be short; and I hope that as little time as possible may be lost in examining and arranging the details of this important measure, and that, whatever reasons we may have to look for voluntary offers, we shall not rely on those offers altogether; for, as the representatives of the people, we are bound to provide for their safety, and to provide a sufficient force. Though they may not be disposed to take care of themselves, it is our duty to take care of them. If, therefore, voluntary offers shall not be adequate to the purpose, we must of course resort to compulsory proceedings.

The drilling of the men is, as I have already observed, the principal object to be attended to; but I beg it to be understood that, in my opinion, the poorer classes should be remunerated for the time they may be engaged in discipline. I hope it is so intended, though I have not heard anything of the kind mentioned by my right honourable friend in the opening. The man who is taken from his labour for the public safety, ought certainly to be paid for his time; and this would serve to reconcile such persons to a practice which, otherwise, would be justly considered a very great hardship.

As to the trouble which the nobility and gentry may

be called upon to submit to, in this general armament, I cannot do them the injustice of supposing that they would not submit to it with alacrity, or that questions of mere personal convenience would, in such a crisis as the present, have any weight with them.

In the execution of this measure, I do not like the idea of waiting for the slow progress of a ballot. I think that unless the volunteers should, within a certain date, comply with the condition prescribed, their consent should not be waited for. In those parishes where the voluntary offers should not be promptly made, the compulsory levy should be promptly enforced. This compulsion, however, would not, according to my apprehension, be in any instance necessary, if the Lords-Lieutenant of counties, with the deputies and other persons of respectability, would go round from house to house in their respective districts, and solicit the people to come forward. This I know I am not too sanguine in believing would effectually accomplish, within one month, the ends we have in view without any compulsion whatever, particularly when they are apprised fully of the necessity for their service; when they are encouraged by the advice of their superiors; and when they have the satisfaction of knowing that the legislature have deemed their country's danger demands it.

Much has been said of the danger of arming the people. I confess that there was a time when that fear would have had some weight; but there never was a time when there could have been any fear of arming the whole people of England, and particularly not under the present circumstances. I never, indeed, entertained any apprehensions from a patriot army regularly officered, according to the manner specified in the measure before the House, however I might hesitate to permit the assemblage of a tumultuary army otherwise constituted. From an army to consist of the round bulk of the people, no man who knows the British character could have the least fear—if it even were to include the disaffected; for they would bear so small a proportion to the whole, as to be incapable of doing mischief, however mischievously disposed. There was indeed a time when associations of traitors, systematically organized, excited an apprehension of the consequences of a sudden armament of the populace: but that time is no more, and the probability is now, as occurred in the case of the volunteers, that, if there are still any material number of disaffected, by mixing them with the loyal part of the community, the same patriotic zeal, the same submission to just authority, will be soon found to pervade the whole body, and that all will be equally anxious to defend their country or perish in the attempt; that the good and the loyal will correct the vicious disposition of the disaffected, will rectify their errors, and set right their misguided judgements. We may thus enlist those among our friends who would otherwise, perhaps, become the auxiliaries of our enemy.

Under all these circumstances I feel that the objections urged upon this score are not tenable, and that they ought not to have any weight against a measure which is necessary to the preservation of public order and private happiness.

The bill was read a first time.

Pitt's speeches on the third reading of this bill and on the various measures which succeeded it display in their wealth of technical detail the mastery he had acquired of the whole subject of national defence. The following extracts contain his views on the more important and interesting points.

i. *The maximum of effort needed* [1]

I am ready to admit to the honourable officer,[2] that our regular army is not quite so great as we could wish in this country, but we have provided means for augmenting it to a degree much greater than was ever known in this country; and in addition to all this, we are now providing an immense irregular force, the advantages to be derived from which are admitted and confirmed by the honourable officer himself, being indeed too obvious to be disputed by any one. As far, therefore, as relates to the description and to the extent of our force, Parliament has provided means, which to the honourable officer himself (cautious, honourably cautious, and anxious as he is for the safety of his country) appear sufficient to place this country in a state of absolute safety. All this is undoubtedly matter of great consolation; but at the same time it will not justify us in diminishing our anxiety, or in relaxing our efforts, for its completion, because there must remain some interval before all these plans are completely arranged and organized and brought to that state of perfection at which I hope they will, however, soon arrive; but even supposing that all the measures which I have stated were brought to perfec-

[1] Speech of July 22, 1803 (*Speeches*, vol. iv, p. 251).
[2] Colonel Crawford.

tion, still it would not dispense us from the necessity of adopting other means of defence, particularly in two points of view.

Suppose all the objects attained at this moment, yet the foundation of our security would not be these objects, however completely attained. Against the arduous and most desperate struggle in which we may be engaged, all these kinds of strength can only give us this kind of security, that if we are not wanting to ourselves, if we have not forgotten our national character, but remember who we are, and what we are contending for, the contest will be glorious to us and must terminate in the complete discomfiture of the enemy and ultimate security to this kingdom. But if there remain any measure, by the adoption of which our safety may be yet rendered, not only more certain, perhaps, but more easy; by which our defence can be secured with less effusion of blood, less anxiety of mind, less interruption of the industry of the nation, less, I will not say of alarm, but of the evils, the inconveniences, the agitation that necessarily belong to a great struggle of this kind, however short, or however certain its issue may be;—in a contest of such a nature it certainly would be most unwise to run any hazard of protracting it, or to neglect any means of shortening it still more if possible;—if, upon these grounds, I say, it can be pointed out to me that there are any means by which our regular army could be immediately increased and all our regiments completed, I should say that, although we are safe without it, yet our interest, our prosperity, and every object that can influence us, would require that such a measure should be adopted.

ii. *The need of trained officers* [1]

I certainly feel, as I ought to do, great distrust of my own opinion upon military subjects, and I always state those opinions with great deference ; but I believe that it is universally admitted by all officers, that new recruits poured into an old corps, which has a number of experienced officers, will much sooner acquire a knowledge of discipline and become good soldiers, than they will if they are left in a corps by themselves, whatever pains may be taken in their instruction. Taking that as an established point, I was therefore surprised and disappointed when I heard my right honourable friend the Secretary at War, instead of proposing to diffuse the 40,000 men of the army of reserve over the thirty-nine or forty battalions that are in England, in which case they would have all the advantages of all the officers of those old corps—instead of this, he talks of dividing them among thirteen battalions, by which means all the advantage which they would derive from the instruction of a great number of old and experienced officers would be very much diminished.

I know it may be said that the commissions in the army of reserve will in a great degree be filled up from the half-pay list, which certainly contains a great number of officers perfectly well qualified to instruct and discipline any men placed under their command. But in the first place, it must be recollected that the half-pay list would not furnish any non-commissioned officers, who are certainly the most essential in training raw recruits. There

[1] Speech of July 22, 1803 (*Speeches*, vol. iv, p. 254).

is, however, another consideration which strikes my mind, and which I believe has not yet been suggested to the House. Our situation in point of security will certainly be improved by the adoption of the measure which is now before us; but it must be recollected that, while it improves, it alters our situation. If we had voted only the army of reserve, undoubtedly it might be filled with able and experienced officers from the half-pay list; but we must recollect that, in addition to the army of reserve, we have voted an army of between three and four hundred thousand men.

That we shall have no difficulty in procuring the men who are to compose this force, I am perfectly satisfied, because the spirit of the country is now raised in the capital, and will from thence rapidly pervade all the extremities of the Empire. That spirit was first kindled in the north, from thence it has extended to the metropolis, and is now catching from town to town, from village to village, and very shortly the whole kingdom will, I am convinced, manifest one scene of activity, of animation, and of energy, displaying in its native lustre the character of Englishmen. That the men, therefore, will be procured with the greatest facility, I have not the smallest doubt; but we shall then want the means of preparing and drilling them, with all the accuracy that the shortness of the time will admit. Does it not then occur to the House that we shall have infinitely more use for the services of officers not attached to regiments? Does it not occur to gentlemen, that, in addition to the noblemen, the gentry, and the yeomanry of the country, many of whom will serve as officers, it would be advisable, to every three or four officers of this description, to add one or two from the half-pay list? Would not the adoption of this plan greatly accelerate the training and perfecting of this new force? It therefore does appear most clearly to me, that by allowing a greater number of battalions of the line to receive the army of reserve, you would have a greater number of officers on the half-pay to discipline the irregular force.

iii. *The protection of London* [1]

I know very well that the manly feelings and, if I may say so, the obstinate courage of my right honourable friend,[2] will not let him believe that the French would offer us such an insult as to come over here to fight us for our capital. I am sure I shall not be suspected of depreciating or of not placing due confidence in the army, in the navy, or in the courage of the people of England; on the contrary, I am firmly convinced that the enemy will find us to be invincible. But it must be admitted that in war there are accidents depending sometimes upon a day or an hour, in which, with the bravest and most numerous army, the enemy, by hazarding an operation for which in any other service a general would be broke or shot, but which a French general would attempt, because he knows he would be broke or shot if he did not, might obtain an advantage, the consequences of which might be most serious if some such measure as that recommended by the honourable officer

---

[1] Speech of July 22, 1803 (*Speeches*, vol. iv, p. 259).
[2] C. P. Yorke, Secretary at War.

was not adopted. We unfortunately know that attempts of this kind may be made, however rash or desperate, for those who will make them know that they will not appear so to Buonaparte. The proud despot of France will, however, have reason to tremble on his usurped throne, when the people of France find that they have sacrificed hundreds of thousands of men to gratify his ambition and his revenge. With respect to that despot himself, he would, I am sure, feel as little hesitation in sacrificing a hundred thousand Frenchmen, as he would millions of Englishmen if he had them within his grasp.

In arranging, therefore, the plan of national defence, we ought not to estimate upon probabilities merely. It is not enough for us to say that if he is eccentric and mad, he will pay the price of his madness and folly; we must take care that we do not pay for it first; we must not now disdain to adopt precautions which were formerly thought unnecessary. I cannot, therefore, agree with the short and decisive opinion of my right honourable friend, who, when the honourable officer recommended it to Government to fortify London, replied, 'I say, do not fortify it.' I must enter my protest against such language. He says, he would not affront the people of England by supposing that, while they have 80,000 seamen on board their fleet and have such an army as is now on foot, it could be necessary to fortify the capital. Why, Sir, in the first place as to the navy, we must remember, that although we have 80,000 seamen, a great part of them are detached on service in different quarters of the world, and consequently could not in any degree prevent an invasion at home. I am certainly not denying that the enemy would find great difficulty and danger in transporting his army to this country, but it is by running desperate risks that he can alone hope for success. We may have a proud navy of ships of the line and frigates—I will not now stop to inquire whether that navy might not have been in readiness sooner—but I can conceive a case in which ships of that kind would not be sufficient to meet an innumerable flotilla of boats issuing from all the ports, harbours, and creeks on the opposite coast of France, and covering the Channel for several miles in length. Whether, in order to meet a force of this kind, it would not be wise to multiply the smaller sort of our naval force and to mount them with guns of heavy metal and with carronades, I do not know; I hope something of this kind has been done already. It is admitted, indeed, that our navy, great and powerful as it is, cannot be relied on with absolute certainty to prevent an invasion; because if it could, there would be no occasion for all the precautions which we are adopting.

But it is said, we ought not to fortify London because our ancestors did not fortify it. Why, Sir, that is no argument, unless you can show me that our ancestors were in the same situation that we are. Look back to the days when the genius, the wisdom, and the fortitude of Elizabeth defeated the proud and invincible Armada, fitted out by Spain to conquer us—and I trust that the invincible battalion from France will meet with the same fate—we must admit that not only the situation of this country, but of all Europe, is changed; and it is absurd to say that, when the circumstances are changed, the means of defence should be precisely the same. We might as well be told that, because our ancestors fought with arrows and with lances, we ought to use them now, and that we ought to consider shields and corslets as affording a secure defence against musketry and artillery.

iv. *The magnitude of the danger* [1]

Englishmen must look to this as a species of contest from which, by the extraordinary favour of Divine Providence, we have been for a long series of years exempted. If we are now at length called upon to take our share in it, we must meet it with just gratitude for the exemptions we have hitherto enjoyed, and with a firm determination to support it with courage and resolution. We must show ourselves worthy, by our conduct on this occasion, of the happiness which we have hitherto enjoyed and which, by the blessing of God, I hope we shall continue to enjoy. We ought to have a due sense of the magnitude of the danger with which we are threatened; we ought to meet it in that temper of mind which produces just confidence, which neither despises nor dreads the enemy; and while on the one hand we accurately estimate the danger with which we are threatened at this awful crisis, we must recollect on the other hand what it is we have at stake, what it is we have to contend for. It is for our property, it is for our liberty, it is for our independence, nay, for our existence as a nation; it is for our character, it is for our very name as Englishmen, it is for everything dear and valuable to man on this side of the grave.

[1] Speech of July 22, 1803 (*Speeches*, vol. iv, p. 262).

Parliament has now provided ample means for our defence; it remains for the executive Government to employ them to the best advantage. The regular army must be augmented to that point to which the means are now given to raise it; the militia must be kept high in numbers and unbroken in spirit; the auxiliary force must be as promptly raised and disciplined as the nature of things will admit; nothing must be omitted that military skill can suggest to render the contest certain as to its success and short in its duration. If Government show the same determination to apply all those means that Parliament has shown in providing them; if the people follow up the example which the legislature has set them, we are safe. Then I may say, without being too sanguine, that the result of this great contest will ensure the permanent security, the eternal glory of this country; that it will terminate in the confusion, the dismay, and the shame of our vaunting enemy; that it will afford the means of animating the spirits, of rousing the courage, of breaking the lethargy of the surrounding nations of Europe; and I trust that, if a fugitive French army should reach its own shores after being driven from our coasts, it will find the people of Europe reviving in spirits and anxious to retaliate upon France all the wrongs, all the oppressions, they have suffered from her; and that we shall at length see that wicked fabric destroyed which was raised upon the prostitution of liberty, and which has caused more miseries, more horrors to France and to the surrounding nations, than are to be paralleled in any part of the annals of mankind.

v. *A permanent system of defence* [1]

Now, Sir, in reference to the state of Europe, let us see how this measure operates upon our future safety. Unless we can be perfectly sure, and indeed I know not any degree of foresight and sagacity that should tempt us to suppose that it would not be folly and presumption to be sure—unless, I say, we can be perfectly sure that at the end of the present war (and when that period shall arrive we have no means to calculate or ascertain) we shall see Europe and France reduced to such a state, that we may return to our own system ; unless we shut our eyes and are wilfully blind to our destruction, we may find ourselves obliged for years to make the country a more military nation than it has ever been before thought necessary. Now, if this be the case, there are only two ways by which it can be effected; either by laying the foundation of a large supply in peace that may be brought forward in a prepared state upon a sudden emergency, or by creating a large force which, though disembodied when its services are not necessary, may be reproduced as occasion shall require. Those who look back to the public feeling at the commencement of the present war, cannot surely forget how desirable it would have been, had we attained that state at which we have only now arrived, after several months of anxiety and protracted danger. With this experience will you then have a regular force which is only efficient while embodied, or a force which may be produced for the necessary

[1] Speech of June 18, 1804 (*Speeches*, vol. iv, p. 355).

occasion without the constitutional objection to a large regular army? Even the very persons, who are jealous of a standing army in peace, recommend it in war; and the present measure [1] is such as may be easily efficient when necessary, and facilitates the filling up of the regular force. Upon every ground of public safety and economy, it is particularly recommended to those who would have a large force in war and a small one in peace. It is the means of a provisional force, which is attended with no expense in peace, and may in time of war be rapidly brought forward for the emergency.

A right honourable gentleman [2] says, it is not wise to change the character, manners, and habits of the people. The general principle is right; but if it be necessary to have a large force, I ask, what is so little likely to interfere with the habits and manners of the people as the present measure, which establishes no permanent force and only requires a month's exercise in the year? To hear him, one would suppose it would operate so great a change, that the plough was to stop, and the country was to be converted into a nation of Spartan soldiers; and yet the measure is neither more nor less than to raise by a milder mode that very number of men which the Parliament thinks necessary, I mean 16,000 in England, and 3,000 in Ireland, being the amount of the present deficiency; and when that is completed, to raise annually a force of 12,000. Now, whether this is likely to produce a change in the genius and habits of the nation, I leave to the understanding of the House.

[1] The Permanent Additional Force Bill.   [2] Addington.

vi. *The new era* [1]

In proposing to the House the permanent establishment of the army of reserve, though certainly on a very modified system, I am sensible that objections may be readily started against the proposition. But, Sir, let it be remembered that the times in which we live are not ordinary times. When we are called to encounter extraordinary and unprecedented dangers, we must lay our account to submitting to extraordinary and unprecedented difficulties. If we are called on to undergo great sacrifices, we must bear in mind the interesting objects which these sacrifices may enable us to defend and to secure. I need not remind the House that we are come to a new era in the history of nations; that we are called to struggle for the destiny, not of this country alone, but of the civilized world. We must remember that it is not for ourselves alone that we submit to unexampled privations. We have for ourselves the great duty of self-preservation to perform; but the duty of the people of England now is of a nobler and higher order. We are in the first place to provide for our security against an enemy whose malignity to this country knows no bounds: but this is not to close the views or the efforts of our exertion in so sacred a cause. Amid the wreck and the misery of nations, it is our just exultation that we have continued superior to all that ambition or that despotism could effect; and our still higher exultation ought to be, that we provide not only for our own safety, but hold out a prospect to nations now bending

[1] Speech of April 25, 1804 (*Speeches*, vol. iv, p. 334).

under the iron yoke of tyranny of what the exertions of a free people can effect, and that, at least in this corner of the world, the name of liberty is still revered, cherished, and sanctified.

vii. *A 'mosquito' fleet*[1]

It has been truly said by my honourable friend[2] that the naval defence of the land is our national passion, in which we indulge all the excesses of instinctive pride. With this generous propensity, let us look to the collective strength of the enemy on the opposite coast,[3] which seems to realize the fictions of ancient story. Can it be supposed, with this view before us, we can for a moment forget all the advantages of our insular situation; the glories of our maritime strength; the navy which has extended our commerce, which has established our authority, which has raised us to the rank we enjoy amongst surrounding empires, and which has conduced to our command and aggrandizement in every quarter of the earth? Can we, I say, in the moment of danger, fail to remember this grand source of public security? In such a crisis as this, am I, with all the indifference of a cold comparison, to be referred to the commencement of the former war with France, when she was torn by civil dissensions—when she was encompassed by hostile nations in array against her—when all Europe was leagued for her destruction? Is that period to be assimilated to the present, when we are to meet her single-handed, without the co-operation of one ally; and are

---

[1] Speech of March 15, 1804 (*Speeches*, vol. iv, p. 299).
[2] Wilberforce.
[3] See *infra*, p. 339.

we to limit our exertions to what they were at the time when circumstances were thus totally different? Yet it will be recollected that then the navy of this country, at least, was so far prepared, that scarcely one fleet ventured to forsake the ports of France that did not supply new laurels to the gallant defenders of their country on the tempestuous element by which we are surrounded. The enemy, who have lost their internal trade, their exterior commerce, their fisheries, the very foundation of their navy, have, in the prosecution of a gigantic enterprise, created an artificial marine of prodigious extent; and are we not to proportion our means to the new circumstances in which we are placed, to the new perils to which we are exposed? And are we to have the ardour of all our generous passions dissipated by the application of this 'cold comparison'? I trust, therefore, I shall not be accused of disgraceful fear, of idle panic, if I contend our exertions ought at this moment to exceed all former precedent, because the dangers by which we are encompassed exceed all former peril. Unless I am much mistaken, the kind of minor marine I have recommended is a force easily prepared, neither of tedious nor expensive construction.

But gentlemen have argued as if I wished to lay aside the floating castles by which this country is protected, and to disband the British navy. I was sorry to hear an honourable admiral[1] deviate into this gross misapprehension. True it is, I have expressed some confidence in gun-vessels, for a particular purpose; but have I ever been insane enough to express a doubt that for the

[1] Sir Edward Pellew.

blockade of Brest, Toulon, Ferrol, and the various ports occupied by the ships of the enemy, our men-of-war and our frigates should not be employed? Even should the flotilla of the enemy venture toward our coasts, I have no doubt that a wide destruction and general confusion will be occasioned by the annoyance they will receive from our regular navy. But some will probably escape among the vast multitude; and am I culpable in recommending that this minor navy should be prepared, under such an emergency, to render certain that security which would otherwise be only probable? Our first defence, then, is by our larger ships; our next in the shallows by our flotilla; the third expedient is, to prevent the landing of the enemy; and the fourth and least convenient is, when they have gained a footing on English ground, to meet them in the field of slaughter. Will gentlemen, who affect to despise these gun-vessels, not admit that between the ports of Harwich and Portsmouth there are numerous banks and shallows where ships of the line are incapable of approaching the shore? I am not ashamed to say, before professional gentlemen, however eminent, that if we neglect to provide against contingencies by the kind of force to which I have now adverted, we do not do all in our power to conduce to the national safety.

Terms of derision have been employed to render this species of marine defence contemptible, and it has been called a 'mosquito fleet'.

viii. *A Case of Treason?* [1]

In the summer of 1804, a resident of Banffshire, named James Morison, refused one day to allow his servant, Garrow, who was a private in the Banffshire Volunteers, to attend on the morrow an inspection of the corps, on the plea that he must finish thatching his barn. Garrow finished the work during the night and again applied for leave next morning. It was again refused, and Garrow, having attended the inspection, was at once dismissed without payment of the wages due to him. No action at law could be brought against Morison, except for recovery of the wages, but the Lord Advocate of Scotland (Mr. C. Hope) wrote an official letter to the local Sheriff Substitute, in which he described Morison's conduct as atrocious, and expressed the hope that he would be made to feel his guilt by the public opinion of the county. On June 22, the question whether the Lord Advocate had exceeded his powers and done Morison an injustice was debated in the House of Commons; and Pitt expressed himself as follows:

It is contended, that the conduct of the learned lord was not only unnecessarily severe, but that he stepped out of his province in this particular exercise of it. Sir, if we are to draw any analogy between this and other acts, I think occasions may occur, where it may be as necessary to prevent the thinning of those ranks that were to oppose the enemy as it was to prohibit the departure of men who intended to swell the ranks of the enemy. As to Morison's conduct, I see not upon what grounds of justice it can be defended. It is acknowledged, that he discharged this man, although he had done the work he was ordered to perform, and that at

---

[1] Speech of June 22, 1804 (*Parliamentary Debates*, vol. ii, p. 815).

a time of the year when he must have remained six months out of employment; and in aggravation of this inhumanity he has the dishonesty to refuse him the payment of his wages. As to the argument that his attending that muster was of no consequence, that I must peremptorily deny. What, when it was to be inspected by the commanding officer of the district, and that at a time when, from every information that had been received, an attempt at landing might have been hourly expected from the enemy! Placed in the arduous and responsible situation that the learned lord was, was it not natural that he should employ all the reasonable means in his power to discountenance the possibility of such practices in others? Here was no sentence, no trial. Suppose that the signal was actually flying that the enemy were landing, was this Mr. Morison to say to his servant, 'No; you shan't march to oppose the enemy, you shall stay and thatch my barn'? Why, Sir, if such were the conduct of one of those agricultural philosophers, I should consider such apathy, at such a moment, as something bordering on disaffection, I had almost said treason. If the learned lord had shown such apathy in providing for the defence and security of the country, he would ill deserve the high situation he holds, and which I trust he will long continue to hold, if not disabled by a vote of this House.

4

Before Trafalgar

June 20, 1805 [1]

IN the spring of 1804 the Addington Ministry at last fell, and in May Pitt returned to power. Recognizing that the nation was unanimous in its determination to resist Napoleon, and aware of the lack of talent in the ranks of his own followers, he at once attempted to form a coalition Government. But George III obstinately declined to have any dealings with Fox, and, though Fox patriotically urged his friends to join the Government, they declined the responsibilities forbidden to their leader; and the Prime Minister, his health already dangerously weakened, was compelled to face Napoleon with what was wittily described as the Administration of William and Pitt. He resolutely squared his shoulders to bear, practically alone, the whole gigantic burden.

In its early stages the war moved slowly. Napoleon at once seized the strategic points in the neutral territories of Naples and Hanover; and opened his campaign, extended and elaborated in later years, for the commercial starvation of these islands by closing the ports under his control to British goods. At the same time he set on foot his equally grandiose designs for the invasion of England. They were supposed originally to have aimed at the construction of a huge navy of 130 ships of the line, which, supported by the Spanish, Dutch, and Genoese fleets, was to obtain the command of the sea by sheer weight of numbers. But this plan would have taken years to carry into effect, and Napoleon soon concentrated on more immediate measures. He began the

[1] *Parliamentary Debates*, vol. v, p. 527.

construction of an enlarged naval harbour and an arsenal at Antwerp; and all along the coast of Belgium and France, as far as Dieppe, he collected the 'Army of England', some 100,000 strong, with its head-quarters at Boulogne. To cover the passage of the army a flotilla of gunboats was constructed, and fortified bases prepared for their protection. It was soon apparent, however, that small craft were useless in rough weather or against the watchful British fleet, and that the crossing could only be achieved if the enemy could be decoyed or driven from the Channel. 'Give me the Channel for three days,' he said, 'and the business is done.'

It was the Admiralty's task to render this impossible. Maintaining a squadron in home waters to watch Napoleon's flotilla, they dispatched Nelson to Toulon and Cornwallis to Brest, where the two main French fleets lay safe in harbour. Napoleon's main idea, constantly modified in detail, was that the Toulon fleet should slip out, sail up the Atlantic coast, liberating the lesser French squadrons at the various ports *en route*; drive off Cornwallis by superior numbers, and, thus effecting a junction with the Brest fleet, proceed in overwhelming force to the Channel.

For nearly two years the British fleets patiently rode out the storms of the Atlantic and the Mediterranean. At last, at the end of March 1805, taking advantage of the wind and of the looseness of the blockade, designed by Nelson to tempt him out to a decisive engagement, Villeneuve escaped from Toulon, and, evading Nelson, who expected him to make for Egypt, slipped past Gibraltar and, joining the Spanish fleet at Cadiz, steered for the West Indies. His instructions were to cruise in those waters for a month, attacking British possessions and commerce, and then to re-cross the Atlantic and carry out the plan for the freeing of the French and Spanish[1] fleets and the descent upon the Channel.

[1] Spain declared war on Great Britain in December 1804.

On the news of Villeneuve's escape the naval administration of the Government was vigorously criticized in the House of Commons. On June 20 a hostile motion was proposed by Grey, who, having painted the military aspect of the war in gloomy colours, proceeded to describe its naval aspect in the following terms:[1]

'We have added three ships of the line to our navy. France by extraordinary exertions has, in the course of last year, added fleets to hers. The navy of France cannot now be estimated at less than forty-eight ships of the line; the Dutch have eleven sail; Spain in all has sixty-one sail; but, allowing a great number to be unfit for service, I believe I am within the mark when I say that Spain contributes to the navy of France twenty-five ships of the line fit for service. Thus France has in all eighty-three ships of the line at her disposal, being eight less than the force we now have. This disproportion, indeed, is greatly increased by the superiority of skill and discipline possessed by our seamen. But still we see that France, within so short a space, has made advances towards us altogether unexpected. She has contrived, too, by well-combined plans and through the want of vigour and intelligence in our Government, to send to sea considerable expeditions. Occupying large divisions of our fleets in blockades along her whole line of coast, she has equipped armaments that have escaped our vigilance, have gone to our distant colonies, committing depredations, if not to the extent they might have done, depredations highly prejudicial to our interests and disgraceful to the nation. It certainly is an extraordinary spectacle at the end of two years of a war undertaken to limit the aggrandizement and reduce the power of France, and that too under circumstances, particularly as to the naval state of France, peculiarly favourable, that we now see her more powerful than ever on the Continent, growing formidable on the

[1] *Parliamentary Debates*, vol. v, p. 498.

ocean, threatening our foreign possessions with a powerful armament, of which, though we are ignorant of the destination, we are almost certain that it will go to some quarter where we have not an adequate force to oppose it. The circumstances attending the sailing of the Toulon fleet and its junction with that of Cadiz are of themselves sufficiently extraordinary to call for inquiry. The Toulon fleet sailed twice without being met by our fleet in the Mediterranean, which not only shows our want of intelligence, but the want of a convenient station on that sea from which to observe the movements of the enemy, a circumstance, by the way, which may serve to illustrate the importance of Malta, to which, at the beginning of the war, so much was attached. It sailed twice, however, without interruption, and having effected a junction with the Spaniards at Cadiz on the 9th of April, proceeded to sea again. And is it not an extraordinary circumstance that now, on the 20th of June, we should be ignorant of the destination of so large an armament, which sailed from Cadiz on the 9th of April, to strike a blow at some of our foreign settlements? Indeed, so extraordinary is this affair, that the House ought not to separate till it be investigated.'

To this attack on the Admiralty and on Nelson, Pitt briefly replied as follows:

The right honourable member next adverted to the state of the navy. It was true that there was in ships of the line a very trifling increase, but when it was considered how many had been necessarily laid up in the docks to be repaired, he was sure that the exertions of the noble lord lately at the head of the Admiralty,[1] to expedite this important branch of the public service,

[1] Dundas (Lord Melville).

were entitled to the gratitude of the country. Equally entitled to approbation was his zealous activity in providing stores of every description, and his diligence in hastening the fitting out of that inferior species of naval force which the peculiar circumstances of the country required.

He denied that the escape of the French squadrons at all evinced want of knowledge or activity on the part of the Admiralty. On every one of the stations where the squadrons of the enemy were, they had been blockaded, and, if by accident the blockade was raised, there was no proof of the least blame attached to any one individual. It was quite impossible, great as was the amount of our naval force, to have squadrons in all parts of the world to which a hostile fleet might by accident direct its course. He vindicated the conduct of the Admiralty as to the first sailing of the Toulon fleet. It was not then ascertained that they had gone out of the Mediterranean. On the contrary, there was then reason to suppose that they had in view an object much nearer than any attempt either on our West-India islands or the Brazils,[1] though he was not at liberty to speak with greater freedom on the subject. . . . Every reasonable precaution had been taken on the part of Government; but no vigilance, however active, could at all times prevent the escape of an enemy, continually on the watch to elude us.

The sequel is well known. Villeneuve, hotly pursued by Nelson to the West Indies and back again to Europe, was met on his return by Calder, with fifteen British

[1] Egypt.

ships to his twenty-one, off Cape Finisterre (July 22, 1805). The action was indecisive, but the French admiral, discouraged and irresolute, put in to Corunna, and presently, abandoning the move on Brest, retreated to Cadiz. The great plan had thus finally broken down; it remained to destroy the chance of its resumption. Barham, the vigorous old admiral, on whose appointment at the age of 80 to succeed Dundas at the Admiralty Pitt had insisted, ordered a strong concentration off the Spanish coast, a measure which agreed with Pitt's own intentions. Nelson, now back in England, was sent out to take command, and on October 21 he made British sea-power finally unchallengeable and an invasion of England practically impossible by the Battle of Trafalgar.

5
The Concert of Europe
June 21, 1805 [1]

TRAFALGAR secured England from invasion, but it was only on land that the war could be brought to a final issue, and it was a difficult task to construct yet another coalition of continental Powers against Napoleon. As before, however, Napoleon himself lightened the difficulty by his restless aggressions. His arbitrary treatment of Holland and Switzerland, his occupation of Hanover and Naples, his kidnapping on neutral soil, and hasty execution, of the Duc d'Enghien (March 21, 1804), convinced the ardent young Czar, Alexander, who had welcomed the French Revolution as a triumph of liberty, that the new master of France was no less despotic and far more unscrupulous than the monarchs of the *ancien régime* While, therefore, Pitt was still working out an acceptable basis for a new league, the Czar proposed (June 26,

[1] *Parliamentary Debates*, vol. v, p. 542.

1804) a definite alliance, of which the primary object was ' to deliver from Napoleon's yoke the peoples whom he oppressed '. But, delayed by disputes as to the future settlement of Europe, the Anglo-Russian Convention was not signed till April 11, 1805. Sweden, meantime, came forward as a third member of the League.

It was a still more tedious business to bring Austria into line. Alexander pressed on one side, Pitt on the other, with the offer of an advance of four months' subsidy into the bargain. But the final push came from Napoleon. In the previous December he had accepted from the hands of the Pope himself in Notre Dame the imperial crown of France. Now, on May 26, in Milan Cathedral, he crowned himself King of Italy with the iron crown of the Lombard kings; and promptly proceeded to annex the Genoese Republic to the French Empire. Thus provoked, Austria at last decided to draw the sword once more, and in July the Third Coalition was definitely formed. Prussia, as usual, stood aloof, and so prejudiced, and ultimately wrecked, its chances of success.

While negotiations with Austria were in progress, Napoleon again put forward proposals of peace. Pitt rejected them, but, in the debate of June 21, on a vote of credit to enable Pitt to subsidize our continental allies, Fox maintained that the policy of 'arousing Europe' was misguided, because Europe believed that we were fighting for our selfish interests. 'Whatever we might say', he said,[1] 'of our disinterestedness, whatever of moderation and forbearance, Europe had a different opinion, which might possibly be wrong; but we had a character to gain or retrieve on the occasion.' He therefore urged that a favourable reply should be returned to Buonaparte's overtures, and that England and Russia should conclude a separate peace with France without consulting the wishes of the other Powers.

[1] *Parliamentary Debates*, vol. v, p. 540.

Pitt opened his reply by explaining the object of the vote of credit.

That object is to form such a co-operation with the continental Powers, as will ultimately lead to a secure and lasting peace. Now what I conceive the House to have distinctly agreed in is that a general concert would be far better than if any attempt had been made at a separate pacification. That is the general opinion, and even the opinion of many of those who do not exactly agree with me. But from what the honourable gentleman has now said, I think that he has abandoned this principle so far as to say that a separate peace would be better than any concert formed for the purpose either of peace or of war. His observations seemed to go this length, that all attempts at releasing ourselves from our present situation were improper, because it might happen that our affairs might be made worse. This is a mode of reasoning that would lead all the Powers on the Continent to remain supine under the oppression of France, and never attempt to oppose her schemes of ambition and aggrandizement. Why? Because in opposing these schemes, they run a risk of making matters worse. But are they to wait till the power of France is much more increased and much more confirmed; till their own resources are much more reduced than they are at present, and till the power of resistance is gone? This would indeed be exposing themselves to a certainty of having their affairs made worse. Surely the honourable gentleman can never intend to carry the opinion to this extent.

But then he said that we ought to wait till they were

ready, and not to place ourselves in the odious character of the disturbers of Europe. If I were at liberty to enter upon a statement of facts, I might perhaps satisfy even the honourable gentleman on that head. This I am not at liberty to do. However, if we were at peace with a country and endeavoured to excite other nations against it for views and purposes of our own, undoubtedly this would be to expose ourselves to the odium to which he alluded. But I cannot conceive what odium could attach to you, when you were unjustly attacked, if you endeavoured to bring others to your assistance, especially if their interests were equally concerned. No odium, then, could justly be attached to us on this account. It might be, perhaps, invidious to involve other nations in war, when our own interest alone was concerned; but in the present case, our own interest and that of the Continent are closely connected, as the security of both in a great measure depends upon their co-operation. If we therefore can open the eyes of the continental nations to their true interests, if we can clearly show them that not only their interests but their salvation depend upon their joining us in opposing an enemy whose object it is to destroy us both, then surely it is not only not unjust, but it is even meritorious, to secure their co-operation if possible.

But it ought to be observed, that *this* may in point of fact be the case, though I only mean to put it hypothetically. The Powers of the Continent may have doubts as to their ability for prosecuting the war. Now may it not happen that these doubts may arise from their being much more powerful in any other way than in their finances? In this case we may have the ability to remove all these doubts. Is not this altogether fair and desirable? If we are enabled to remove their objections, and to hold out an expectation that they will be supplied where they are most deficient, would it not be both for their interest and our own to do so?

When the honourable gentleman recurred to the idea of a peace guaranteed by the other nations of Europe, it is above all things to be considered, what is the situation of those Powers who are to give the guarantee, and what are their means of preserving it. If they were in such a state of weakness as not to be able to punish a violation of the treaty, what effectual purpose would their guarantee serve? Viewing the subject in this light, it appears to me necessary that there should be some concentred system agreed on between us and other Powers, before we can properly explain ourselves to France with respect to that sort of peace which we may think necessary for our own security and the security of Europe. To establish this sort of concert among the other nations is certainly a subject of much delicacy and difficulty, and it is therefore not at all surprising that the negotiations are not now in such a state of maturity as to allow of a communication respecting them.

The honourable gentleman seems to misunderstand the spirit of the answer which was given by His Majesty to the overture of peace on the part of France. Nothing could have been more loose or general than the terms of that overture, and certainly the answer was not disdainful or scornful; it was all that the country, under the existing circumstances, could say, for it stated our desire of peace, but at the same time the necessity we felt of consulting the other nations of Europe with whom we were in confidential intercourse. The French overture stated no specific terms upon which peace could be granted, but the messages of the French Government to the legislative body lay down as a *sine qua non* of peace, that we shall agree not only to the Treaty of Amiens, but to their construction of that treaty on the particular points which occasioned the present war. It will be recollected that the cause of the present war, as has been expressly stated, proceeded from the general encroachments of France upon all other nations, accompanied by a peremptory demand that we should relinquish that which, in the opinion of our Government and in my private opinion, the country could not, under all circumstances, be called upon to relinquish by the treaty. I do not know how far the judgement of the other nations of Europe may be induced by the arts and misrepresentations of France to consider the cause of this country as unjust, but I consider, and I trust the House does, that the war was on our part most strictly just.

There was one proposition of the honourable gentleman to which everybody must agree, namely, that peace should, if possible, be concluded upon reasonable terms. This general proposition is most undeniable, but the difference still exists as to what terms are to be considered reasonable. The honourable gentleman seems to consider that, in order to make the terms reasonable, they should be such as the enemy would accept of.

This is a most strange conclusion. At a time when we are at war professedly for the purpose of defending ourselves against the schemes of inordinate ambition which France has manifested, it would be extraordinary to make the criterion of a reasonable peace that which would please France.

I am ready to allow that the alliance of Russia alone would not promise such efficacious or powerful co-operation as would make it worth while to protract the war on account of any hope it would hold, or even equivalent for the large vote of credit which is demanded; but it is my opinion that even the limited co-operation of a few of the Powers, and for a short time, may be of material service in the course of the war, in protecting those points which the enemy appear particularly anxious to attack.

The vote of credit was carried without a division.

6

The Last Speech
November 9, 1805 [1]

THE Third Coalition soon collapsed. It was destined that, while Pitt lived, the balance of war should hang evenly between his country and Napoleon. On the day before Trafalgar destroyed Napoleon's last chance of winning the command of the sea, he had dealt the first of the two shattering blows which destroyed Pitt's last chance of crushing him on land.

[1] Stanhope, *Life of Pitt*, vol. iii, p. 364 (1879 edition).

The strategic plan of the Coalition was to attack Napoleon on all sides. The main Austrian and Russian armies were to make a combined advance through Central Europe upon France, while minor movements—which eventually came to nothing—were to be undertaken by the allies in Hanover and South Italy. The plan was ruined by the vacillating attitude of Prussia. As long as a possibility existed of her finely-trained army taking Napoleon's side, the Russians hesitated to advance, and an Austrian army under Mack impatiently pushed on alone up the valley of the Upper Danube. Napoleon, meanwhile, had executed a sudden change of front. The failure of his designs at sea confirmed the purpose he had formed in case the invasion of England should prove impossible. It was on August 20 that Villeneuve retired to Cadiz. On the 24th the cavalry of the 'Army of England' broke camp. On the 26th the main body began its lightning march across Europe. On October 17 Mack capitulated with the greater part of his army at Ulm. On November 13 Napoleon entered Vienna.

News of Ulm reached Pitt on November 2. It was countered on the 6th by the tidings of Trafalgar, but the victory seemed at the moment robbed of almost all its value by the loss of Nelson. Pitt, however, was full of hope. If Prussia would only join the Coalition, Napoleon, he believed, might yet be caught and crushed, and already, at the end of October, he had dispatched a last appeal to Berlin. His offer was magnanimous. He would pay on generous terms for every man Prussia put into the field against Napoleon. He would assist her to legitimate territorial acquisitions on the Continent. And, at the close of the war he would surrender all the oversea conquests of England, except Malta and the Cape. By this act alone he proved, if proof were needed, the truth of the assertion, which had been the dominant refrain of all his speeches on the war for twelve years past, that England was not fighting for her own material gains but for liberty, and not only the liberty of England, but of Europe and the world.

It was fitting that Pitt's last speech should consist of a final declaration, in a few clear words, of the cause to which the best part of his short life had been devoted, as if he were handing on the vindication of that cause as a legacy to future generations of his countrymen. At the Lord Mayor's banquet on November 9, the Lord Mayor proposed his health as the 'Saviour of Europe'. His reply was very brief:

> I return you many thanks for the honour you have done me; but Europe is not to be saved by any single man. England has saved herself by her exertions, and will, as I trust, save Europe by her example.

His trust was justified, but not till the new spirit of nationality had revivified Europe. The only Europe that Pitt was allowed to know was not yet ready to be saved by any example of national devotion. On December 2, less than a month after the Guildhall speech, Napoleon routed the main Austro-Russian army with overwhelming loss at Austerlitz. As far as the continental Powers were concerned, the war was at an end. The Czar Alexander obtained an armistice and at once retreated into Russia. Austria hurriedly purchased peace by the surrender of her provinces in Venetia and on the Adriatic coast. And what of Prussia? Her action before Austerlitz had been typical of her traditions. The violation of an outlying portion of Prussian territory on the march to Ulm had induced Frederick William to yield at last to the pressure of Russia; but, in striking contrast to the spirit of Pitt's offer, the condition of her alliance with

Russia, embodied in a secret article, was her acquisition of Hanover. Pitt's repudiation of this condition, which no minister of Hanover's legal sovereign, George III, could possibly accept, restored the influence of the Napoleonic party in Berlin, and Austerlitz was fought and lost before Prussia had taken any step to act on her alliance. The chance of taking Napoleon on the flank, while he was occupied with the Russians and Austrians on his front, was thus neglected. It is true that a few years later Prussia, her national pride awakened, played a great part in the Wars of Liberation. It is true that Prussian armies took their fair share in paralysing Napoleon's power at Leipzig and finally destroying it at Waterloo. But it is also true that, but for Prussian selfishness, the results of Leipzig, if not of Waterloo, might have been achieved in 1805, and Europe might have been saved from ten years of wholesale bloodshed and destruction.

After Austerlitz, Prussia was an easy victim. Napoleon shrewdly offered the same tempting bait of Hanover as the price of an ignominious alliance, and on December 15 the Treaty of Schönbrunn was signed. Less than a year later, Napoleon, realizing that his new ally was untrustworthy, dangerous, and friendless, threw off the mask. Jena and its sequel were the result and the reward of Prussian policy.

Pitt, however, to the very last, hoped against hope that the statesmen of Berlin would realize that they could not always be exempt from the danger which threatened all Europe: he hoped against hope that the Prussian armies might at the eleventh hour turn the scale. But no such gleam of light appeared on the dark horizon, growing darker and darker still as autumn deepened into winter; and towards the end of the year his health began to fail under the almost intolerable suspense. It had been already strained wellnigh to breaking-point by the burden of the long struggle. For twelve years, with one brief interval of doubtful peace,

England alone of all the Powers had carried on the war continuously. For most of those years the responsibility for British policy had lain chiefly on Pitt, for the last two years on him alone. And now the actual breaking-point was reached. The tidings of Prussia's secret deal with Russia for the acquisition of Hanover intensified the anxiety caused by Ulm; and, as the news of Austerlitz filtered through, his agony of mind deepened. Even then his courage did not fail him. He still refused to abandon hope of Prussia. On the last night of his life he asked which way the wind blew, and was glad to hear it was blowing from the east, since it would bring a messenger more quickly from Berlin. The arrival of the news he longed for might have saved his life, a decisive change of fortune on the Continent might have prolonged it for many years. But no news came, and in the early hours of January 23, 1806, he died. His last words were clearly audible: 'My country! How I leave my country!'

At the present time (April 1915) no epitaph on William Pitt could sound to the ears of his countrymen more appropriate than the words spoken by Pericles of the Athenians who had died for Athens in the war with Sparta: *The whole earth is the sepulchre of famous men; and their story is not graven only on stone over their native earth, but lives on far away, without visible symbol, woven into the stuff of other men's lives. For you now it remains to rival what they have done, and, knowing the secret of happiness to be freedom and the secret of freedom a brave heart, squarely to face the war and all its perils.*

INDEX

Aachen (Aix-la-Chapelle), xl.
Aboukir, 274.
Acre, 246, 274.
Addington, Henry, 234, 302, 305, 308, 331, 338.
Additional Force Bill, 310, 331.
Adriatic, the, 190, 351.
Aix-la-Chapelle, Peace of, 242.
Alexander I (of Russia), xliii, xliv, 302, 343, 344, 351.
Alien Act, 68, 70.
Alkmaar, Convention of, 247.
Alps, the, xx, xl, 190, 249, 288.
Alsace, 173.
Amboyna, 179 n.
America, United States of, xliv, 1, 4, 155, 262.
American colonies, loss of, ix, xii, xiii, 3.
American colonists, 4, 82.
American Congress, 4.
American War, ix, xi, 1–8.
Amiens, Treaty of, 303–5.
Amsterdam, 134.
Ancien régime, the, xvii, xxxii.
Anglo-Dutch Alliance (1788), xxv.
Anglo-Russian Convention (1805), 344.
Antwerp, xxiv, xxv, xliii, 46, 339.
Armed Neutrality League, 288, 298.
'Army of England', Buonaparte's, xliii, xlvi, 339, 350.
Army of Reserve Act, 310.
Assignats, 130–2.
Auckland, Lord, 61.

Austerlitz, battle of, xxxix, xli, xliii, 351, 352, 353.
Australia, x, xlii.
Austria, xi, xv, xix–xxiv, xxviii, xxx, xli, xliii, 36, 39 n., 44, 48, 63, 74, 92, 103, 104, 112, 116, 122, 123, 135, 136, 151 n., 173, 174, 178, 189, 190, 198, 233, 246, 247, 250, 253, 254, 257, 265, 269, 271, 273, 274, 284, 288, 291, 292, 344, 351, 352.
Austrian Succession, War of the, 242 n.
Avignon, 254.

Bahama Islands, 3.
Baltic, the, xv, 299.
Banda, 179 n.
Bank of England, 190, 234.
Barham, Admiral, 343.
Barras, xliii, 260, 265.
Basle, 135, 137, 153, 156, 157.
Bastille, the, xvi, xxvii.
Batavian Republic, 134.
Belgium, xxi–v, xxviii, xlvi, 39, 72, 104, 116, 135, 145, 173 ff., 198, 249, 339. (*See* Austrian Netherlands, Liège, Luxemburg.)
Benasco, 268.
Berlin, 134, 135, 350, 352, 353.
Boulogne, xlvi, 339.
Bourbon-Hapsburg alliance, xi.
Bourbons, the, xi, xvi, xviii, xxvii, xxxv, xxxviii, 279, 284–6.
Brazils, the, 342.
Breda, 91.

Index

Brest, 299, 335, 339, 343.
Brissot, xix, xxvi, 120, 260.
Brumaire, 247.
Brussels, 39.
Budgets, Pitt's: 1792, 15-23; 1793, 78-91; 1798, 232-44.
Buonaparte, Jerome, King of Westphalia, xli.
Buonaparte, Joseph, King of Spain, xli.
Buonaparte, Louis Napoleon, King of Holland, xli.
Buonaparte, Napoleon, xxxii–xlviii, 135-7, 173, 189, 190, 198, 200, 233, 246-80, 288, 289, 302-4, 326, 338, 339, 343, 344, 349-52.
Burke, Edmund, xvi, xxxii, xlii, 149.

Cadiz, 200, 339, 341, 343, 350.
Caesarism, xxxi, xlvi.
Cairo, xxxiv, 246.
Calder, Admiral, 342.
Cambon, xxix, 131.
Camperdown, battle of, 200.
Campo Formio, Treaty of, xliii, 190, 200, 265, 271.
Canada, x, xii, xiv, xlii, 2 n., 82.
Canning, George, 121, 248.
Cape Comorin, xliv.
Cape Finisterre, 343.
Cape of Good Hope, 135, 179 n., 180, 199, 256, 305, 350.
Cape St. Vincent, 190.
Carnot, 104.
Catharine II (of Russia), xviii.
Ceylon, 179 n., 180, 304.
Chandernagore, 218.
Channel, the English, xii, xliii, 200, 300, 327, 339.
Charlemagne, xl, xli.
Charles, Archduke, 173.
Chatham, William Pitt, Earl of, ix, 2 n.

Chauvelin, 24, 25, 32, 34, 35, 46-9, 59, 60, 65, 145, 146, 252.
Clifden, Lord, 105.
Clive, Lord, xlii.
Coalition Government, 8.
Coalitions with foreign Powers: the First (1793), 103, 104, 116, 135, 190; the Second (1799), 247, 288, 302; the Third (1805), 344, 349, 350.
Commercial Treaty with France (1786), xiii, xvi, xxii, xxvii, 8-14, 18, 34, 62, 67, 70, 294, 295.
Committee of Public Safety, xxxiii, xl.
Condé, 110.
Constitution of 1795, xxxiv; of 1799, xxxv.
'Continental System', the, xliii.
Copenhagen, battle of, 302.
Cornwallis, Lord, 339.
Corsica, 135.
Corunna, 343.
Crawford, Colonel, 321.

Danton, xxvi, 24.
Danube, the, 350.
Defence Act, 310-11.
Delacroix, 173, 174.
d'Enghien, Duc, 343.
Denmark, 155, 173, 183, 288, 296, 297, 302.
Dieppe, 339.
Directors, the, xxxiv, xliii, 200.
Directory, the, xxxiv, 136, 137, 154, 158, 159, 161, 162, 173, 174, 176, 183-5, 187, 198, 203, 208, 214, 215, 220, 223-5, 246, 247, 261, 265, 266.
Dominica, 3.
Dumouriez, General, 39, 61, 146.
Dundas, Henry (Viscount Melville), 85, 200, 247, 341, 343.
Dunkirk, 4, 104.

Index 357

East India Company, x.
Egypt, xxxiv, xxxviii, xliv, 190, 233, 246, 258–9, 262, 271–5, 302, 304, 305, 339, 342.
Elba, 304.
Erskine, Thomas, 248, 254, 255.
Executive Council, the, xxvi, xxxii, 47, 64, 72.

'Family compact,' xi.
Ferrol, 305.
First Consul, xxxv, xxxix, 247, 276, 304.
Flanders, 69, 104.
Fleet, Mutiny in the, 189–98.
Florida, 3.
Fort Louis, 110.
Fox, Charles James, xvi, xxvii, xxviii, 1, 5, 7, 77, 92, 103–5, 111, 117, 137, 170, 338, 344.
Francis II (of Austria), 247.
Frederick William II (of Prussia), xviii, 63, 351.
French Revolution, xv, xvi, xix–xxi, xxiii, xxiv, xxvii–xxxii, xxxiv, xxxviii, xxxix, xlviii, 33, 68, 71, 132, 248–50, 252, 257–67, 270, 277–80, 343.

Garrow, Private, case of, 336–7.
Geneva, 233.
Genoa, 260, 269, 270, 338.
Genoese Republic, 344.
George III, xviii, 8, 25, 52, 247, 302, 338, 352.
German States, the, xli, 135.
Germany, xlvii, 150, 178, 188, 253, 254, 262.
Gibraltar, 188, 339.
Girondins, the, xix, xx, xxii, xxxi, xlvi, 120, 136.
Goree, 3.
Grenada, 3.
Grenville, Lord, 24, 35, 60, 174, 253.

Grey, Charles, 289, 291, 292, 340.
Guadeloupe, 127 n., 135.

Hague, The, xxv, 61, 62, 146.
Hainault, 40.
Hanover, 338, 343, 350–3.
Hanoverian troops, 82.
Hapsburgs, the, 135, 269, 271.
Harwich, 305.
Hastings, Warren, xlii.
Hawkesbury, Lord, 313.
Hayti, 126 n.
Helvetic Republic, 233, 304.
Hill, Sir Richard, 126.
Hohenlinden, battle of, 288.
Hohenzollerns, the, 135.
Holland, ix, xiv, xvi, xxii, xxiv, xxv, xxvii, xli, xlvi, 1, 4, 32, 42, 45, 51, 69, 91, 116, 122, 125, 134, 135, 145, 150, 179, 188, 191, 214, 219, 248–50, 252, 254, 262, 288, 305, 338, 340, 343. (*See* Batavian Republic, United Provinces.)
Hollandsch Diep, the, 91.
Hope, Charles, 336.
Howe, Lord, 135.
Hussey, Mr., 229.

Île de France, xliv.
India, xii, xlii, xliv, 2 n., 4, 85, 86, 110, 180, 218, 256, 259, 260, 262, 302.
India Bill, 8.
Institute, the (French), xxxvi.
Ionian Islands, 190, 304, 305.
Ireland, ix, x, xxvi, 187, 190, 198, 233, 247, 262, 275, 302, 331.
Italy, xxxiv, xl, xlvi, 123, 134, 135, 153, 173, 178, 188, 189, 246, 247, 254, 262, 266–8, 288, 305, 344, 350. (*See* Genoa, Lombardy, Venice, &c.).

Index

Jacobin clubs in England, xxv, xxvi, xxvii, 121 n.; in India, 260.
Jacobins, the, xx, xxxiv, 38, 57, 99, 103 ff., 121, 127, 149, 151 n., 257, 260, 264, 273, 275, 277, 283.
Jamaica, 3.
Jemappes, battle of, xx, xxviii.
Jena, battle of, 352.
Jervis, Sir John (Earl St. Vincent), 190.
Jourdan, General, 173.
Joséphine, Empress, xxxvii, xxxix.

Kabul, xliv.

La Fayette, Marquis de, 115, 151.
Lameth, M., 151.
Laurence, Dr., 299.
Leipzig, battle of, 352.
Leoben, 198.
Leopold II (of Austria), xviii, 63.
Liège, xx, 135 n., 174.
Lille, 198, 200, 215, 220, 266.
Lodi, battle of, 136, 137.
Lombardy, 136, 174, 267, 268, 344.
London, xlv, 65; fortification of, 325-8.
Louis XIV (of France), xl, xlviii.
Louis XVI (of France), xviii-xx, xxvi, 24, 48, 66, 73-5.
Louisiana, xlii.
Louvet, xxx.
Low Countries, the, xxvi, xxxi, 44, 46 (*see* Netherlands).
Lunéville, Treaty of, 288, 305.
Luxemburg, 135 n., 174.

Mack, General, 350.
Maestricht, xxv.
Mainz, 105.

Malacca, 179 n.
Malmesbury, Lord, 173, 174, 182-4, 189, 199, 200, 211, 215, 223, 225, 266.
Malta, 233, 246, 258, 289, 302, 304, 305, 341, 350.
Marat, xxix, 99, 100.
Marengo, battle of, xxxix, 288.
Maret, xxxi, 60.
Marie Antoinette, xviii, xxix.
Martinique, 135, 179, 218.
Masséna, 247.
Mediterranean, the, 104, 135, 233, 275, 302, 339, 341, 342.
Milan, 267, 268, 344.
Mincio, the, 268, 269.
Minorca, 3.
Miquelon, 218.
Modena, 267, 269.
Monge, French Minister of the Marine, 48, 75.
Mons, xx, 40.
Montserrat, 3.
Moreau, 173, 288.
Morrison, James, 336-7.
Moselle, 178.
Mulhouse, 233.
Münster, Treaty of, xxv, 45, 158.
Murat, Joachim (King of Naples), xli.

Naples, xli, 247, 304, 338, 343.
National Assembly, the, xvii, xx, xxi, 57, 64.
National Convention, the, xxi, xxvi, xxxi-iv, 40-3, 46, 47, 51, 65, 67, 110, 116, 125, 126, 130-2, 136.
Neerwinden, battle of, 92.
Nelson, Lord, 233, 234, 302, 339, 341-3, 350.
Netherlands, the Austrian, xx, xxi, xxiii, xxvii, 38, 39, 125, 135, 174, 177, 178, 221, 250, 255, 256.

Index

Nevis, 3.
Newfoundland, 3.
Nice, xx, 136, 178.
Nile, battle of the, 233, 234, 274.
Nootka Sound, 85 *n*.
Nore, the, 191 ff.
North, Lord, 3, 5, 7.
North Sea, 191.
Northern Powers, League of, 288 ff., 302.

Pacific, the, xiv.
Papal States, the, xli, 254.
Paris, xvii, xviii, xx, xxv, xxix, xxxiii, xxxv, xxxvi, xli, xliii, 51, 64, 104, 136, 174, 182-4, 189, 200, 211, 220, 246, 247, 276, 344.
Paris, Peace of (1763), 2.
Paul I (of Russia), 246, 288, 289, 302.
Pavia, 268.
Peel, Robert, 234.
Pellew, Sir Edward, 334.
Philip II (of Spain), xlv, xlviii.
Pichegru, General, 134.
Piedmont, 136, 304.
Pillnitz, Declaration of, xviii, xix, 63 *n*.
Pius VII, xxxviii, xli, 233, 344.
Poland, xi, xx, xxiii, xxviii, 112, 115, 116, 135, 144.
Pondicherry, 218.
Portland, Duke of, 7.
Portsmouth, 335.
Portugal, 213, 214, 247, 254.
Press Bureau, Buonaparte's, xxxvii.
Providence, 3.
Prussia, xi, xiv, xv, xix, xxviii, xxx, xli, 32, 36, 48, 63, 74, 92, 104, 112, 116, 122, 123, 134, 135, 150, 151, 247, 252-4, 289, 344, 350-3.

Quesnoi, 110.
Quiberon, 135.

Red Sea, xliv.
Reichenbach, Convention xxiii.
Reubel, 260.
Réunion, xliv.
Rhine, the, xviii, xx, xl, xli, 92, 116, 135, 173, 178, 190, 2
Robespierre, xxx-xxxiii, 1 120, 125, 132, 133, 260.
Rome, 233, 267, 269.
Romilly, Sir Samuel, xxxii.
Russia, xi, xiv, xxiii, xxviii, xliii, xlvii, 112, 116, 233, 2 246, 247, 253, 273, 274, 2 289, 296, 297, 343, 344, 34 53.

St. Domingo, xlii, 179, 218, 2
St. Helena, xliv.
St. Kitts, 3.
St. Lucia, 3, 135, 179, 218.
St. Pierre, 218.
Sardinia, xx, 136.
Savoy, xx, 36, 38, 57, 136, 17
Scheldt, River, xxiv, xxv, 43- 71, 72, 145, 249.
Schönbrunn, Treaty of, 352.
Scotland, xxvi, 167, 170, 1 236.
Sebastiani, Colonel, 305.
Senegambia, 3.
September massacres, the, xx 99.
Seringapatam, 302.
Sheerness, mutiny of the Nc fleet at, 191 ff.
Shelburne, Lord, 1, 5, 7.
Sheridan, Richard Brinsley, 29
Sinclair, Sir John, 200.
Sinking Fund, 16.
Smith, Adam, 18.
Smith, Sir Sidney, 246.

South Africa, xlii. (*See* Cape of Good Hope.)
South America, xxiii, 299.
Spain, ix, xi, xiv, xli, xlii, 1, 4, 42, 47, 85, 86, 122, 123, 134, 150, 151, 190, 191, 214, 219, 254, 299, 300, 327, 338, 339, 340, 341.
Spithead, mutiny of the fleet at, 191 ff.
Stadtholder, the (of Holland), xiv, 116, 134, 150.
States-General (of Holland), the, 45, 116.
Suez, Isthmus of, xliv.
Sweden, xv, 288, 296, 297, 344.
Swiss Guard, xx.
Switzerland, xlvi, 233, 246, 257, 258, 304, 343. (*See* Helvetic Republic.)
Syria, 246.

Talleyrand, xxii, xliii, 255.
Tallien, 132, 260.
Temple, Lord, 200.
'Terre Napoléon', xlii.
Terrorists, the, xxxiii, 99, 100, 106 ff., 116, 132, 136.
Texel, the, 191.
Thugut, 247.
Tierney, George, 284, 285.
Tilsit, xliii.
Tippoo Sahib, xliv, 260, 302.
Tobago, 3, 110, 179, 187, 218.
Toulon, xxxiii, 104, 135, 151, 200, 220, 233, 299, 305, 339, 341, 342.
Trafalgar, battle of, 338, 343, 349, 350.
Traitorous Correspondence Act, 121.
Trinidad, 199, 219, 256, 304.
Triple Alliance (between England, Prussia, and Holland), xiv, xv, xxiii.
Triumvirate, the, xxxv, 266.
Tuileries, the, xx.
Turkey, xi, xv, 144, 246, 247, 272, 274, 275.
Tuscany, 267, 269.

Ulm, battle of, (1) in 1800 : 288. (2) in 1805 : xxxix, xliii, 350, 351, 353.
'United Empire Loyalists', 82 *n*.
United Provinces, the, 52, 76.
University, the Imperial, xxxvi.
Ushant, 135.
Utrecht, Treaty of, xxiii, xxv, 219 *n*.

Valenciennes, 92, 103, 147.
Valmy, battle of, xx, xxviii.
Vancouver Island, 85 *n*.
Varennes, xviii.
Venice, 190, 267, 269–71, 351.
Versailles, xvii ; Treaty of, 14, 68.
Vienna, 135, 190, 350.
Villeneuve, Admiral, 339, 340, 342, 343, 350.

Wales, 167.
Waterloo, battle of, 352.
West Indies, xii, 68, 126, 127, 135, 187, 218, 219, 339, 342.
Whitbread, Samuel, 113, 248.
Whitworth, Lord, 305 *n*.
Wilberforce, William, 117, 127 *n*., 333.
Windham, William, 313.
Würzburg, battle of, 173.

Yorke, C. P., 325.

Zurich, battle of, 247.

Printed in England at the Oxford University Press

```
DA        Pitt, William
522           War speeches
P45
1915
```

PLEASE DO NOT REMOVE
CARDS OR SLIPS FROM THIS POCKET

UNIVERSITY OF TORONTO LIBRARY

CPSIA information can be obtained
at www.ICGtesting.com
Printed in the USA
BVHW04*1417090718
521168BV00004B/9/P

9 780332 135625